THE BIG RED WINE BOOK

Campbell Mattinson

Hardie Grant Books

Published in 2008 by
Hardie Grant Books
85 High Street
Prahran, Victoria 3181, Australia
www.hardiegrant.com.au

All rights reserved. No part of this publication may be reproduced, stored in a retrieval system or transmitted in any form by any means, electronic, mechanical, photocopying, recording or otherwise, without the prior written permission of the publishers and copyright holders.

The moral right of the author has been asserted.

Copyright © Campbell Mattinson 2008

ISBN 9 781 740 66 605 3

Cover and text design by Letterbox
Typeset by Megan Ellis
Printed and bound in Australia by Griffin Press

10 9 8 7 6 5 4 3 2 1

Every effort has been made to incorporate correct information and statistics. The author and publisher regret any errors and omissions and invite readers to contribute up-to-date or relevant information to Hardie Grant Books.

Welcome to *The Big Red Wine Book*	05
How I taste my reds	08
The Big Red Wine Book awards	10
The top 100 red wines at $20 or less	14
How this book works	17
SHIRAZ	19
PINOT NOIR	125
CABERNET AND BLENDS	151
MERLOT, GRENACHE, ITALIANS, SPANIARDS, AND BLENDS	209
Wine glossary	245
Winery contact details	249
Wine index	261

WELCOME TO THE BIG RED WINE BOOK

Australian red wine is an outrageously fun place to spend your time. It's why I often felt as I travelled around and tasted wines to compile this book that I was living in a toyshop. Our reds are more diverse and interesting than they've ever been – I can guarantee you that there's never been a better time to drink Aussie red wine.

The fun hasn't always been so diverse. For a great part of the twentieth century, Australian wine was a story of heavy, fortified wine – tokays, muscats, sherries, vintage ports and tawnies. In the 1950s, things slowly started to change as Australia began a thirty-year shift toward table wines. For a lot of this time the table wines we drank were white wines (indeed, in the 1980s, six out of every seven bottles of wine sold in Australia were whites), though over the past twenty years red wines have gained dramatically in popularity.

If you walked into an Australian bottle shop as recently as 1990, the red wines available would almost entirely be made of cabernet sauvignon, shiraz, grenache and blends of the three. There were other grape varieties around, but a lot of them weren't much good, or were severely under-appreciated. There would have been very little sparkling red or pinot noir available, and pretty much zero Italian or Spanish varieties.

Fast forward to today, and the choices are massive. Not only that, but the choices are better than ever. Until a few years ago I was unconvinced of the quality of the Italian grape varietals being grown and made in Australia, such as sangiovese, nebbiolo and barbera. I thought they were overpriced and over-hyped, an exercise in sucking in the wine consumer via lots of glossy magazine articles. Today, this is no longer the case; many of these wines are excellent, and some of them are world class. Indeed, it's a good time to explore them, because as these vines grow older, and more mature, and our winemakers gain further experience at making the wines, the quality is rapidly rising. These are exciting times for the so-called 'alternative varieties' of Australian red wine.

As indeed they are for Australian (and New Zealand) pinot noir. I still come across people at parties who grind their fingers into my breastbone and demand to know, 'What's the point of pinot noir? It's pissy and weak – why wouldn't you just make shiraz!' This always makes me both laugh and recall a statement made by wine doyen James Halliday: 'There was a time when it was thought in Australia that if you were male and you liked drinking pinot noir, then there was something wrong with your chromosomes. Thanks to the movie *Sideways* and, more particularly, to the availability of much better quality pinot noir, we're thoroughly coming out of that.'

As indeed we are. Pinot noir is one of the fastest growing segments in Australian wine.

A warning: UK wine writer Matthew Jukes reckons that Australian pinot noir is the best value pinot noir in the world. The great pinot noirs of the world traditionally come from Burgundy in France, but Australian pinots are now lapping at their shores in quality at far lower prices (if that sounds difficult to believe, especially considering pinot noir's notoriously high prices, please bear in mind that top Burgundian pinot noir is the most expensive wine in the world). The warning is that world markets tend to balance themselves out before you'd like them to; when the world wakes up to the quality and value of Australian pinot, it's likely that the prices will adjust, accordingly, upwards.

Of course, the more robust styles of Aussie red – usually from the Barossa Valley, McLaren Vale and central Victorian regions – are still the most popular of all, and hallelujah to that. Walk into any decent bottle shop or barn (or, as I usually do, internet wine shop) at any time of the year, and there you'll find a collection of them, ready for you to sink your teeth into. I'm extraordinarily lucky; people send them to me for free. But I also buy lots of wine, because I'm a wine drinker first and a wine writer second, and it continues to stagger me just how cheap some wine is.

Indeed, in the last week of putting this book together, I drove to my nearest Dan Murphy's liquor store. I needed a fix of the real world. I wanted to buy a dozen different wines, all reds, all of them for $20 or less. I thought it might take me a while; it took me less than ten minutes. I picked up a Fox Creek Shadow's Run Shiraz Cabernet for $11.40, a Wirra Wirra Scrubby Rise red for $12.35 and a Banrock Station Reserve Sparkling Shiraz for the unbelievable price of $8.55. All of them, once I got them home, were fantastic drinks – indeed, that Banrock Station sparkling red could well be the best value 'always available' wine in Australia, and was an easy choice as this book's Bargain Sparkling Red of the Year.

What this wine shop visit did was reinforce two things for me. It underlined what a fantastically lucky red wine country we live in. Also, it made me painfully aware of how much wine is out there; what a raging maze of choice there is.

Which made me, once again, peer admiringly at the Aussies who wrote on wine in the 1960s and 1970s. Back then, there were probably only a few thousand different wines made in Australia each year and bugger-all in New Zealand. It would then have been relatively simple to taste them all (if you were keen enough), and to feel like you knew everything you needed to know about the Aussie wine scene. Today, though, with over 25,000 different wines made in Australia each year (as a calculated guess) and many thousands more in New Zealand, it is impossible for anyone to come close to tasting them all properly. I've been writing about wine for nine years and publishing a website and a monthly newsletter devoted to wine for the past six years, and all through that time and across all the travel that covering wine properly demands, I've met many wonderful experts on wine, but no one who can taste and cover it all. The 'industry' is simply too big.

Which is why I really wanted to write a book solely devoted to red wine. There is so much choice out there; it was time to narrow it down to the wines I really loved to drink, and (in all honesty) to the wine styles that, as a reader, I liked to read about. There are days when I love a glass of white wine, but I almost never read about them; I just drink them. Reds, though, I like to drink, taste, read about and write about – I just love 'em. (I've also been known, just quietly, to utter the words, 'If you can see through it, it's not a real wine' and on milder days, 'This white wine is lovely, but do you have any real wines?')

I've been talking to wine-loving folks seven days a week for the past nine years; I know I am not alone. There are a lot of people passionate about enjoying a good bottle of red – it's high time us red wine lovers had our own book.

Welcome then to the results of my constant mucking about in the red wine toyshop. There are traps out there and indeed a lot of overpriced crud, but there is also a world of joy. Any day of the week, for any occasion, for any amount of money – this book tries its darnedest to make sure that you're always drinking a seriously good red.

Cheers!
Campbell Mattinson

HOW I TASTE MY REDS

I'm not going to be so arrogant as to tell you how to drink red wine – I'm sure you're travelling very nicely all by yourself, thank you very much. What I am going to do, though, is give a quick summary of how I drink and prepare the red wines I drink, in the hope that it may prove useful to some.

DECANTING
The first thing I do, before I've started tasting or drinking, is decant most bottles of red. I am a serial decanter. Decanting is simply the act of getting air into the wine – as an attempt to coax more flavour and fragrance from it (that is, get the most out of it for the money you've paid).

Now, when I say that I decant most reds, I don't necessarily leave them around for long periods. What I mean is that I pour the wines into a clean jug and then straight back into the bottle. They've been cooped up in the bottle; most reds benefit from being able to quickly stretch their legs. Just like with people: the bigger the red wine (that is, the more intense the flavour) the more likely the wine will benefit from being decanted. Stretch the legs of those big wines!

Of course, if it's a rosé or lighter style I may give the decanting a miss, but then for the grippier, more tannic reds I may actually let them sit in a decanter for an hour or two before tucking into them.

TEMPERATURE OF THE WINE
The other thing I do from the outset is assess the wine's temperature. When I hear people disagreeing over the quality of a particular wine, the first thing I ask is: what temperature did you drink the wine at? The temperature of a red wine affects the way it tastes massively. Most red wines taste ugly if they're too cold (it usually makes the wine taste more bitter and hard) and just as ugly if they're too warm (it makes the alcohol leap out, shrouding the wine's true flavours).

Most red wine should be consumed at room temperature. The problem is that room temperature in Australia can mean anything from about 12 degrees to 35 degrees Celsius, depending on the time of the year and where you are. Most red wines tastes best at between 14 or 18 degrees.

This means that in summer, I stick my reds in the fridge for 30 minutes or so before I start drinking them. If it's really warm in the house, I store the bottle in the fridge while I drink a glass of it.

In winter, I do the opposite – I warm bottles up. Bear in mind that I live in a particularly cold area; but the principle is worth noting. Come to my place in winter and you will see bottles of wines sitting a safe (and reasonable) distance from the open fire!

GLASSES

I drink from a heap of different glasses, but all of them curve in at the top, rather than splaying outwards at the top. It simply concentrates the smell of the wine and so makes drinking the wine more enjoyable. A fair amount of our sense of taste is bound up in our sense of smell (strange but true), one reason why food tastes different when we've got a blocked nose. Those big balloon-like glasses, which you see some people drinking red wines from, are not for extra-large servings (you still only fill them with a normal serving size), but it's simply to create a big space for the wine's aromas to gather in. It's for this reason – I swear it's true – most red wines taste better in bigger glasses (you get more for your money).

THE BIG RED WINE BOOK AWARDS

The Big Red Wine of the Year (and Big Red Shiraz of the Year)

Mount Langi Ghiran Langi Shiraz 2005
($55)

When I tasted the $27 Langi Cliff Edge Shiraz I immediately wanted to give it the wine of the year title, I liked it that much. It's a magnificent wine at a fair price, and if you can't go the whole hog, jump for that. The Big Red Wine of the Year though, is the $55 Langi Shiraz. Its quality speaks for itself: it melts in your mouth, has complexity dripping from its inside sleeves, has the structure to age very long term and has flavour that goes on and on. I compared it against $10 wines and $500 wines; it won the day. (See page 75.)

The Big Red Winery of the Year

Wirra Wirra

Samantha Connew is the chief winemaker, and she's got the place singing. I suspect she's incapable of making an ordinary wine. All of Wirra Wirra's wines are now leaders in their class – they are a small winery in McLaren Vale and yet, remarkably, they have five wines in this guide scoring over 90 points and two super wines in the Top 100 list of red wines priced at $20 or less. For glugging down on a weeknight; for savouring on a Saturday night; for cellaring – Wirra have a top red wine to suit. No wonder they have been grabbing a good deal of international attention of late. It is a pleasure to award them the Big Red Winery of the Year.

The Big Red Winemaker of the Year

Peter Gago

Peter Gago has presided over the grandest of Australian red wine ships – Penfolds – through difficult times. The Australian wine industry itself has been in flux, and Penfolds has been through a range of ownership changes and internal restructurings. If the wines were lacklustre, he'd have an excuse; and yet with the release of the 2005 reds, he's got them looking brilliant. This is the powerful end of red winemaking, done incredibly well. When you taste the 2005 reds (and early signs are that the 2006s look outstanding too) you see that Gago and his team didn't make this award possible; they made it inevitable.

The Big Red Boutique Bargain of the Year (and Bargain Shiraz of the Year)

Torzi Matthews Schist Rock Shiraz 2007
($17)

The only problem is that there's not much of it. It is a great wine at a great price – as good a bargain as I have seen in Australian wine over the past ten years. Loaded with flavour and style, it is the perfect red wine package. It tastes better than a lot of $35 reds. Please, get in fast – this will not last. (See page 110.)

The Big Red 'Widely Available' Bargain of the Year

Gramp's Shiraz 2005
($15.95)

It was a toss-up between this and the Jacob's Creek Reserve Shiraz 2005, two fantastic reds that you can often pick up at remarkably good prices; I am sure that a lot of other wine producers weep at this quality being sold at these prices. The 2005 Gramp's Shiraz follows on from a string of excellent releases; this one is thick with dark, chocolaty, fruit and oak flavour. (See page 52.)

The Big Red Bargain Cabernet Sauvignon of the Year

Lake Breeze Cabernet Sauvignon 2005
($22)

I guess $22 is stretching the meaning of the word bargain, but the quality of this wine certainly makes it so. It combines full-bodied deliciousness with syrupy smoothness with structural integrity – it is great red wine drinking, full stop. A worthy winner. (See page 176.)

The Big Red Super Premium Cabernet Sauvignon of the Year

Wynns Coonawarra Estate John Riddoch Cabernet Sauvignon 2005
($75)

Shiraz rules the Australian red wine roost but when you taste a wine like this, it's clear that cabernet really is king. This is the most serious of red wines in the most glorious of guises. Winemaker Sue Hodder and her winemaking and vineyard team should be incredibly proud. Bold, muscular, tannic and intense – and yet perfumed, lengthy, exotic and delicious. This wine has the lot. (See page 205.)

The Big Red Bargain Sparkling Red of the Year

Banrock Station Reserve Sparkling Shiraz NV
($12)

This is great. I mean it. It is better than many, many wines at more than twice the price. It is satisfying and sweet-fruited and massively slurpable; it should come with a money-back guarantee, because they'd never have to refund to anyone. (See page 26.)

The Big Red Pinot Noir of the Year

PHI Lusatia Park Vineyard Pinot Noir 2006
($54)

I know it's not inexpensive but in the wider world of quality pinot noir it is laughably so. I would even argue that this is an incredible bargain. It is powerful, perfumed, structured and remarkably long-flavoured – I know of a couple of French pinot noir lovers who have bought more than a dozen bottles of this, such is their excitement. Australian pinot has arrived; this is proof. (See page 144.)

The Big Red Grenache of the Year

D'Arenberg Derelict Vineyard Grenache 2006
($30)

Great grenache is an incredibly difficult achievement; D'Arenberg have done it here. They've mixed rich, varietal flavour with structure and balance, the end result is a wine that drinks wonderful young, but which will cellar gorgeously for many years; even decades. The price is extremely reasonable. (See page 219.)

The Big Red Super-Premium Sparkling Red of the Year

Castagna Genesis Sparkling Syrah 2005 ($75)

This marks a new era of Australian sparkling red. It's stylish, dry, elegant and yet profound – it's a head-turner. Expect to taste sweet dark fruit in a very dry style: perfect. I just wish there was more of it to go around; it's extremely limited. (See page 36.)

The Big Red Sweet Red of the Year

Brown Brothers Dolcetto Syrah 2007
($15.95)

The best part about my job is that it gives me the ability to make people smile, and I've made more people smile with this red over the past few months than via any others means (no matter how hard I push my line of corny jokes). I even served this to my mother-in-law with the words: 'If you don't like this, I resign.' She loved it. So do many others. It is sweet, yes, but it's zippy and fruity and affordable. Chill it lightly in winter; more heavily in summer. (See page 213.)

The Big Red 'Heart of Australia' Red of the Year

Mount Pleasant Philip Shiraz 2005
($16)

This is a special award. Australia is a great country and wines that bring its landscape to life are vitally important. This widely available red from Mount Pleasant brings both the Hunter Valley and Australian red wine to life in the most gorgeous way. Even better, it's pretty much guaranteed to appeal to all kinds of different wine tastes. This is a great vintage of a great wine; it really does bring the big red heart of Australian wine to life. (See page 77.)

The Big Red Rising Star of the Year

Vinea Marson

The days are still early at Mario Marson's Vinea Marson winery in Heathcote, but his 2006 releases announce that a star is most definitely on the rise. Over the past ten years the old hierarchy of Australian wine has been challenged (and in many cases over-thrown), and it has been because of outfits like this. Nebbiolo, syrah and sangiovese, all exquisitely flavoured. These wines will become highly sought after in a very short space of time.

The Big Red Wine of the Future Award

Innocent Bystander Sangiovese Merlot 2006
($19.95)

Australian wine has a great history of blending varieties in a unique way – our famed cabernet shiraz blends the perfect example. With so many more grape varieties available in Australia today, there is a great need to keep the experimentation going – it keeps things interesting, and you never know when a classic new style is about to be discovered. Blends of sangiovese and merlot are not new in Italy, but they largely are in Australia – and Innocent Bystander has produced a ripper. This is the savoury-sweet, easy-drinking future of Australian red wine drinking. (See page 226.)

THE TOP 100 RED WINES AT $20 OR LESS

1	Torzi Matthews Schist Rock Shiraz 2007	$17	94 pts
2	Meerea Park Shiraz 2007	$15	93 pts
3	Mount Pleasant Philip Shiraz 2005	$16	93 pts
4	Gramp's Shiraz 2005	$15.95	93 pts
5	Hoddles Creek Estate Pinot Noir 2006	$17.95	93 pts
6	Cape Mentelle Marmaduke 2005	$14	92 pts
7	Richard Hamilton Hut Block Cabernet Sauvignon 2006	$17.95	92 pts
8	Wirra Wirra Catapult Shiraz Viognier 2006	$20	92 pts
9	Curly Flat Williams Crossing Pinot Noir 2005	$20	92 pts
10	Mike Press Cabernet Sauvignon 2006	$10	92 pts
11	Howard Park Mad Fish Premium Red 2005	$18	92 pts
12	Longhop Old Vine Shiraz 2007	$15	92 pts
13	Jacob's Creek Reserve Shiraz 2005	$15.95	92 pts
14	Innocent Bystander Sangiovese Merlot 2006	$19.95	92 pts
15	Taylors Cabernet Sauvignon 2006	$18	92 pts
16	Richard Hamilton Gumprs' Shiraz 2006	$17.95	92 pts
17	Tollano Bin TR16 Shiraz 2006	$18	92 pts
18	Rockbare Shiraz 2006	$19	92 pts
19	Poacher's Ridge Vineyard Louis Block Merlot 2005	$18	92 pts
20	Tahbilk Cabernet Sauvignon 2004	$18	92 pts
21	Heartland Cabernet Sauvignon 2006	$17	92 pts
22	Maglieri Shiraz 2006	$20	92 pts
23	Izway Mates GMS 2005	$19.95	92 pts
24	Innocent Bystander Shiraz 2006	$19.95	92 pts
25	Water Wheel Shiraz 2006	$18	92 pts
26	Hardy's Oomoo Shiraz 2006	$18	92 pts
27	De Bortoli Gulf Station Pinot Noir 2006	$18	92 pts
28	Gramp's Grenache 2006	$15	92 pts
29	Campbell's Bobbie Burns Shiraz 2005	$18	92 pts
30	Alkoomi Shiraz Viognier 2005	$20	92 pts
31	Baileys of Glenrowan Shiraz 2006	$19	91 pts
32	Tim Adams Fergus 2006	$19	91 pts
33	Wynns Coonawarra Estate White Label Shiraz 2006	$19	91 pts
34	Seppelt Cabernet Sauvignon 2005	$18.95	91 pts
35	D'Arenberg Vintage Fortified Shiraz 2006	$19	91 pts
36	Picardy Merlot Cabernet Sauvignon Cabernet Franc 2005	$20	91 pts

37	Katnook Estate Founder's Block Cabernet Sauvignon 2005	$20	91 pts
38	Innocent Bystander Pinot Noir 2006	$19.95	91 pts
39	Galli Estate Tempranillo Grenache Mourvedre 2006	$19	91 pts
40	Ingoldby Cabernet Sauvignon 2004	$18	91 pts
41	Fox Gordon By George Cabernet Tempranillo 2005	$20	91 pts
42	Woodstock Shiraz 2005	$20	91 pts
43	Charles Cimicky Trumps Shiraz 2005	$18	91 pts
44	Coriole Nebbiolo Rosé 2007	$18	91 pts
45	Yalumba Y Series Shiraz Viognier 2006	$12.95	90 pts
46	Lake Breeze Bernoota Shiraz Cabernet 2005	$20	90 pts
47	Heartland Shiraz 2006	$17	90 pts
48	Woodstock Cabernet Sauvignon 2005	$20	90 pts
49	O'Leary Walker Pinot Noir 2006	$18.50	90 pts
50	Banrock Station Reserve Sparkling Shiraz NV	$12.50	90 pts
51	Taylors Eighty Acres Cabernet Shiraz Merlot 2005	$16.95	90 pts
52	Warburn Estate Premium Reserve Cabernet Merlot 2006	$9.50	90 pts
53	Seppelt Victoria Shiraz 2005	$18.95	90 pts
54	Penny's Hill Red Dot Shiraz Viognier 2006	$14	90 pts
55	Mountadam Shiraz 2006	$18	90 pts
56	Penley Estate Hyland Shiraz 2005	$19	90 pts
57	Kurtz Boundary Row Shiraz 2005	$20	90 pts
58	Penfolds Koonunga Hill Shiraz Cabernet 2005	$14.95	90 pts
59	Over the Shoulder Cabernet Merlot 2005	$18	90 pts
60	Kalleske Clarry's Red 2006	$19	90 pts
61	Metala White Label Shiraz Cabernet 2005	$19	90 pts
62	Cascabel Tempranillo 2007	$20	90 pts
63	Peter Lehmann Cabernet Sauvignon 2005	$19	90 pts
64	Hoddles Creek Estate Cabernet Sauvignon 2006	$19	90 pts
65	Fox Creek Baron Shiraz 2006	$17	90 pts
66	De Bortoli Gulf Station Shiraz Viognier 2006	$18	90 pts
67	Peter Lehmann Clancy's 2005	$17	90 pts
68	Annie's Lane Cabernet Merlot 2005	$20	90 pts
69	Xanadu Dragon Cabernet Merlot 2006	$16	90 pts
70	Angus The Bull Cabernet Sauvignon 2006	$19	90 pts
71	Balnaves of Coonawarra The Blend 2005	$19	89 pts
72	Brand's of Coonawarra Laira Cabernet Sauvignon 2004	$19	89 pts

73	Red Knot Shiraz 2006	$14.95	89 pts
74	Taylors Eighty Acres Shiraz Viognier 2005	$16.95	89 pts
75	Wine by Brad Cabernet Merlot 2005	$18	89 pts
76	Moondah Brook Shiraz 2005	$18	89 pts
77	Rutherglen Estates Durif 2006	$19.95	89 pts
78	Kangarilla Road Cabernet Sauvignon 2006	$17	89 pts
79	Riddoch Cabernet Shiraz 2004	$17	89 pts
80	Majella The Musician Cabernet Shiraz 2006	$19	89 pts
81	Reilly's Barking Mad Shiraz 2006	$13	89 pts
82	Plantagenet Omrah Shiraz 2005	$17	89 pts
83	Glaetzer Wallace Shiraz Grenache 2006	$20	89 pts
84	Langmeil Hangin' Snakes Shiraz Viognier 2006	$19.50	89 pts
85	Fox Creek Shadow's Run Shiraz Cabernet Sauvignon 2006	$12	89 pts
86	Chapel Hill Sangiovese 2005	$20	89 pts
87	Elderton Friends Cabernet Sauvignon 2005	$18	89 pts
88	Coriole Sangiovese 2006	$20	89 pts
89	Anvers Razorback Road Shiraz Cabernet Sauvignon 2005	$20	89 pts
90	Wirra Wirra Scrubby Rise Red 2006	$16.50	88 pts
91	Ravensworth Sangiovese 2006	$18.50	88 pts
92	Mike Press Shiraz 2006	$10	88 pts
93	Jacob's Creek Reserve Cabernet Sauvignon 2005	$15.95	88 pts
94	David Hook The Gorge Shiraz 2006	$18	88 pts
95	Black Chook Sparkling Shiraz	$18	88 pts
96	Angove's Long Row Cabernet Sauvignon 2006	$9.95	88 pts
97	Black Chook Shiraz Viognier 2006	$18	88 pts
98	Woodlands Cabernet Merlot 2006	$20	88 pts
99	Rosemount Diamond Label Cabernet Sauvignon 2005	$15	88 pts
100	Jim Barry Three Little Pigs Shiraz Cabernet Malbec 2004	$19	88 pts

HOW THIS BOOK WORKS

SELECTION OF WINES
All the wines reviewed in this book are here for a reason. They are here because their quality got them here, or their value, or the public interest in them, or because you just need to know about them. There's somewhere over 500 new release reviews and a similar number of reviews of back vintages – but this is by no means the extent of the wines I drink and taste each year. I never keep a proper count but I would taste somewhere between 4000 and 10,000 red wines each year, depending largely on my travel schedule (and how many colds I catch for the year). Rest assured then that if there seems to be a lot of wines scoring highly in this book, it's because they've been carefully selected.

That said, as much as possible I try not only to taste the wines that make it through to the reviewing process, but to drink them at dinner (or in front of the TV) as well. This isn't always possible but I almost never have anything less than three bottles of red open at dinner – a perk of the occupation. Wines tastes different when they're alongside a number of other wines, compared to when it's just you and the wine and your loved ones. This is partly why I'm suspicious of the results of wine shows; all the wines are being tasted in an unnatural environment, remote from the way we actually drink wine. I like to review wines in the same setting as I drink them.

THE SCORES
The written review of each wine is the best guide to whether or not you will like it; but the scores are there to help too. Don't get too hung up on the scores though. Wine is not a blood sport – it's not to be calculated, it's to be enjoyed. I am quite happy buying and drinking wines that score 85 points – if they're to my taste, and are being sold at good prices. That's a good lead-in to a basic explanation of how I score wines:

95–100
Exceptional. Money is the only deterrent to me filling my house with it. Fit for a special occasion.

91–94
Excellent. Better than excellent. Hunt out a good price, and buy up.

87–90
Very happy with the way these wines taste. Could take a wine as good as this just about anywhere.

84–86
Reasonable drinking. For a night at home or for casual quaffing. Price has to be good to tempt me to buy.

83
The cut off mark to what I'm prepared to drink. Red wine is good for you but consuming lots of alcohol isn't; it's wise to be at least a little choosy. An $8 wine that scores 83 is worth considering. A $25 wine that scores 83 is not.

0–82
OK. But life is too short to bother.

BACK VINTAGE REVIEWS
The idea of this is to give a quick idea of some prior vintages – particularly if it's a wine people are likely to cellar. My rule was that I'd give an idea in five words or less (sometimes I'd stretch to six – shhh, don't tell the editor) plus a drinking window and a score.

THE REVIEWS
There are two different ways to review a wine: to comment on its quality, or to try to describe the wine in words (this is where all the flowery 'onion cake dipped in liquefied plums' malarkey tends to slip in). The comment is the most important bit, because it lets you know whether the reviewer thinks the wine is any good or not. The description part has its role too: it's an attempt to let you make your own mind up, by describing the flavours. Does it sound like the kind of wine you enjoy? The reviews in this book try to cover both ways of reviewing. You'll also notice a couple of other little signposts:

**THE DRINKING WINDOW
(eg DRINK 2008–2012)**
This is an indication of the best years in which to drink the wine. It's a calculated guesstimate.

THE VALUE RATING ◆
This is an assessment of the quality versus the price. Logically, less expensive wines have a better chance of gaining the maximum five stars, but in a world where some wines cost more than $1000 per bottle, an awesome wine at $50 can still be judged as a bargain. Anything from three stars and above is good buying.

THE AUCTION RATING ★
This is an acknowledgement that wine (particularly internet-based) auction houses are booming. It also acknowledges that a lot of people have an interest in wine investment. Most wines either rarely appear at auction, or are too new to the market to have yet appeared. These wines are simply denoted as N/A.

The higher number of stars, the better the wine is likely to perform at wine auction. Three stars or above means there is a very good chance that the wine will either hold its value or increase in value (if it was to appear later at auction).

As with all auction results: nothing is guaranteed. These ratings are purely indicative only.

CAMPBELL'S CHOICES
OK, I confess – this is an admission that for all the words, scores and ravings, sometimes the absolute best recommendation is a simple thumbs up, 'nuff said'. These choices are personal; they're simply the reds I'll be picking up the next time I'm in the bottleshop, or scanning the restaurant wine list.

THE BIG RED WINE BOOK AWARDS

This year's award-winning wines, as shown on pages 10 to 13, are highlighted throughout the book.

SHIRAZ

Shiraz is the lovechild of all Aussie red wine drinkers. It's cuddly, intense, plump with fruity flavour and if you want to drink, rather than think, it is the wine to grab every time. But it's more than that, too. One of the extraordinary things about shiraz is that it's the grape they make Penfolds Grange with (in all its huge, silky magnificence) and the wine they also use to make spicy, almost pinot noir–like wines in the cooler regions of Victoria – and New Zealand too. You name the style of red you like, and shiraz can do it successfully. No wonder we love it so much.

TOP TEN OF THE YEAR
1. Mount Langi Ghiran Langi Shiraz 2005
2. Penfolds RWT Barossa Shiraz 2005
3. Castagna Genesis Syrah 2005
4. Clonakilla Shiraz Viognier 2007
5. Giaconda Warner's Vineyard Shiraz 2005
6. Shaw and Smith Shiraz 2006
7. Tyrrell's Four Acres Shiraz 2007
8. Tahbilk Reserve Shiraz 2002
9. Penfolds St Henri Shiraz 2004
10. Meerea Park Hell Hole Shiraz 2006

Alkoomi Jarrah Shiraz 2003

The Frankland River region of Western Australia is a beautiful place to grow shiraz grapes. Alkoomi grows some of the region's oldest vines.

2003 RELEASE
It's the tannin structure that I have a problem with here. It's tough and drying, with flavours of hung game wafting through more attractive notes of blueberry and five-spice. The fruit flavours are excellent, the flow through the finish not so good. **DRINK** 2009–2013.

Price	$35
Region	Frankland River
Value	♦♦
Auction	★★★
Score	87

Alkoomi Shiraz Viognier 2005

A few years ago the odd winemaker predicted that shiraz viognier blends would stop being quirky one-offs and would fast become a 'category' of wine, *á la* sparkling wine or fortified. The prediction was reality in the blink of an eye.

2005 RELEASE
Worthy of serious consideration. Flooded with pure, polished, blackberried flavour, jaunts of black pepper and five-spice keeping its savoury edge keen. Chewy, plummy, fruity tannins too. The viognier seems here to heighten aroma and little else – thankfully. Beautiful. **DRINK** 2008–2014.

Price	$20
Region	Frankland River
Value	♦♦♦♦♦
Auction	N/A
Score	92

Allira Shiraz 2006

The Strathbogie Ranges are on the north-east side of Central Victoria. It's not one of the sexiest places in Australian wine, but grapes from the region are used in brands far and wide; it's good dirt for wine.

2006 RELEASE
Good quaffer. Good amount of chewy, plummy fruit, matched to ripe, clean, chewy tannins. Overt eucalypt flavour too. **DRINK** 2008–2009.

Price	$13
Region	Strathbogie Ranges
Value	♦♦♦
Auction	N/A
Score	84

Amberley Shiraz Viognier 2005

Quality has shot up over recent years, though the wines are generally on the sweet side – even the reds. The bottles are very nicely packaged.

2005 RELEASE
Real crowd-pleaser. Silken and soft, fragrant and sweet, the viognier sliding all over the cherry-cola flavours of the shiraz. Indeed, I thought the sweet, apricot-like viognier influence was a bit much, but when I served it at dinner the assembled throng raved. I love it when that happens.
DRINK 2008–2009.

Price	$18
Region	Margaret River
Value	♦♦♦♦
Auction	★★
Score	87

Andrew Thomas Kiss Shiraz 2006

The idea here is that you pronounce shiraz as 'shirahhhz', as in kiss shirahhhz. The wine itself, though, is no joke – over the past few years it has proven itself to be among the best shiraz wines in Australia.

2006 RELEASE
Andrew Thomas manages to get a lot of rich, sumptuous, seductive oak into his wines, without them seeming overdone. This is a great example. It's rich with spicy, creamy oak, and yet the medium-bodied, cherry-like fruit has mopped it up and taken it in its stride. Minerals, earth, lavender – there's a bit going on here. This is terrific. Drink it young, or drink it at eight years plus (from vintage).
DRINK 2008–2018.

PREVIOUS
2003 Medium-weight, savoury-sweet style. 2007–2015. 94 pts.
2004 Oak-driven, gamey, medium-weight. 2007–2014. 92 pts.
2005 Classic Hunter red. 2012–2020. 96 pts.

Price	$48
Region	Hunter Valley
Value	♦♦♦♦
Auction	N/A
Score	94

Andrew Thomas Sweetwater Shiraz 2006

Andrew Thomas specialises in Hunter Valley shiraz and semillon – the region's two wine stars. No wasting anyone's time – just the best. It's a lead others should take.

2006 RELEASE
Medium-bodied styles like this cellar like a charm; I can guarantee that this one will too. Mind, it's a super drink right now, ripped with such sweet-savouriness that you can't help diving back for more. It's wines like this that make my job such fun. **DRINK** 2008–2016.

Price	$28
Region	Hunter Valley
Value	♦♦♦♦
Auction	N/A
Score	93

Angove's Long Row Shiraz 2006

There are times when I think that the days of good quality, sub-$10 red wines are over; these Angove's wines prove that they are not.

2006 RELEASE
There's a nice amount of musky, vanillin oak here, enough to keep this red berried, minty shiraz in glossy style. There's a swagger of fine soft tannin too, keeping it in shape, and while there's some stalky bitterness on the finish the overall flavours are excellent, and the value high.
DRINK 2008–2009.

Price	$9.95
Region	South Australia
Value	♦♦♦♦
Auction	N/A
Score	86

Annie's Lane Shiraz 2006

I'm a firm believer that the Clare Valley is better at cabernet and blends than it is at shiraz; here's another example.

2006 RELEASE
Presents itself nicely without wowing you. Firm tannins, medium-weight plummy flavour, eucalyptus-like accents and a satisfying finish. Its alcohol shows in a warm afterburn, and while it's good quaffing it generally fails to excite – or not at twenty bucks anyway. On discount I might change my mind. **DRINK** 2008–2012.

Price	$20
Region	Clare Valley
Value	♦♦♦♦
Auction	★★
Score	86

Anvers Shiraz 2005

This is made from grapes grown in the Willunga sub-region of McLaren Vale. It was matured in American oak, but only ten per cent of that oak was new. Nine hundred and fifty dozen were made.

2005 RELEASE
Close to the groove. It tastes of raisins, tar, malt and porty blackberry, the acidity high and a little jarring for what is a ripe, chocolaty, full-bodied style. It finishes warm but not too warm, its tannins ripe and mouth-filling.
DRINK 2008–2012.

Price	$28
Region	McLaren Vale
Value	♦♦♦
Auction	N/A
Score	88

Baileys of Glenrowan 1904 Block Shiraz 2004

There's an element of rarity factored into the price of this wine – there aren't a lot of vines in the 1904 Block, and you can't go back in history and plant more. I routinely prefer the (cheaper) 1920s Block shiraz.

2004 RELEASE
I've seen some good reviews of this (yes, I do look) but I reckon it lacks X-factor. It tastes old-fashioned, leathery, blackberried and coffeed, the freshness of it already starting to feel lost. Mind, there's a good amount of flavour, and it finishes soundly. **DRINK** 2010–2016.

Price	$52.95
Region	Glenrowan
Value	♦ ♦
Auction	★ ★ ★
Score	89

Baileys of Glenrowan 1920s Block Shiraz 2006

Baileys is one of north-east Victoria's most important wineries. It's a large estate planted with 100 per cent red wine grape varieties. Talk about a winery after my own heart. They have also started maturing this partly in French oak – a great move.

2006 RELEASE
It tastes lovely. It's plush with dark fruit flavour, iodine, blackberry, hay and mint swishing about with coconut and cedarwood oak flavour. Flavours of aniseed hang about the edges, and it's then terrifically structured and succulent through the finish. Love it. **DRINK** 2012–2020.

Price	$31.95
Region	Glenrowan
Value	♦ ♦ ♦ ♦
Auction	★ ★ ★
Score	94

Baileys of Glenrowan Shiraz 2006

Baileys have lightened off on the tannin for this wine, making it less of a 'baby version of the 1920s Block Shiraz', and more of an everyday drinker. The strategy has worked nicely here.

2006 RELEASE
Lap this one up! It's tremendous value. This is a sign of a more robust, more attractive Baileys of Glenrowan – maybe even the start of a new era for the historic old war horse. Pretty floral aromatics, flavours of blackberry, violets and minerals, toasty oak and a fruity, chalky, punchy finish. Lovely mouthful of fragrance and flavour. **DRINK** 2008–2011.

Price	$19
Region	Glenrowan
Value	♦ ♦ ♦ ♦ ♦
Auction	★ ★ ★
Score	91

Balgownie White Label Shiraz 2005

Central Victoria is renowned for its shiraz, but Balgownie's rarely reaches the highs of its cabernet sauvignon. For me, it's a highly enjoyable wine, but for earlier consumption.

2005 RELEASE
Good currunty, minty, vanillin flavour, but a little on the stinky side, and lacking the structure to really get me excited. Good, but ho-hum. Given an hour or two in the decanter (which it needs), rounds of plummy, peppery flavour sally forth, making for a satisfying drink.
DRINK 2008–2013.

PREVIOUS
2000 Coffeed, sweet, lovely. 2006–2010. 90 pts.
2001 Floral, soft, gluggable. 2004–2010. 90 pts.
2002 Jammy, dark, luscious. 2009–2014. 92 pts.
2003 Musky, floral, beautiful. 2005–2010. 90 pts.
2004 Savoury, gamey, earthy. 2006–2012. 89 pts.

Price	$31
Region	Bendigo
Value	♦ ♦
Auction	★ ★
Score	87

Balnaves of Coonawarra Shiraz 2005

I used to say that I wasn't much of a fan of Coonawarra shiraz (despite the copious amounts of Wynns White Label shiraz I've drunk over the years). Balnaves and Majella have made me see the truth.

2005 RELEASE
I loved the 2004 release but, admittedly, it was quite high in alcohol. This sheds that issue and maintains the joy, here conveyed along a deep channel of spicy, meaty, cherry-plummed deliciousness. There are even some notes of smooth, fleshy mulberry in there – no wonder I kept drinking and drinking it. This is a stellar drink.
DRINK 2008–2014.

Price	$24
Region	Coonawarra
Value	♦ ♦ ♦ ♦ ♦
Auction	N/A
Score	93

Bannockburn Range Shiraz 2005

Geelong might be known for its pinot noir (rightly so) but as with the Yarra Valley, its future will have as many good shiraz wines as pinot noirs.

2005 RELEASE
Should I be worried about the bitterness in the aftertaste? For the most part this is an expansive, impressive wine, full of complexity and interest, blackberried fruit flavour and stylish notes of cedarwood, ash, stalks and cherries. The bitterness does, however, put a question mark next to the wine. **DRINK** 2011–2018.

Price	$65
Region	Geelong
Value	♦♦♦
Auction	★★★
Score	90

Banrock Station Reserve Sparkling Shiraz NV

Seppelt might rule the sparkling red roost, but for bargain sparkling red drinking this Banrock is impossible to beat.

NV RELEASE
It's a mighty good drop – every time I look at a bottle I can't help imagining that it's saying 'come hither' to me. It offers a fluffy, sweet-centred, generous rush of flavour – redcurrant, chocolate and mulberry mostly, though there might even be a splash of dried herbs too. Really, the individual flavours aren't the thing here; it's about the smooth texture, the oomph, and its fabulous value. **DRINK** 2008–2010.

Price	$12.50
Region	South Australia
Value	♦♦♦♦♦
Auction	N/A
Score	90

Barossa Old Vine Company Shiraz 2003 & 2004

Produced off vines that are now 100 years old. Matured in mostly French oak. Made by the Barossa's Langmeil winery.

2003 RELEASE
I'd never heard of it either – but I've now drunk two bottles of this and I still can't fathom the price tag. Developed, warm leathery flavours meet coffeed oak, its black dense fruit still both evident and abundant. Alcohol sticks out. Finish is awash with spirity, menthol-like flavours. **DRINK** 2009–2015.

2004 RELEASE
Much better. Fresh, groomed flavours of black coal and blackberry, its cedary, toasty oak flavours almost completely melted into the thick dark swathe of the wine. This is an intense, inky beast, as bold as it is black and beautiful. **DRINK** 2013–2022.

Price	$100
Region	Barossa
Value	♦♦
Auction	★★
Score	88 (2003)
	94 (2004)

Battely Syrah 2005

The Battely property was once known as the Brown Brothers Everton vineyard (back in the early 1980s). It had a very high reputation. The property was lost to vines for nearly a decade, but Russell Bourne has revitalised it, and is now producing extremely high quality wine from it.

2005 RELEASE
Packed with sweet fruit flavour – aniseed, raspberry, blueberry – but lifted to higher realms by exotic notes of graphite, cedar and toast. Brightness and oomph galore. Fruity, ripe, flavoursome tannins. Really, it's just a beautiful wine. **DRINK** 2008–2015.

PREVIOUS
2002 Complex mix of herbs and ripeness. 2006–2014. 91 pts.
2003 Warm, pruney, complex. 2007–2011. 88 pts.
2004 Bright, bold, stylish. 2007–2018. 96 pts.

Price	$52
Region	Beechworth
Value	♦♦♦♦
Auction	★★★
Score	93

Battle of Bosworth Shiraz 2005

They deliberately raisin a small amount of the grapes for this wine, in an effort to build both softer texture and greater weight. It works, to a degree.

2005 RELEASE
I like the wine. It's rich and sweet and earthy, chocked with warm dark flavour, and clean and dry on the finish. I could easily have opted for higher marks, except that for me it lacked complexity. Am I asking too much of it? Maybe. It sure would drink great with a meaty chunk of pie.

Price	$25
Region	McLaren Vale
Value	♦♦♦♦
Auction	★★★
Score	88

Bilancia La Collina Syrah 2005

This wine is very hard (read: impossible) to track down, and even if you did find some you might find that the price is even higher than $90. Its quality though, is simply compelling.

2005 RELEASE
The kind of wine you take one swig of and say: I don't care what it costs, I want some (and then cry into your credit card later). It smells spicy, perfumed, like a field of flowers, like bright, ripe cherries, blackcurrant, and wood smoke. You drink it, and every detail of it is in sharp relief, like you've just been handed a more powerful lens. It's that good. **DRINK** 2011–2019.

Price	$90
Region	Hawke's Bay, NZ
Value	♦♦♦♦♦
Auction	★★★
Score	96

Black Chook Shiraz Viognier 2006

Black Chook is a collaboration between celebrated winemaker Ben Riggs and the Penny's Hill winery in McLaren Vale. They're certainly putting out some decent juice.

2006 RELEASE
Drink it young, and drink it well. It's tarry and licoricey and strong, its robust flavour punching to all corners of your mouth. Malty oak completes the show, and while it's hardly an exercise in either elegance or finesse, there's lots of good, sweet-centred black-coloured fun here.
DRINK 2008–2011.

Price	$18
Region	South Australia
Value	♦♦♦♦
Auction	N/A
Score	88

Black Chook Sparkling Shiraz NV

There was a time when a whole host of sparkling reds appeared on the market but in recent years activity has slowed down. Great then to see this excellent drop crop up.

NV RELEASE
Yes! This is a great new introduction to the affordable sparkling red ranks. Bless its soul. It's clean, sweet, medium-bodied and fresh, its fruitiness dark and earthy. Neat price too. **DRINK** 2008–2010.

Price	$18
Region	McLaren Vale
Value	♦♦♦♦
Auction	N/A
Score	88

Blackjack Block 6 Shiraz 2005

A couple of years ago the folks at Blackjack noticed that Block 6 of their vineyard produces different flavours to the rest of the vineyards. They then decided to bottle it separately – a great move.

2005 RELEASE
It's such a lively, flavoursome wine that it's almost impossible not to like it. Full vibrant acidity, silken plums, mint, chocolate and pepper, the spiciness of it very much second fiddle to the pure rich darkness of it. A bottle of this with roast meat before settling in to watch the footy – the word 'schtonking!' comes to mind. **DRINK** 2008–2015.

Price	$35
Region	Bendigo
Value	♦♦♦♦
Auction	★★★
Score	93

Blackjack Major's Line Shiraz 2005

The 2004 was the first release and it was a beauty too. It's made from grapes grown on a neighbouring property to Blackjack itself. It's a wine to hunt down.

2005 RELEASE
The Blackjack boys have really hit their straps. This is noice, different, unusual – and deadset yum. Spicy, savoury, minty, peppery and plummy, the whole lot clubbed into a seductive package. **DRINK** 2008–2015.

Price	$25
Region	Bendigo
Value	♦♦♦♦♦
Auction	N/A
Score	93

Blackjack Shiraz 2005

Blackjack has hit the mark in recent years, though for some reason I often prefer the new shiraz wines in its portfolio – Major's Line and Block 6.

2005 RELEASE
It's a good wine but I have a problem with it. My issue is with the oak, which is slick and custardy and much like coconut oil – it got me wondering what this would be like as a face pack. However, it is ripped with smooth, plummy, intense shiraz flavour, and if that slippery-sweet oak can melt into the wine over time, it could deserve a far higher rating. **DRINK** 2009–2016.

PREVIOUS
2002 Stylish blackberry and plum fruitiness. 2005–2012. 91 pts.
2003 Loud with forceful fruit flavour. 2005–2011. 90 pts.
2004 Firm, plummy, minty and bold. 2010–2016. 93 pts.

Price	$35
Region	Bendigo
Value	♦♦♦
Auction	★★★
Score	88

Bleasdale Sparkling Shiraz NV

I vaguely recall a time when the thought of bubbles in red wine repulsed me. These days I can barely get enough of this uniquely Australian style.

NV RELEASE
I guess it's not brilliant quality but the value just gets me excited. This is fun drinking, no doubt. It tastes a bit like liquid black forest cake, its boysenberry and blackcurrant flavour aided by gently creamy oak. There's a slight hint of mint too. It really is bonza drinking. **DRINK** 2008–2009.

Price	$17.50
Region	Langhorne Creek
Value	♦♦♦♦
Auction	N/A
Score	86

Bowen Estate Shiraz 2005

Bowen Estate is still a favourite of red wine drinkers and rightly so; it's an honest outfit of full-flavoured wines. Quality seems more variable than it once did though.

2005 RELEASE
Here's an example of where Bowen Estate seems to be having problems. It is capable of making super shiraz, but while this release is sound and attractive, it simply lacks the quality it once had. This tastes of blackberry, pepper, meat, smoky French oak and raspberries, the soft easiness of it difficult to resist. As a drink, it's good. As a quality statement, maybe not so. **DRINK** 2008–2013.

PREVIOUS
1995 Excellent result from a difficult vintage. 1998–2006. 90 pts.
1996 Lacks ripeness. 1999–2004. 85 pts.
1997 Stylish flavour and nutty oak. 2000–2009. 91 pts.
1998 Rich, blackberried, spicy fruit force. 2001–2012. 94 pts.
1999 Rich, perfumed, gamey. 2002–2009. 87 pts.
2000 Fat plummy flavours; lacks structure. 2003–2007. 88 pts.
2001 Good drink but lacks substance. 2005–2010. 93 pts.
2002 Green and unpleasant. 2005–2009. 82 pts.
2003 Awkward but interesting. 2006–2012. 88 pts.
2004 Savoury, gamey, currenty and good. 2009–2015. 90 pts.

Price	$29
Region	Coonawarra
Value	♦♦♦
Auction	★★★
Score	88

Bremerton Old Adam Shiraz 2004

This wine has garnered some high praise and while I love drinking it too, I'm not sure it's quite as good as the hype. That said, if you see some, grab it!

2004 RELEASE
Even though it's super premium wine this is essentially ready for drinking now too. It's already showing the first signs of development, with leathery flavours giving a lovely mellowness to the heavier rush of kirsch and coffee-like flavour. What the wine is really about though is its ultra-smooth texture, which itself makes you want to suck on this wine for hours. This wine is as soft through the mouth as any wine you will ever come across. **DRINK** 2008–2013.

Price	$40
Region	Langhorne Creek
Value	♦♦♦♦
Auction	★★★★★
Score	93

Bremerton Selkirk Shiraz 2005

Langhorne Creek's ability to produce well-priced reds is rivalled only by McLaren Vale in Australian wine today. Bremerton is a Langhorne Creek leading light.

2005 RELEASE
I guess this will cellar but if you don't drink it in the short-ish term you're mad. It's just so malty and smooth and satisfying as a young wine. It's all about sweet, coffeed oak on currany, plummy fruit flavour, the impact of it full of satisfaction. **DRINK** 2008–2010.

Price	$22
Region	Langhorne Creek
Value	♦♦♦♦
Auction	★★★
Score	89

Bridgewater Mill Shiraz 2005

Sudden demand for Adelaide Hills grapes is putting pressure on the price of the wines. This really should be under $20.

2005 RELEASE
They've backed a truckload of oak up to this, and it's not done the wine any favours. That said, it's quite a yummy wine. Flavours of toast, dark chocolate, raspberries and sour cherries, the tannin structure firm and bunchy. There's a bitterness on the finish that concerns me though. **DRINK** 2008–2011.

Price	$24.95
Region	Adelaide Hills
Value	♦♦
Auction	N/A
Score	87

Brini Blewitt Springs Shiraz 2004

John Brini has supplied grapes to well-known wine brands for years. This is his own label and the grapes are clearly good quality.

2004 RELEASE
Straightforward, plush, ripe shiraz of weight and impact. Flooded with blackberry jam-like fruit flavour and vanillin oak. It's simple, but effective. **DRINK** 2008–2011.

Price	$18
Region	McLaren Vale
Value	♦♦♦♦
Auction	N/A
Score	87

Brokenwood Graveyard Shiraz 2005

The asking price is more of a statement in favour of the Hunter Valley than a realistic sign of the wine's quality, but it no doubt can be an excellent wine.

Price	$100
Region	Hunter Valley
Value	♦♦♦
Auction	★★★
Score	95

2005 RELEASE
Four hail storms hit the vineyard through the 2005 growing season, plus four days over 40° Celsius, plus a dump of 132 mm on 20 February. It's tough growing grapes in the Hunter, and then out pops a wine like this? It's a bright, clovey, musky wine underpinned by vibrant, blackberried, plummy fruit. Look hard and you notice black pepper and beef stock too, but the real thing is the wine's length, which is sound and clear. Top-notch Hunter, no doubt. **DRINK** 2012–2018.

PREVIOUS
1995 Light, gamey, bitter. 2001–2007. 83 pts.
1996 Sweet, developed, lovely drinking. 2004 2011. 89 pts.
1997 Gamey, plummy, tannic and bitter. 2005–2010. 86 pts.
1998 Too much oak, but excellent. 2009–2018. 92 pts.
1999 Gorgeous, medium-bodied, savoury classic. 2008–2014. 95 pts.
2000 Bold, balanced power. 2010–2025. 96 pts.
2001 Dry and tough. 2008–2013. 87 pts.
2002 Ripe, sweet, oaky. 2011–2016. 90 pts.
2003 Surging, fruity, lengthy. 2011–2025. 93 pts.
2004 Balanced and stylish. 2011–2020. 94 pts.

Brokenwood Shiraz 2005

A lot of the time the 'normal' wine in a winery's range is as good or better than the flagship, particularly if the main difference between the two is simply an increase in new oak flavour. This isn't a case of that, but it comes mighty close to Graveyard quality.

Price	$35
Region	Hunter Valley
Value	♦♦♦
Auction	★★★
Score	93

2005 RELEASE
This is one of those pure, perfumed, medium-weight wines that may not win in the intensity stakes but sure holds its head high on the grounds of drinkability. It will cellar like a charm too. It smells of Turkish delight, plums, musk and earth, the tastes following straight on. It's not an ego-driven wine, it's a wine of the land. Full credit. **DRINK** 2008–2017.

Burge Family Winemakers Draycott Shiraz 2005

Rick Burge is one of Australia's deepest wine thinkers; he is simply a fascinating man. His Draycott shiraz is technically his flagship wine, though I often prefer the blends – as I did here.

2005 RELEASE
Nice wine but it wanes and dries out through the finish, robbing it of a sense of true quality. While the flavour lasts it's rich with both cherried, blackberried flavour and savoury, earthy notes, the appeal of it strong, if not lingering. French oak has been cleverly applied, and its medium-weight profile does not lack appeal.
DRINK 2008–2013.

PREVIOUS
2000 Lacks power. 2005–2010. 88 pts.
2001 Intense but balanced. 2005–2012. 94 pts.
2002 Not made.
2003 Deep, complex and generous. 2006–2011. 92 pts.
2004 Gamey, licoricey, blackberried and powerful. 2007–2015. 92 pts.

Price	$36
Region	Barossa
Value	♦ ♦ ♦
Auction	★ ★ ★ ★
Score	88

By Farr Shiraz 2005

I can never remember whether this should be called By Farr Shiraz or Shiraz by Farr. In any case, these are the wines of former Bannockburn winemaker Gary Farr.

2005 RELEASE
A riot of aroma. Spice, cherries, pepper, dandelions, cedary oak – it's all happening here. It looks cloudy in the glass too, the ultimate sign of a 'natural' wine. Expect the unexpected, and be ready to be challenged. Long, sweet, porty length. Oddball but exciting. Drink 2011–2016.

PREVIOUS
1999 Balanced, meaty, persistent. 2006–2011. 91 pts.
2000 Salty, funky, cherried. 2006–2009. 85 pts.
2001 Stalky, savoury, gamey. 2006–2011. 88 pts.
2002 Gamey, drying out. 2006–2011. 88 pts.
2003 Funky, minerally, drying. 2005–2008. 84 pts.
2004 Tannic, smoky, spicy. 2007–2012. 91 pts.

Price	$55
Region	Geelong
Value	♦ ♦ ♦ ♦
Auction	★ ★ ★
Score	94

Campbells Bobbie Burns Shiraz 2004 & 2005

Family company Campbells has been producing great quality shiraz from its Rutherglen property for years, and over the past couple seems to have ramped the quality up a notch. The two releases below are excellent, and a sneak preview of the 2006 (92 points) showed a fuller, richer wine of enormous promise. This is becoming a no-brainer buy.

Price	**$18**
Region	**Rutherglen**
Value	●●●●●
Auction	★★★
Score	90 (2004) 92 (2005)

2004 RELEASE
Great stuff. Balanced, ripe, easy-to-drink but with enough stuffing to keep you interested, and satisfied, all the way to the bottom of the bottle. It tastes of ripe, liqueured raspberries and dark plums, whispers of iodine, saltbush and cedar lingering about the edges. Kudos to Campbells. **DRINK** 2008–2013.

2005 RELEASE
I love the mix of sweet, sun-ripened raspberries and tarry, heavy dark flavour here, the bulk of it tempered by minerally, inky, textural tannin. Stew on it, or gulp it – it's great both ways. **DRINK** 2009–2015.

Cape Mentelle Marmaduke 2005

This is the only red wine in the Cape Mentelle range that isn't grown in Margaret River; but it is made from grapes grown in Western Australia. The quality has been rising steadily, and this is a beauty.

Price	**$14**
Region	**Western Australia**
Value	●●●●●
Auction	**N/A**
Score	**92**

2005 RELEASE
This is almost impossible to beat in the ready-to-drink style. It's so generous, fruity, dark and handsome that one sip and you start wondering how they can sell it so cheap – but who cares! It tastes of raspberries, boysenberries, dates and plums, a lick of vanillin oak adding a delicious smoothness. It had me going back for more! **DRINK** 2008–2010.

Cape Mentelle Shiraz 2005

Shiraz isn't supposed to be Margaret River's bag, but I'm often quite a fan, particularly when elegance is the call rather than brute force (which, when I want it, I get from the Barossa and McLaren Vale). Cape Mentelle generally makes a better fist of Margaret River shiraz than just about anyone.

Price	$36
Region	Margaret River
Value	♦ ♦
Auction	★ ★ ★
Score	92

2005 RELEASE
I was surprised by the level of oak here – it goes against the wine's essentially savoury, nutty, elegant style – but it still manages to be fresh, minty, aniseedy and attractive, vague briary/herbal notes noticeable, but not distracting. Tannins are a little too rigid, but given a few years in a cool, dark place it should mellow and soften into something savoury and nice. **DRINK** 2011–2016.

PREVIOUS
2000 Good, earthy, blackberried wine. 2003–2008. 88 pts.
2001 Gamey and metallic. 2003–2007. 85 pts.
2002 Exotic spice and sweet fruit. 2006–2013. 91 pts.
2003 Long-termer. Complex, spicy, good. 2006–2013. 92 pts.
2004 Very ripe, very peppery, very stylish. 2006–2016. 93 pts.

Carlei Green Vineyards Shiraz 2004

Over the past fifteen years a strong assumption has grown that Heathcote is a great place for shiraz – and red wine in general. A ten-year drought has brought the assumption into question: if it's such a great region, where are all the great wines?

Price	$26
Region	Heathcote
Value	♦ ♦ ♦
Auction	★ ★ ★
Score	92

2004 RELEASE
Strong smell and taste of eucalyptus but once you move through that there's a fantastic flush of rich, ripe fruit flavour, every ounce of it texturally smooth and cuddly. Plums, toast, cedar and clove-like flavours, framed by ripe, dry, finely formed tannins. **DRINK** 2008–2014.

Castagna Genesis Sparkling Syrah 2005

The sparkling red market has stagnated in recent times; in part due to uninspiring sales, and in part due to uninspiring wines. This new wine though, goes straight to the top of the Australian sparkling red tree.

2005 RELEASE
It's rare that top quality shiraz is used to make sparkling shiraz; even rarer that the top quality shiraz used has come from a coolish climate. This wine shows the way forward for sparkling shiraz. It's spicy, ripe, dry, has structure and elegance and – essential for a sparkling red – sex appeal. The thing that sets this apart is that it combines spicy complexity with dry, structured elegance with ripe fruit appeal. **DRINK** 2010–2017.

Price	$75
Region	Beechworth
Value	●●●●●
Auction	N/A
Score	96

Castagna Genesis Syrah 2005

Castagna is a biodynamic estate in north-east Victoria. Its wines are always interesting, and always very high quality. First vintage was 1998. The Genesis Syrah routinely includes a small dash of viognier.

2005 RELEASE
The best Genesis syrah yet released. It's a pearler. I just love the proportion of it: the way it slings to all corners of the mouth, washing flavours of kirsch, smoke, chocolate, concentrated blackberry/blueberry and warm summer cherries. Ropes of tannin keep it firm. Drinking it is an exercise in both indulgence and elegance. There are some who believe that this wine is as good as any syrah/shiraz wine ever made in this country. **DRINK** 2011–2022.

Price	$75
Region	Beechworth
Value	●●●●
Auction	★★★
Score	97

PREVIOUS
1998 Sweet and leathery. 2002–2008. 89 pts.
1999 Peppery, meaty, elegant. 2004–2010. 89 pts.
2000 Structured, spicy, long. 2006–2011. 90 pts.
2001 Complex yet balanced. 2006–2012. 94 pts.
2002 Pretty, powerful, persistent. 2006–2014. 95 pts.
2004 Simply gorgeous. 2007–2016. 95 pts.

Chapel Hill Shiraz 2005

2005 RELEASE
Had to take off my glasses and put my feet on the desk after taking a swig of this. It's so perfectly in the groove, so absolutely what I want to see in a hearty McLaren Vale red. It's smooth, substantial, savoury-sweet and brilliantly long through the finish. Coffee beans, blackberry, classy hazelnut-like oak and impeccable balance. Yes! **DRINK** 2008–2020.

Price	$25
Region	McLaren Vale
Value	♦♦♦♦♦
Auction	★★★
Score	95

Charles Cimicky Trumps Shiraz 2005

Charles Cimicky winery is a quiet achiever. It often produces very good wines, some of them at super good prices. Yet you rarely hear much about them. If you see some of this lying around, grab it.

2005 RELEASE
We're getting into serious red territory here, even though Cimicky produces shiraz wines at far higher prices. This, though, has a force of sweet dark fruit flavour, the strike of it pure and delicious. Coal, toast, blackberry jam, cedary oak, coffee beans – you get the picture. Basically, it's the kind of red you imagine when you think about Barossa shiraz. Intensely flavoured and intensely yum, at an intensely nifty price. **DRINK** 2008–2013.

Price	$18
Region	Barossa
Value	♦♦♦♦♦
Auction	★★★
Score	91

Charles Melton Shiraz 2005

If you ever visit the Barossa search out the Charles Melton cellar door. It's small, charming and personal – it's what makes a cellar door visit worthwhile.

2005 RELEASE
No problems with this one. It's an excellent example of what the Barossa Valley does best: soft and charming and yet rich with dark fruit flavour, the profile of loamy, blackberried, plummy cedary flavour delicious to the last drop. Watch for the tannins on this wine: they are beautifully ripe and sophisticated. My only reservation – and it's a minor one – is that the alcohol shows a touch too keenly as it finishes. **DRINK** 2012–2028.

PREVIOUS
1995 Beautifully balanced. Star of the vintage. 1999–2006. 90 pts.
1996 Moderate oak, medium-weight flavour. 2002–2007. 91 pts.
1997 Blackberried, plummy, savoury finish. 2005 2010. 88 pts.
1998 Rich fruit, savoury style, chewy finish. 2003–2008. 92 pts.
1999 Nice oak, nice fruit, good length. 2007–2012. 92 pts.
2000 Medium-weight, sweet and savoury. 2003–2007. 87 pts.
2001 Fresh leather, red berries, easy-going. 2005–2010. 91 pts.
2002 Brooding and intense, but elegant. 2006–2014. 94 pts.
2003 Perfumed, soft, plummy and easy. 2006–2010. 89 pts.
2004 Brooding, intense, jammy beauty. 2007–2016. 93 pts.

Price	$41.50
Region	Barossa
Value	♦♦♦♦♦
Auction	★★★
Score	93

Chatto Shiraz 2005

Jim Chatto is a gun winemaker plying his trade principally in the Hunter Valley – though he buys grapes from other regions too at times (principally pinot noir from Tasmania). He invariably turns them into distinctive wines.

2005 RELEASE
It really needs an hour in the decanter to show its best. Before then it's clouded with unpleasant farmyard aromas; given some air they dissipate and reveal a delightful wine. It tastes of plums, earth, undergrowth and cedarwood, and it should cellar well. **DRINK** 2011–2018.

Price	$40
Region	Hunter Valley
Value	♦♦♦
Auction	★★
Score	88

Clonakilla Shiraz 2006

This is not the top-of-the-range model, and indeed it's not from the Clonakilla home vineyard. It's made from grapes bought from the Hilltops region of New South Wales, and it offers fantastic buying.

2006 RELEASE
Unusually minty – not a flavour I've noticed in this label before – but it gets away with it. It's satiny, floral and swishly fruited, the palate round, medium-weight, and just damn delicious. Poised, balanced, smooth-textured value.
DRINK 2008–2015.

Price	$25
Region	Hilltops
Value	♦♦♦♦
Auction	★★★
Score	90

Clonakilla Shiraz Viognier 2006 & 2007

The rise in status of this wine over the past ten years has been phenomenal. It is now a contender for the mantle of 'Australia's best red wine'.

2006 RELEASE
Another wonderful release. Just look at the frame of it: it's steely, smoky, struck with gunmetal-like tannins and yet still comes across as both shapely and sophisticated. It's musky, floral, sweet-fruited and raw, the mix of blackberries and cherries as pure as the sky is blue.
DRINK 2014–2023.

2007 RELEASE
Frosts devastated the season so there will be precious little of this. The quality though is stunning. Waves of flavour: cherries, stalks, plums, black pepper, wood smoke and cedar. Divine. **DRINK** 2009–2025.

Price	$75
Region	Canberra District
Value	♦♦♦♦
Auction	★★★★★
Score	95 (2006) 97 (2007)

PREVIOUS
- **1996** Savoury and developed. 2002–2006. 90 pts.
- **1997** Peppery, tannic, complex. 2006–2012. 88 pts.
- **1998** Complexity galore. 2009–2017. 93 pts.
- **1999** Green, stemmy, peppery. 2007–2013. 87 pts.
- **2000** Tastes of tomatoes and smoke. 2009–2016. 86 pts.
- **2001** Blueberried, cherried, beautiful. Modern classic. 2012–2022. 96 pts.
- **2002** Gorgeously fragrant and lengthy. 2012–2020. 94 pts.
- **2003** Slippery-smooth, spicy and long. 2013–2022. 95 pts.
- **2004** Simply feels great in the mouth. 2010–2022. 95 pts.
- **2005** Superlative. Pretty, substantial, complex. 2014–2025. 98 pts.

Clos Pierre Reserve Shiraz 2005

This is largely sold through Dan Murphy's stores. The brand has caused something of a stir since it was released a couple of years back.

2005 RELEASE
There's a fair amount of peppery, savoury flavour but it all seems clumsy to me. The flavour balls through the mid-palate and is distractingly bitter, the tannin drying and hard. I like the style and character, but not the execution. **DRINK** 2009–2013.

Price	$30
Region	Yarra Valley
Value	♦♦
Auction	N/A
Score	85

Cookoothama Darlington Point Shiraz 2005

Cookoothama is a sub-brand of Nugan Estate, in New South Wales' Griffith region. It produces wines from many regions, but this is grown close to home.

2005 RELEASE
What a bolter. This is fresh, smart, bold and generous – there's a richness here that you don't often see in Riverina reds. Plums, olives, mint and vanilla, all in good form. A smooth mouthful of flavour for fifteen bucks!
DRINK 2008–2011.

Price	$15
Region	Riverina
Value	♦♦♦♦♦
Auction	N/A
Score	87

Crackerjack Shiraz Viognier 2005

This is a new wine range put out by the Wingara group, owners of Katnook Estate, Deakin Estate and Riddoch. They've done a good job here – the 2005 cabernet sauvignon (86 points) is excellent value too.

2005 RELEASE
It just scrapes into medium-weight status – this is not a hefty wine by any stretch – but it's juicy, fragrant, evocative of sweet plums and noticeably soft throughout.
DRINK 2008–2010.

Price	$15
Region	Victoria
Value	♦♦♦♦
Auction	N/A
Score	87

Craggy Range Gimblett Gravels Le Sol Syrah 2005

Craggy Range has fast become part of New Zealand's wine royalty. The wines are not cheap, but they are very, very good.

2005 RELEASE
This deserves its luxury status. It's an exotic wine, splashed with a wide array of flavours and smells: smoke, beef, cherries, kirsch, cracked pepper, the full box of spice, grape-stalks, peanuts – there's a lot going on here. It might sound like a hotchpotch, but it's not: it's seamless, silken, and highly seductive. Cue Nigella: this is deeply, *deeply* satisfying. **DRINK** 2013–2019.

Price	$85
Region	Hawke's Bay, NZ
Value	♦ ♦ ♦
Auction	★ ★ ★ ★
Score	94

Craiglee Shiraz 2005

Craiglee is a fabulous vineyard not far from Melbourne airport. Its shiraz is a legitimate icon of Australian wine.

2005 RELEASE
Perfumed, spicy wine, full of fragrance and complexity – though not all of it seems attractive. Some of its aromas seem a little gluey, and its gritty tannin structure borders on being clumsy. Extra time in the bottle should heal both wounds. Lovely blackberried, strawberried fruit flavour, its notes of stalks and pepper a welcome attraction.
DRINK 2012–2017.

PREVIOUS
- **1995** Light-weight, savoury style. 2001–2006. 85 pts.
- **1996** Cool, compact, savoury beauty. 2003–2010. 90 pts.
- **1997** A beautiful Craiglee. Peppery and powerful. 2005–2013. 95 pts.
- **1998** Very good. Medium-weight, savoury, satisfying. 2006–2011. 90 pts.
- **1999** Cool, peppery, balanced and true. 2005–2012. 90 pts.
- **2000** Balanced, peppery, fine. 2006–2014. 95 pts.
- **2001** Tart, sweet-bitter, blackberried. 2007–2011. 87 pts.
- **2002** Fine, spicy, focused. 2006–2015. 94 pts.
- **2003** Dense, thick, licoricey. 2008–2013. 90 pts.
- **2004** Intense, powerful, blackberried. 2012–2022. 93 pts.

Price	$40
Region	Sunbury
Value	♦ ♦ ♦ ♦
Auction	★ ★ ★ ★
Score	91

Dalwhinnie Moonambel Shiraz 2005

The Dalwhinnie shiraz vineyard is one of the best shiraz vineyards in the country. It's been in very strong form of late.

2005 RELEASE
There's a sweet simplicity here but it tastes so beautiful that it needn't matter. In any case, time will look after the complexity angle. A gob full of plums, musk and spice, minerally tannins giving it the frame to grow and develop in its own time. Beautiful. **DRINK** 2011–2018.

PREVIOUS
1995 Strong, oak-driven, minty, tannic. 2007–2015. 90 pts.
1996 Leathery, earthy, minty and drying. 2008–2014. 85 pts.
1997 Stellar wine. Fruit, structure, the lot. 2009–2018. 94 pts.
1998 Gangly and rough, but powerful. 2008–2015. 87 pts.
1999 Too much tannin and oak, but powerful. 2005–2010. 88 pts.
2000 Cool, stylish, cherried and earthy. 2008–2016. 93 pts.
2001 Overdone creamy oak. 2008–2013. 88 pts.
2002 Cherry-plummed and attractive. 2008–2014. 91 pts.
2003 Beautiful smell, beautiful taste. 2006–2013. 93 pts.
2004 Big, stylish, lengthy. 2007–2016. 94 pts.

Price	$52
Region	**Pyrenees**
Value	♦♦♦♦
Auction	★★★
Score	93

Dalwhinnie South West Rocks Shiraz 2005

It took dynamite to clear the rocks enough to plant vines on this site. Dramatic action for an ambitious wine.

2005 RELEASE
I have a problem. I don't like peppermint aromas or flavours in a wine and no matter how good the wine beneath them is, it's a battle for me to get past them. This wine would be great if it weren't so pepperminty. Its plush, voluptuous, smooth train of mouth-filling fruit flavour hits the spot to perfection, but ... **DRINK** 2008–2014.

Price	$65
Region	**Pyrenees**
Value	♦♦
Auction	★★★
Score	91

D'Arenberg Dead Arm Shiraz 2005

I've had a love-hate relationship with this wine; everyone seemed to love the 2002, but no matter how many times I tried it, I just couldn't get excited. The 2004, and most particularly this 2005, have got me properly on board.

2005 RELEASE
This is a powerhouse. It's not just a fruit bomb either; there's complexity here. Currants, raspberries, kirsch, violets, lightly browned toast – this smells and tastes beautiful. The thing I really like is that despite all this might and fruit power, it's still lively and vigorous, like it can't wait to jump out of the glass and please you. I wouldn't be surprised if I rate it higher once it's fully mature. **DRINK** 2015–2025.

Price	$65
Region	McLaren Vale
Value	♦♦♦♦
Auction	★★★★
Score	94

PREVIOUS
- 2000 Massive coffee and licorice flavour. 2003–2011. 92 pts.
- 2001 Long, fruity, tannic monster. 2005–2014. 94 pts.
- 2002 Great depth, great tannin, lacking polish. 2009–2015. 88 pts.
- 2003 Deliciously sweet plums and cedar. 2006–2014. 92 pts.
- 2004 Ripe, sweet, structured. 2009–2019. 95 pts.

D'Arenberg Laughing Magpie Shiraz Viognier 2006

There's a good argument to be mounted that this is the wine that popularised shiraz viognier. I don't like it as an aged wine, but as a young wine it is delicious.

2006 RELEASE
This is drinking beautifully now. It tastes of toast, blackberry jam, coal and cedar and apricots, but you can forget all that and simply expect one thing: deliciousness with an extra serving of loveliness. It's dark, soft, syrupy, vital red wine at its drinkable best. **DRINK** 2008–2010.

Price	$29
Region	McLaren Vale
Value	♦♦♦♦
Auction	N/A
Score	93

PREVIOUS
- 2000 Too sweet and apricotty. 2003–2005. 85 pts.
- 2001 Richly plummy and cherried. 2003–2006. 91 pts.
- 2002 Warm, floral, blackberried. 2004–2008. 91 pts.
- 2003 Gutsy, toasty, sweet. 2005–2008. 91 pts.
- 2004 Blueberried, meaty, delicious. 2006–2010. 92 pts.
- 2005 Spicy, blackberry, excellent. 2007–2009. 92 pts.

D'Arenberg Vintage Fortified Shiraz 2006

If you're after a proper vintage port, this is without a doubt the best value example on the market. This year's is a particularly interesting release.

2006 RELEASE
Gosh it's nice to tuck into this – this is why I look forward to the cooler months. It tastes of chocolate and menthol, sour cherries and plums, its sweetness obvious but totally delicious. If you look hard you see notes of charcuterie, marzipan and burnt sugar. But really – we're talking hedonism here. Its complexity barely matters.
DRINK 2008–2016.

Price	$19
Region	McLaren Vale
Value	♦♦♦♦
Auction	N/A
Score	92

David Hook The Gorge Shiraz 2006

The fact that wines like this are starting to sell well is a sign that Australian wine is growing up; as a wine drinking nation, we've increasingly come to appreciate a broad range of styles.

2006 RELEASE
This is a very sensible wine. Its alcohol is moderate, its flavours are enough without being too much, there's a good dose of spirit-of-the-land earthiness about it and it's both savoury and fruity through the finish. I reckon you'd please a lot of people by serving this; it's like a good quality bottle of Chianti, or a slightly stronger, earthier version of pinot noir. **DRINK** 2008–2016.

Price	$18
Region	Hunter Valley
Value	♦♦♦♦♦
Auction	N/A
Score	88

De Bortoli Estate Grown Shiraz Viognier 2006

Want to know how close Aussie shiraz viognier can be to the wines and styles of France's (northern) Rhône Valley? Drink a bottle of this.

2006 RELEASE
Viognier can get in the way of good shiraz at times but no such problem here. It's a cool-climate shiraz but it's bursting with life, spice and flavour. Plums, boysenberry, meat, smoke, pepper and a whole host of other ingredients. It all comes in plush, smooth form, though the finish is coiled with cellar-worthy tannin. A terrific Yarra shiraz. **DRINK** 2012–2017.

Price	$35
Region	Yarra Valley
Value	♦♦♦♦♦
Auction	★★★
Score	94

De Bortoli Gulf Station Shiraz Viognier 2006

2006 RELEASE
A few years back a winemaker said to me that shiraz was for winedrinkers who like to roll over and have their tummies tickled. It's cuddly and fruity and as a drinker you don't have to work hard to enjoy it. Adding viognier to the show is supposed to make this statement even more apt. Except that it's not at all true of this wine: this is a complex, taut style of wine, in need of food for its tannins to soften, and worthy of contemplation. It's a thinking drinker's shiraz. For that, the price is a steal. **DRINK** 2008–2013.

Price	$18
Region	Yarra Valley
Value	♦♦♦♦♦
Auction	N/A
Score	90

De Iuliis Charlie Shiraz 2006

Hunter Valley reds have been in the doldrums for quite some time but in the past five years they've undergone a quiet revolution. They're riper, cleaner, juicier and more immediately drinkable. De Iuliis has been part of the change.

2006 RELEASE
You'll find it hard not to like this. It's perfumed and plummy and sweet, yet marked by that irrepressible yank of Hunter earthiness. There's even a spot of minerality here, marking its class. Sweet and yet savoury, solid in the mouth and yet immensely drinkable. The new Hunter. **DRINK** 2008–2020.

Price	$25
Region	Hunter Valley
Value	♦♦♦♦
Auction	N/A
Score	92

De Iuliis Limited Release Shiraz 2006

The great recent vintages for Hunter Valley reds are supposed to be 2003, 2005 and 2007. The notoriously wet Hunter, though, has benefited greatly (in a wine sense) from the drought, so that there hasn't been a dud Hunter red vintage in years. I'm fast becoming a big fan of the 2006s.

2006 RELEASE
Over the last few vintages I've thought winemaker Mike De Iuliis has been a little heavy-handed with his oak usage, and it's true that there's a fair whack of it here too. But boy, with this 2006, does he get away with it! The is a fabbo red. It's smooth and luscious and blessed with the most glorious creek of earthy, spicy flavour – though soft-centred fruit power is always the wine's main card. **DRINK** 2008–2020.

Price	$40
Region	Hunter Valley
Value	♦♦♦♦
Auction	N/A
Score	95

Donny Goodmac Shiraz 2006

This is made in limited quantities, and might be hard to track down. Get yourself on the mailing list by emailing thepig@donnygoodmac.com.au and ask them if they know where to find some. It's $30 per bottle, but $290 for a dozen. It's $50 per bottle quality.

2006 RELEASE
Rarely do you find a wine with all the components so well balanced, and at the same time so charming. You could call this the perfect Australian shiraz. It's not too big, but not thin and wimpy either. It's a medium-bodied, plum-centred, cherried red wine, exotic notes of five-spice, sandalwood, cedar, sap and toast pitching it just right. It drinks like a champion now, and yet it will age. It's brilliant. **DRINK** 2008–2020.

Price	$30
Region	Pyrenees
Value	♦♦♦♦♦
Auction	N/A
Score	95

Dowie Doole Shiraz 2005

I like what this mob are on about. They make good wines and talk honestly about them, rare in wine today. Every now and then they even criticise one of their own – a sure sign of good, grounded folk.

2005 RELEASE
If big, glycerol, chocolaty McLaren Vale reds are your thing, then you're gonna like this one. It's seen the boxes and popped ticks into all of them. Plums, earth and coffee flavours are welded together by a whack of creamy, chocolaty oak. Lots of flesh on this baby's bones. It's also got a gentle leatheriness which is most attractive. **DRINK** 2008–2014.

Price	$25
Region	McLaren Vale
Value	♦♦♦♦
Auction	N/A
Score	90

Dutschke GHR Four Vineyards Shiraz 2005

An excellent addition to the Dutschke range. I like this more than some of the higher priced wines in the range.

2005 RELEASE
Like sucking on malted blackberries after they've just re-asphalted the road. It's got lots of sweet fruit power and lots of tarry, oak-and-fruit packed oomph. Its warm black finish is entirely appropriate to the style of the wine. If you like big reds, this really delivers. **DRINK** 2008–2013.

Price	$25
Region	Barossa
Value	♦♦♦♦
Auction	★★★
Score	91

Elderton Estate Shiraz 2005

I was a big fan of the 2004 and was keen to taste this. I wasn't disappointed.

2005 RELEASE
It's almost old-fashioned and it's almost modern too, two reasons why it's a great red for winter drinking. It does have a bit too much coffeed oak flavour but it also has more than enough blackberried, coal-like flavour, and because of its sling of firm, supple tannins and fresh, juicy finish it's difficult to view it as anything other than more-ish. Barossa shiraz drinkers: this wine will not disappoint. **DRINK** 2008–2014.

Price	$27
Region	Barossa
Value	♦♦♦♦
Auction	★★★
Score	91

Elderton 'Friends' Shiraz 2005

Elderton is one of the hardest working wineries in the Barossa I reckon; they put their hand up for all sorts of things, in all sorts of admirable ways. Name your price, and they've got a wine to suit.

2005 RELEASE
I'm tempted to call this a simple quaffer but it's better than that. It boasts an excellent burst of blueberried, blackberried flavour, and while it doesn't hold on long through the finish the ride is certainly enjoyable. It's getting harder and harder to find good Barossan reds for less than twenty bucks, but here we have one. **DRINK** 2008–2010.

Price	$18
Region	Barossa
Value	♦♦♦♦
Auction	★★★
Score	88

Euroa Creeks Shiraz 2006

Euroa is a flat warm landscape but its soils are interesting and the climate reliable; it should be an excellent place to grow shiraz. The only rein on the area is access to water. This hand-picked, handmade wine was matured in large 500 L oak. They only bottled 150 dozen of it.

2006 RELEASE
Lots of juicy acidity and lots of rich flavour. It's a crowd pleaser but it's also got underlying substance. Juicy blackberry and dark cherry flavours, integrated chocolaty oak, a grainy earthiness and a long, succulent, structured finish. Look hard and you notice the odd herbal character – presented in the most attractive manner. I'm a big wrap for this; it will age majestically. **DRINK** 2011–2018.

Price	$28
Region	Euroa
Value	♦♦♦♦
Auction	N/A
Score	92

Evans and Tate Shiraz 2004

Evans and Tate was a massively ambitious endeavour that all turned out sour – and ended up in liquidation. The expanding McWilliam's family wine company eventually snapped it up towards the end of 2007.

2004 RELEASE
There's a lot of good drinking here. It's soft and plush and undemanding, coffeed, malty oak swimming over the top of blackberried fruit flavour. A bit old-fashioned maybe, but very well put together, and certainly not lacking in flavour. If you ever see the price of this slashed, hook into it by the case. **DRINK** 2008–2014.

Price	$22
Region	Margarct River
Value	♦♦♦
Auction	N/A
Score	89

Fairbank Syrah 2004

This has been around for a while but it's such a good wine that I just had to give it a run here.

2004 RELEASE
The thinking drinker's sex symbol. A-class quality. Quite an amazing wine really. Brilliantly firm, concentrated and complex, its dark, blackberried heart shot with minerals and eucalypt. The balance, the oak handling, the strength, the tannin – it's all of the highest quality. It will live for a very long time. If you see some, pop a couple of bottles in the cellar for the long haul. **DRINK** 2012–2024.

Price	$25
Region	Bendigo
Value	♦♦♦♦♦
Auction	N/A
Score	94

Fox Creek Red Baron Shiraz 2006

2006 RELEASE
A new-ish wine on the Fox Creek scene and a good one. This is a warm, raisiny, blackberry-flavoured wine, bright and plush and with a decent amount of fruit weight. Oak adds toasty-vanillin flavours and it feels good in the mouth, all slippery and smooth. **DRINK** 2008–2010.

Price	$17
Region	McLaren Vale
Value	♦♦♦♦♦
Auction	N/A
Score	90

Fox Creek Reserve Shiraz 2005

There's a rich, beefy style of red that can be perfect for certain kinds of business dinners – big impressive reds with soft centres. A couple of decades ago Grange was that wine, but with its current $500 price tag you need an exceptionally good reason to go there. Enter a wine like Fox Creek Reserve Shiraz, a wine with pedigree, oomph, and just the right flavour profile.

2005 RELEASE
Very good Fox Creek reserve without being a great one. There's a lot of slippery, vanillin oak here but it's more or less well tamed, the fruit behind it reminiscent of leather, coffee, toast and dark red plums. It's also fresh through the finish and nicely persistent. I would drink it young.
DRINK 2008–2015.

PREVIOUS
2000 Savoury appeal; easy drinking. 2005–2009. 87 pts.
2001 Deep, controlled, classy wine. 2005–2014. 92 pts.
2002 Smooth blackberries, raisins and vanilla. 2007–2014. 92 pts.
2003 Not made.
2004 Good fruit, far too much oak. 2006–2012. 90 pts.

Price	$70
Region	McLaren Vale
Value	♦♦♦♦
Auction	★★★
Score	92

Fox Creek Shadow's Run Shiraz Cabernet Sauvignon 2006

Fox Creek is renowned for its reserve shiraz, but this inexpensive blend is a gift to red wine drinkers.

2006 RELEASE
Exactly as an easy-drinking shiraz cabernet should taste. This is a totally reliable bargain buy. It tastes of blackberries, mint, dust and chocolate, its fresh juiciness making it both refreshing and satisfying at once. It's a great quaffer. **DRINK** 2008–2011.

Price	$12
Region	McLaren Vale
Value	♦♦♦♦
Auction	N/A
Score	89

Gemtree Uncut Shiraz 2006

This is made from the grapes of 40-year-old vines growing on Tatachilla Road in McLaren Vale.

2006 RELEASE
Really nice red wine. Big on flavour and smooth of texture, its blueberried, blackberried heart smooching into chocolaty, vanillin oak. It's at the big end of town, but it still manages to be nicely balanced, courtesy, I suspect, of some gentle handling in the winery. It's open fermented and only minimally filtered, leaving all the goodness of McLaren shiraz intact. I've seen the odd retailer sell this for just under $20, at which it represents extraordinary value. **DRINK** 2008–2014.

Price	$22
Region	McLaren Vale
Value	♦♦♦♦♦
Auction	★★★
Score	92

Geoff Merrill Shiraz 2004

Geoff Merrill is one of the great personalities of Aussie red wine. He consistently produces very fine drops.

2004 RELEASE
It's edging towards 'dry port' territory but boy it's a nice drink, flush with dark blackberry and plum-like fruit flavour and only lightly kissed by oak. There's a crushed herb flavour here too that I like quite a lot – but which makes me think it will drink better young than with age. **DRINK** 2008–2013.

Price	$25
Region	McLaren Vale
Value	♦♦♦♦
Auction	N/A
Score	90

Giaconda Warner's Vineyard Shiraz 2005

Giaconda may be best known for its chardonnay, but personally I prefer the shiraz. It's not just because red wines are real wines either.

2005 RELEASE
This will evolve into a great wine. It has structure and class dripping from every pore. It's both a pretty wine and a big wine, with toasty, fragrant, strident oak and layers of ripe, meaty, spicy fruit weight. What makes it so great? It has complexity of flavour, power through the mouth, great persistence and terrific tannin structure. It is a complete wine. **DRINK** 2014–2024.

PREVIOUS
1999 Pretty, savoury, floral. 2004–2009. 87 pts.
2000 Soft and generous. 2005–2012. 90 pts.
2001 Complex and floral. 2008–2013. 92 pts.
2002 Tannic, ripe, weighty. 2008–2014. 94 pts.
2003 Not made.
2004 Tight, smoky, complex. 2007–2017. 96 pts.

Price	$85
Region	Beechworth
Value	♦♦♦♦
Auction	★★★★★
Score	97

Gilligan Shiraz Grenache Mourvedre 2006

Gilligan is a small operation but the wines have become steadily better over the past five years. This is the best so far.

2006 RELEASE
Bonza drink. Epitome of what this blend is all about. There's an excellent whack of warm, soft, vibrant flavour, the impression of it running to all corners of your mouth. This is McLaren Vale red wine on excellent show. Spice, blueberry, blackberry jam – but not at all overcooked. Lively! Really good. **DRINK** 2008–2013.

Price	$25
Region	McLaren Vale
Value	♦♦♦♦♦
Auction	N/A
Score	92

Glaetzer Bishop Shiraz 2006

Ben Glaetzer took over the reigns at Glaetzer wines a few years back – no small feat considering that his father and uncle are Barossa winemaking legends – and now makes the wines fresher, lower in obvious oak, and arguably more interesting to drink.

2006 RELEASE
It needs a couple of hours in the decanter but it's an intelligently restrained wine. It tastes of warm, inky blackberry and ironstone, the tannins almost metallic in their minerally, rock-strewn character – though there's still a softness to them that is beguiling. Is the alcohol just a touch shrill? There's plenty to think about here, partly why it's so easy to keep going back for more. **DRINK** 2012–2019.

Price	$30
Region	Barossa
Value	♦ ♦ ♦
Auction	★ ★
Score	92

Gramp's Shiraz 2004 & 2005

Gramp's is both an Orlando brand and part of Orlando history – though I'm not supposed to use the word Orlando anymore. Orlando is owned by French company Pernod Ricard, and the umbrella now in favour is Jacob's Creek.

2004 RELEASE
This will be near the end of its retail run but you might find the odd bottle around. I've been banging on about it for months. It's an uncompromising red – chock-a-block full of dark, porty blackberry and coffeed, American oak flavour. Big-oaked, big flavour Barossan shiraz at a bargain price. **DRINK** 2008–2011.

2005 RELEASE
Yee-ha, we have another winner – I like it even more than the 2004. It's old-fashioned black Barossan shiraz at its bountiful best. Smooth blackberry and blood plums, carried on a wave of coffee and vanilla. Replica of the 2004 except that the flavour carries longer, thicker and juicier. **DRINK** 2008–2011.

Price	$15.95
Region	Barossa
Value	♦ ♦ ♦ ♦ ♦
Auction	★ ★
Score	91 (2004)
	93 (2005)

Grove Estate Cellar Block Reserve Shiraz 2006

Tim Kirk of Clonakilla fame buys Hilltops region shiraz grapes from the Grove Estate vineyard, as good an endorsement as any that the quality is good. One taste of this though and you have all the endorsement you need.

2006 RELEASE
Lots to love here – of the kind worth sharing. It's full-bodied but elegant, ribbed with spicy flavour, long through the finish and charming in the silken, soft, polished way it goes about seducing you. Spicy, dark-cherried fruit, integrated cedary oak, an obvious sense of cool-climate finesse and lots and lots of ageing potential.
DRINK 2008–2018.

Price	$36
Region	Hilltops
Value	♦♦♦♦
Auction	N/A
Score	93

Hardy's Oomoo Shiraz 2006

It's had the odd miss but this has generally been a value-killing star since its launch a handful of years back. It often outguns far more expensive wines.

2006 RELEASE
Perfect quaffer. Absolutely perfect. Ripe, dark, pure and tasty. Flavours of chocolate, blackberry, ground spice and earth, its chewy, juicy tannin making it feel in the mouth like a far more aspirational wine. It's a screaming bargain.
DRINK 2008–2014.

Price	$18
Region	McLaren Vale
Value	♦♦♦♦♦
Auction	N/A
Score	92

PREVIOUS
2001 Sweet coffee, rich blackberry, excellent. 2003–2006. 88 pts.
2002 Chocolaty, dark-fruited flavour. 2004–2006. 89 pts.
2003 Balance, flavour and weight. 2005–2007. 89 pts.
2004 Great value. Rich and smooth. 2005–2006. 90 pts.
2005 Balanced, easy-drinking quality. 2006–2008. 89 pts.

Hardy's Tintara Shiraz 2005

Hardy's has been a McLaren Vale stalwart since 1876. It is the most important McLaren Vale producer. This is the bottle with the orange front label.

2005 RELEASE
There's a saltiness to this wine that I find distracting, but otherwise it's rich, flavoursome and satisfying. Plums, tar, prunes and toast make up the flavours, gentle vanillin oak attempting to keep the texture soft. It almost succeeds. Indeed it's almost a very good wine, and does offer good value. **DRINK** 2008–2012.

Price	$18
Region	McLaren Vale
Value	♦♦♦♦
Auction	★★★
Score	87

Heartland Director's Cut Shiraz 2006

Ben Glaetzer makes the Heartland wines with much of the grapes sourced from the Langhorne Creek region. Glaetzer's uncle, John Glaetzer, is famous for having championed the region during his long period of red winemaking at Wolf Blass.

2006 RELEASE
If you're into the bigger styles this mouth-coating red will be right up your alley. You take a sip and it spreads deep and wide through your mouth, its intense, plummy, chocolaty flavour pouring on the charm. There's a lot of fine, filigreed tannin and a weave of toasty, creamy oak – it really hits the spot. A masterfully managed monster. **DRINK** 2008–2014.

Price	$28
Region	Langhorne Creek Limestone Coast
Value	♦♦♦♦
Auction	N/A
Score	93

Heartland Shiraz 2006

If you haven't cottoned on to the Heartland range yet it's time to familiarise yourself with it. They're hearty reds, stylishly packaged, and invariably sharp value.

2006 RELEASE
Winemaker Ben Glaetzer crams a whole lot of rich, fruity grunt in this range; exactly why it's moved so quickly up the popularity charts. This release shows its alcohol but is otherwise warm and cakey, full of blackberried flavour and moderate in its toasty oak influence. It's a red for the middle of winter, made in the monumental style. **DRINK** 2008–2012.

Price	$17
Region	Langhorne Creek Limestone Coast
Value	♦♦♦♦
Auction	N/A
Score	90

Hewitson Ned and Henry's Shiraz 2006

Dean Hewitson once worked for Petaluma, but since he branched out on his own he's gone from strength to strength. I don't know that I've ever tasted a wine of his that I didn't enjoy.

2006 RELEASE
There's such a thing in wine as 'grapeyness', which might sound like a statement of the bleeding obvious but refers to the fact that most wine tastes 'winey', but the odd one tastes 'grapey'. It's usually a very attractive trait in a wine. This wine has it, especially in the velvety softness of the tannins. They taste like red grape skins. The wine as a whole is all about rich fruit, with oak playing very little role. It's not a look-at-me wine, but it is very good.
DRINK 2008–2014.

Price	$25
Region	Barossa
Value	♦♦♦♦
Auction	★★★
Score	91

Houghton Gladstones Shiraz 2003

There was a great buzz about the initial Gladstones shiraz release, made from the 1999 vintage. Since then it has faded largely from view; as indeed have many of the super-premium red wines in the Hardys Wine Company portfolio.

2003 RELEASE
The bottle of this I tasted from showed a gangly, awkward wine full of aggressive, drying tannin, undercut by gamey, raspberried flavours. There was lots of toasty, cedary oak too, and a wide array of various herbs and spices. Complex, it certainly was – it was fascinating. Cohesive, it wasn't. It's always difficult to pass judgment on such wines; time will be the true judge. My score here is a bet each way.
DRINK 2011–2016.

Price	$60
Region	Great Southern
Value	♦♦
Auction	★★★
Score	90

Houghton Shiraz 2003

Frankland River is an inland sub-region in southern Western Australia (part of the larger Great Southern region). It has the ability to produce intensely spicy, vibrant, persistent shiraz wines that rival the very best.

2003 RELEASE
There's a lot of spice here and a lot of drying tannin too, and while the dose of cherry-plummed flavour is reasonably good, it's just not intense enough to carry the style. It's an awkward wine. It's savoury and spicy, but ultimately unconvincing. **DRINK** 2008–2014.

Price	$28
Region	Great Southern
Value	♦ ♦ ♦
Auction	★ ★
Score	87

Howard Park Leston Shiraz 2005

Leston is a single vineyard wine made from Howard Park's Margaret River plantings.

2005 RELEASE
Margaret River shiraz comes across as bulkier, and less spicy, than Great Southern shiraz, a difference often highlighted in Howard Park's single vineyard series. There's some rum and raisin flavour here matched to chocolaty, cedary oak, supporting tannins equal to the thickness of the flavour. This is a red to sink your teeth into. **DRINK** 2008–2016.

PREVIOUS
2001 Full, plummy, grippy. 2006–2012. 91 pts.
2002 Complex, medium-weight, satisfying. 2004–2010. 89 pts.
2003 Smooth, polished, medium-weight and lovely. 2005–2010. 90 pts.
2004 Flamboyant, cedary and black cherried. 2006–2014. 90 pts.

Price	$40
Region	Margaret River
Value	♦ ♦ ♦
Auction	★ ★ ★
Score	93

Howard Park Scotsdale Shiraz 2005

Howard Park has significant Margaret River digs but it was founded in the Great Southern region of Western Australia. Many of its best reds are still made from Great Southern grapes. Scotsdale is one of its Great Southern vineyards.

2005 RELEASE
It's a melodious, lip-smacking wine, the type that can easily have you skipping around the house singing merrily – or maybe that's just me. The thing is, it's tasty, spicy, smooth and dark, but it's sophisticated too. Filigreed tannin, bass notes of olive and aniseed, cedary oak and excellent length. It's one of my favourite wines of the year.
DRINK 2012–2018.

PREVIOUS
2001 Blackberry nip and pepper; seriously good. 2004–2011. 93 pts.
2002 Elegant, pure, balanced. 2004–2010. 92 pts.
2003 Firm, polished, balanced. 2008–2015. 93 pts.
2004 Fruit and oak at odds. 2007–2012. 86 pts.

Price	$40
Region	Great Southern
Value	♦♦♦
Auction	★★★
Score	95

Ingoldby Shiraz 2005

I was surprised to find that the Ingoldby cabernet is in fine form; the same cannot be said of the shiraz. Foster's – the owners of Ingoldby – need to either can this label, or beef it back up to its former reliable status.

2005 RELEASE
Not a bad red but nothing much going for it either. Dilute raspberry flavours just edge into darker blackberry, the drinkability of it good but the level of satisfaction low. It's sound, pure and clean, but there are many other reds at the same price that give it a severe touching up.
DRINK 2008–2011.

Price	$18
Region	McLaren Vale
Value	♦♦
Auction	★★
Score	84

Innocent Bystander Shiraz 2006

Australian wine internationally tends to be portrayed as big, fruity and sweet. It can (gloriously) be that, but it can be so many other things too. This shiraz is the kind of (relatively) inexpensive wine Australia needs to get into the mouths of Europeans – to indicate how remarkably diverse Australian wine is.

2006 RELEASE
Here's a wine about savouriness, tannin, complexity and length, its peppery, meaty aspects ably caressed by succulent cherry flavours. Its tannin structure is dry, obvious and lengthy, but never overly assertive or distracting. There's even a sense of steely minerality, the likes of which are usually associated with higher priced wines. Winemaker Steve Flamsteed should be damn proud of this wine. **DRINK** 2009–2014.

Price	$19.95
Region	Yarra Valley
Value	★★★★★
Auction	★★★
Score	92

J & J Shiraz 2006

This wine won the Edinburgh Cellars trophy for Best Dry Red Still Wine for a wine under $20. It's 15.6 per cent alcohol, and is described by its makers as 'a real man's drink'.

2006 RELEASE
The incredible thing is that this wine is $20. It tastes like an attempt at a wine double that price. It's massively rich, syrupy, porty, sweet and soft, the flavour so thick it has reached saturation point. It's all mid-palate power; it falls away through the finish. It also seems very low in acid. It won't cellar, but for short term drinking (if you like massive flavoured wines) there's fun for the taking here. **DRINK** 2008–2010.

Price	$19.95
Region	McLaren Vale
Value	★★★★
Auction	★★
Score	88

Jacob's Creek Centenary Hill Shiraz 2002 & 2003

Orlando's Centenary Hill shiraz now comes under the Jacob's Creek banner, a curious move indeed. This release may not be convincing, but it's usually a sure bet in the big, rich red style.

Price	$39.95
Region	Barossa
Value	♦♦♦
Auction	★★★
Score	93 (2002)
	88 (2003)

2002 RELEASE
Almost a boomer. Banged up with dark, blistering fruit flavour, the way it whacks through your mouth an experience in itself. This is thick with dark shiraz fruit flavour, no holds barred. The only reason my grading hasn't reached for the stars is the overt mintiness of it, and the feeling that its coconuty oak is a touch out of balance. It's superbly fruited though. **DRINK** 2009–2017.

2003 RELEASE
Sweet and easy. Neither the oomph or the persistence of flavour to warrant higher scores, but it's still a good drink. Sweet coffee, rum and raisin flavours carry through to a finish that reminds strongly of licorice ice-cream. **DRINK** 2008–2012.

Jacob's Creek Reserve Shiraz 2005

When Jacob's Creek first launched a 'reserve' range of reds there was some scepticism. Now it's established as a wine always worth checking out.

Price	$15.95
Region	South Australia
Value	♦♦♦♦♦
Auction	★★
Score	92

2005 RELEASE
If it's sheer concentration you're after then this isn't the go; if you want power with finesse, softness with balance, and satisfying flavour with only moderate oak input – then this is impossible to pass by. I was staggered when I first tasted it. It's a more successful wine than many at twice the price. Plums, blackberries, perfect acidity, moderate tannins and a long, clean, fruity finish. Commercial winemaking at it best. **DRINK** 2008–2013.

Jacob's Creek Shiraz 2006

It might be the biggest name in commercial red wine – though Yellow Tail is fast impinging – but the value for money is still bang on.

2006 RELEASE
It's still kicking goals. It's fleshy and soft enough in its texture, flavours of earth-splashed cherries and olives leading to a slightly minerally finish. There's tannin here but not a lot of it – it is highly successful at providing good, clean, medium-weight red wine drinking.
DRINK 2008–2010.

Price	$10
Region	Australia
Value	♦♦♦
Auction	★★
Score	85

Jim Barry McRae Wood Shiraz 2004

The 2003 South Australian vintage was a tough one but Jim Barry's McRae Wood Shiraz made it look easy. I was hoping the 2004 would follow on the form.

2004 RELEASE
All about softness. Indeed, if the wine's warm, brandied alcohol wasn't shooting out through the finish – distracting you from the wine's overall appeal – this would be a bonza wine. It's full of plush, plummy, minted fruit flavour, creamy oak sliding it delightfully across your tongue. The problems lie with the disjointed alcohol, and jagged acidity. So close, but so far. **DRINK** 2008–2013.

Price	$48
Region	Clare Valley
Value	♦♦♦
Auction	★★
Score	88

John Duval Wines Entity Shiraz 2005

John Duval is one of only four people who can claim to have been responsible for the making of Penfolds Grange – from 1986 to 2002. He now buys high quality Barossa Valley red grapes, and turns them into high quality red wines under his own name.

2005 RELEASE
Black Barossan shiraz on full show. Big, plush, syrupy wine with toasty, sawdusty oak and oodles of dark, plummy, liqueurous fruit power. It's a hefty, almost porty wine but the flavours are delivered to your tongue in fine, fresh condition. **DRINK** 2008–2018.

Price	$43
Region	McLaren Vale
Value	♦♦♦♦
Auction	★★★
Score	93

Kaesler Old Vine Shiraz 2006

Kaesler winemaker Reid Bosward makes big wines off ancient Barossan vines. The wines take no prisoners, but are generally of very high standard. This wine is so dense it tastes like port.

Price	$60
Region	Barossa
Value	♦ ♦ ♦
Auction	★ ★ ★
Score	94

2006 RELEASE
Thick, expansive, sweet and coffeed. A riot of flavour hits your mouth as soon as you take a slug of it. Smoke, graphite, sweet syrupy plums, mocha, chocolate, woodspice – it's one with the lot. Mammoth flavour, layer upon layer. **DRINK** 2008–2018.

Kilikanoon Covenant Shiraz 2005

Kilikanoon's spiritual home is the Clare Valley and it's where most of its best wine comes from, white and red. This is a sound example.

Price	$40
Region	Clare Valley
Value	♦ ♦ ♦
Auction	★ ★ ★
Score	93

2005 RELEASE
Soft as suede. As saturated in colour and flavour as ink. Masses of plums, blueberries, mint, creamy vanilla, brandy and caramel. Warm to hot on the finish, but the seduction is well complete by then. Not complex, but voluptuous. **DRINK** 2008–2014.

Kilikanoon Parable Shiraz 2005

Kilikanoon jumped into the limelight a handful of years back when it took the Clare Valley Wine Show by storm, taking out a host of trophies. The wines have always been voluptuous, syrupy and full of immediate, saturated appeal. Have they become too big and raisiny?

Price	$40
Region	McLaren Vale
Value	♦ ♦ ♦
Auction	★ ★ ★
Score	91

2005 RELEASE
It smells like raisins dipped in brandy, the warm alcohol lifting right up out of the glass. It's an attractive introduction. The palate offers more of the same, its sweet, chocolaty richness shot with musky oak and brandied plums. It sure ain't hard to like it; it's great fun. In pure quality terms though, the alcohol takes over the finish, distorting the natural progress of the wine's flavours. **DRINK** 2008–2013.

Kilikanoon Testament Shiraz 2005

I haven't kept up with developments at Kilikanoon over the past couple of years and it surprised me to see a super premium Barossan shiraz in the range; it's excellent too. It's made from grapes grown in the Greenock sub-region of the Barossa Valley.

Price	$40
Region	Barossa
Value	♦♦♦
Auction	★★★
Score	94

2005 RELEASE
Now this is a salacious red. Pouring it into your mouth is like running a hot knife through butter; it's that soft! Blood plums, chocolate, raisins, smoke, molten caramel – that's what it tastes like. It's not a sweet wine but it has a sweet fruit profile, and I dare say that if you served this at a Saturday night dinner party you'd evoke ooos and ahhhs galore. **DRINK** 2008–2014.

Kurtz Boundary Row Shiraz 2005

Steve Kurtz has been in and around the wine business all his life, and has worked for a range of large wine companies. He broke out on his own a couple of years ago, and hopes his children will follow on in the family wine business.

Price	$22
Region	Barossa
Value	♦♦♦♦
Auction	N/A
Score	90

2005 RELEASE
Have to applaud this one. It manages to offer seriously dark, red wine flavour while at the same time keeping the alcohol level in check, the full force of it all about beautiful Barossan blackberried fruit flavour. There are also notes of coffee, spice, blackcurrant and toast, but it's really just a big mouthful of dark fruity flavour. Nice and soft too. Lacks the length required to deserve higher marks. **DRINK** 2008–2013.

Lake Breeze Bernoota Shiraz Cabernet 2005

Lake Breeze reds are reliably good, and reliably good value. Lots of good flavour and smooth creamy oak.

Price	$20
Region	Langhorne Creek
Value	♦♦♦♦
Auction	N/A
Score	91

2005 RELEASE
It delivers exactly what we've come to expect of Lake Breeze: rich blackcurrant flavour, a dash of Aussie eucalypt, creamy vanillin oak and the odd leafy cabernet note. It's all mid-palate punch and probably lacks a little length – a point I only realised near the end of the bottle. **DRINK** 2009–2015.

Langmeil Hangin' Snakes Shiraz Viognier 2006

There's about five per cent viognier in this and normally I would have said that's too much in a style like this. They've got it working pretty well though.

2006 RELEASE
If someone told me that they hated this I'd laugh and shout, I KNEW YOU WERE GOING TO SAY THAT (even if I didn't). But it is a polarising style. It tastes sweet, rich and warm, its aniseedy, raspberried, candied characters mixing happily with sweet, dark, blackberried fruit flavour. The viognier is apricotty and obvious, but its exuberant fruit sweetness floats well with the sweetness of the shiraz. Lighter than the other Langmeil reds, but in a good way. **DRINK** 2008–2013.

Price	$19.50
Region	Barossa
Value	♦♦♦♦
Auction	N/A
Score	89

Langmeil Orphan Bank Shiraz 2005

Interesting story to this one. It's made off vines in excess of 100 years of age, though a section of these vines was recently dug up and replanted to another site in the Barossa ... long story, but it's amazing that it was possible. The name of the wine refers to this rescued patch of vines.

2005 RELEASE
Obvious coconut oak and obvious alcohol heat – both detractors to the wine. Otherwise it's a display of slightly overcooked grapes, the flavours tarry, pruney, lacking in vibrancy and charm. That said, it does not lack intensity. Vague notes of orange peel and dried herbs come forward as it opens in the glass. All guts, no glory. **DRINK** 2009–2014.

Price	$50
Region	Barossa
Value	♦♦
Auction	N/A
Score	86

Langmeil The Freedom 1843 Shiraz 2005

The price is high but it's often the way with wines made from historic vineyards – there aren't many that can top the age of this one.

2005 RELEASE
A slinky, smooth, seductive wine, noticeably high in both acid and alcohol and carrying distinct notes of truffle oil – a trait that is bound to polarise drinkers. If that sounds yum, no doubt you will love this wine, because the saturation of dark fruit flavour is delivered so smoothly it tastes like the wine equivalent of a voice-over to a Valvoline commercial. Loam, tar, blackberries, leather, aniseed – this is big on fruit-rich delivery. **DRINK** 2009–2019.

Price	$100
Region	Barossa
Value	♦♦♦
Auction	★★
Score	94

Lazy Ballerina Shiraz 2006

This has been one of the real finds of recent years. Young bloke James Hook makes the wines out of the Redheads studio in McLaren Vale, a hotpot for interesting young wine folks.

2006 RELEASE
What a beauty. This is a super wine, at a super price. It tastes like a big mouthful of chocolate and blackberry and smoky oak, but before the words 'fruit bomb' jump to mind it's also blessed with a lovely run of sophisticated tannin. Fantastic. **DRINK** 2008–2018.

PREVIOUS
2004 Structure, richness and length. 2006–2014. 94 pts.
2005 Depth, class and impact. 2006–2014. 93 pts.

Price	$24
Region	McLaren Vale
Value	●●●●●
Auction	N/A
Score	94

Leaping Lizard Shiraz 2006

Leaping Lizard is produced by the excellent Ferngrove winery, though nowhere on the bottle is that fact revealed.

2006 RELEASE
I thought long and hard about this. It has cool herbal flavours but it also tastes of sweet, liqueured raspberries, just enough to get me over the line. I could happily drink this – though don't expect a blast of rich, chocolaty flavour. It's a spicy, savoury wine, and reasonable value all told.
DRINK 2008–2009.

Price	$14
Region	Western Australia
Value	●●●
Auction	N/A
Score	84

Leasingham Bin 61 Shiraz 2005

This and Leasingham Bin 56 are two of the wines I cut my teeth on. I've been disappointed in this label of late, but it looks as though the label may have turned the corner.

2005 RELEASE
There is a nice lick of vanillin oak sitting on top of plush, savoury, plummy fruit flavour, the archetypal Bin 61 flavour profile. All tastes good. There's quite a bit of acidity here too though, and the flavour doesn't really flow easily through the finish. In short, I'd buy and drink it, but I wouldn't go out of my way. **DRINK** 2008–2013.

Price	$22
Region	Clare Valley
Value	●●●
Auction	★★
Score	87

Lindemans Limestone Ridge Shiraz Cabernet Sauvignon 2004 & 2005

This has long been a favourite of the corporate set, though in recent years the production volume has simply been too high. They're reining it back, and the quality is up.

2004 RELEASE
Lots of dark berry and cassis-like smells burst from the glass. The palate is then sturdy, plummy, toasty and simple in its currenty fruit profile. Seventy per cent shiraz, thirty per cent cabernet. Nice balance of structure, fruit flavour and oak. **DRINK** 2014–2020.

2005 RELEASE
Mighty good. Big bloom of fruity fragrance and flavour. Generous doses of raspberry, plums and blackcurrant, the finish then awash with chalky, lengthy tannin. Made from vines planted in 1967, and blessed with attractive overtones of milk chocolate and violets. This is a terrific return to the quality arena. Only 12.9 per cent alcohol! **DRINK** 2014–2025.

Price	$55
Region	Coonawarra
Value	♦♦♦♦
Auction	★★★★
Score	92 (2004)
	95 (2005)

Lindemans Reserve Shiraz 2005

A couple of years ago there was a cracking wine under this label, and this is impressive too.

2005 RELEASE
The score may not be all that high but this is fabulous red wine buying. It tastes of plums, cherries and minerals, and has enough structure for the flavour to run along solid rails. Chewy, flavoursome and good. **DRINK** 2008–2010.

Price	$13
Region	Padthaway
Value	♦♦♦♦♦
Auction	N/A
Score	87

Longhop Old Vine Shiraz 2006 & 2007

Domenic Torzi makes this wine and is also one half of the Torzi Matthews Frost Dodger team. I hear he has another couple of wine projects well advanced too.

2006 RELEASE
Fifteen bucks for this? Get outta here! It's lashed with licorice, raspberry and plum-cake flavours, the attack of rich, sweet fruit like a vice grip to your throat. It's a perfumed monster of a wine. Amazing value. Big red in every sense of the word. **DRINK** 2008–2009.

2007 RELEASE
I thought the 2006 was good but this is a significant step up. It's a classy wine. It's rich with flavours of toast, blackberry, raspberry and kirsch, raisiny sweetness helping to plump out the core of it. This is one juicy little sucker.
DRINK 2008–2012.

Price	$15
Region	Adelaide Plains
Value	♦♦♦♦♦
Auction	N/A
Score	89 (2006)
	92 (2007)

Longview Yakka Shiraz 2006

Longview is one of the rising stars of Australian wine. Its shiraz is on the money, its nebbiolo a field of promise. It's easy to suspect that the Adelaide Hills is about to enter a grand era.

2006 RELEASE
It's tempting to call this a whopper except that it's also got the hallmarks of an elegant, finesse-matters red wine. It's big on bold blueberried fruit flavour, but it's also nuanced with flavours of chicory, hay, cedarwood and smoke. I guess it's the best of all worlds. Lively, life-giving, handsome red wine. **DRINK** 2011–2018.

Price	$35
Region	Adelaide Hills
Value	♦♦♦♦
Auction	★★★
Score	93

Luke Lambert Syrah 2006

This is a tiny Yarra Valley operation – so tiny that Lambert refers to his winery as a tiny corrugated-iron shed, complete with a dirt floor. Nothing tiny about the quality. The wines are terrifically packaged too.

2006 RELEASE
Desperately needs to be decanted, preferably for a couple of hours. It's so tight and controlled that it needs a lot of air to relax. It's exotic: it tastes of violets, black and red cherries, woodspice and pepper. It's stylish; not only in its flavours, but in the way it stretches out through the finish, like a spirited ovation. It really needs to be cellared but it's a super wine – in quality and interest. **DRINK** 2011–2017.

Price	$33
Region	Yarra Valley
Value	♦♦♦♦♦
Auction	N/A
Score	93

McWilliam's Hanwood Estate Shiraz 2006

Big volume wine routinely offering big value.

2006 RELEASE
Give it a little time to breathe (maybe thirty minutes) and it smells really good. Turkish delight, raspberries, a touch of sawdusty oak and stewed mulberries. The flavours are pretty much similar, if not quite as enchanting. It finishes with a burst of ripe fruit sweetness. I've heard it said that you can pick this up for less than ten bucks; if true, you are onto a world-level bargain. **DRINK** 2008–2009.

Price	$10
Region	South Eastern Australia
Value	♦♦♦♦
Auction	N/A
Score	87

Mad Fish Gold Turtle Shiraz 2005

A lot of good things get said about Great Southern shiraz but there aren't a lot of good examples to use as evidence. Here's one – it's a belter.

2005 RELEASE
You could blow me down with a feather! The quality of this made my jaw drop (and it had nothing to do with the fact that I'd just taken another big heavy mouthful). If this doesn't cellar like dream I'll be amazed, frankly. Dark cherries, plums, spice, gravel, understated creamy oak – I promise you, you cannot go wrong with this. It is class-ee. **DRINK** 2011–2016.

Price	$25
Region	Great Southern
Value	♦♦♦♦♦
Auction	★★★
Score	93

Maglieri Shiraz 2006

This brand has become somewhat lost in the bulging Foster's wine portfolio, so I was surprised to discover that it still tastes damn good. A hearty shiraz, likely to be found on discount.

Price	$20
Region	McLaren Vale
Value	♦♦♦♦♦
Auction	★★
Score	92

2006 RELEASE
A blast of ink and chocolate and blackberry – it's just the ticket for those nights when only a robust red will do. There's creamy vanillin oak swooshing all through the wine too, giving the wine a melt-in-your-mouth personality; I reckon you'd be hard pressed to find an Aussie red wine lover who doesn't like this. Big, smooth, warm and generous. **DRINK** 2008–2014.

Majella Shiraz 2005

A friend was telling me recently that he prefers Majella's shiraz over its cabernet. I thought he'd gone nuts until I looked at my ratings over the years – I almost agreed with him. The auction market agrees too; Majella shiraz often outguns Majella cabernet for re-sale value.

Price	$33
Region	Coonawarra
Value	♦♦♦♦♦
Auction	★★★★
Score	94

2005 RELEASE
What a beauty. Dense, luscious, finely boned and fleshy. It's got the lot. Structure and charm. Flavours of chalk, plums, chocolate and cedar. Minty oak rears its head, but only just. It's a very fine wine. **DRINK** 2010–2018.

PREVIOUS
1997 Perfectly balanced oak, fruit tannin. 2003–2009. 91 pts.
1998 Lots of oak, lots of fruit. 2004–2011. 92 pts.
1999 Cherries, plums and spice. 2005–2010. 90 pts.
2000 Approachable, bold, syrupy. 2003–2010. 92 pts.
2001 Plummy and bold. Enormously enjoyable. 2004–2010. 91 pts.
2002 Sweet, generous, tannic. 2005–2011. 91 pts.
2003 Licorice, cherries, lighter-bodied. 2006–2011. 88 pts.
2004 Plush and plummy. Deadset delicious. 2007–2012. 92 pts.

Marius Symphony Shiraz 2005

Roger Pike is the man behind Marius and since launching a few years back he's produced a string of hits. There seems little doubt that he is a fabulous grower of red grapes.

2005 RELEASE
Chocka-block with warm, chocolaty fruit and oak flavour. This is a great example of a dark, slippery smooth shiraz. Puff-chested, coffeed and powerful. I think you get my drift. It's good. **DRINK** 2008–2012.

Price	$35
Region	McLaren Vale
Value	♦♦♦♦
Auction	N/A
Score	92

Marius Symposium Shiraz Mourvedre 2006

There's an argument in wine that shiraz lacks complexity by itself, and needs something blended with it – even if it's in minute quantities. This explains why viognier has become such a common blender with shiraz. Here mourvedre works excellently.

2006 RELEASE
What a lovely array of flavours. Blue- and blackberried fruit, lots of dark, minerally tannin, an earthy leatheriness (courtesy of the mourvedre) and lots of mouth-filling, seductive, chocolaty oak. Excellent length. A great winter wine, full stop. **DRINK** 2008–2016.

Price	$30
Region	McLaren Vale
Value	♦♦♦♦
Auction	N/A
Score	94

Mayer Big Betty Shiraz 2006

Not all that long ago shiraz was one of the Yarra Valley's ugly ducklings. Not any longer – now it's part of the avant-garde.

2006 RELEASE
This took a long time to come around – if you're thinking of opening a bottle to drink, do so at least two hours before time. It's stinky to the point of off-putting at first, but given time to breathe a thoroughly enthralling wine opens up before you. Chocolate, raw steak, thick plummy fruit goodness, dark pepper and an assortment of dried herbs – it sounds like a meal more than a wine, but it's all in there. Art-house shiraz. Delectably fine, swaggering tannin. **DRINK** 2012–2019.

Price	$30
Region	Yarra Valley
Value	♦♦♦
Auction	N/A
Score	94

Meerea Park Alexander Munro Shiraz 2006

The bar is being pushed ever higher at Meerea Park.

2006 RELEASE
There's a rich core of sweet fruit here, shot as it is by trademark notes of Hunter earthiness. It tastes of plums, malt, iodine, minerals and red earth, and there seems little doubt that it will mature majestically. **DRINK** 2012–2020.

Price	$60
Region	Hunter Valley
Value	♦♦♦♦
Auction	★★★
Score	94

Meerea Park Hell Hole Shiraz 2006

Maybe it's the name but ever since it first appeared – with the 2003 vintage – it's been a wine I've looked forward to tasting. It's a single vineyard wine made from the Howard 'Somerset' vineyard, planted in the 1960s. It is one of the Hunter's best vineyards.

Price	$55
Region	Hunter Valley
Value	♦♦♦♦
Auction	★★★
Score	96

2006 RELEASE
I liked this wine so much that I felt like a better person the moment I started drinking it. It's perfumed and musky and outrageously plummy, its earthy, spicy foundations evident, but discreet. A fine flourish of scented flavour bursts through the finish; as do superfine tannins. Wow. Classic Hunter, in the best possible way. **DRINK** 2012–2020.

PREVIOUS
2003 Big, savoury, stylish and long. 2007–2017. 94 pts.
2004 Cedary, licoricey, tannic. 2010–2016. 94 pts.
2005 Fragrant, fruity and savoury. 2009–2017. 95 pts.

Meerea Park Shiraz 2006 & 2007

I'd not heard of this wine until recently but it's quickly become a house favourite. Extraordinary value in my books. Worth hunting around for.

2006 RELEASE
Great stuff. A medium-weight, savoury wine with an attractive cherry-plummed heart, flecked also with spice, earth and cedar. To boot, it's flushed with an impressive churn of grapey, ripe tannins. I can't fault it. I love it. **DRINK** 2008–2017.

2007 RELEASE
Son of a gun. This is as good – or maybe even better – than the outstanding 2006. The tannin structure of it, the easy-going complexity, the blush of ripe, bright, vibrant fruit – it's all going on. A mouthful of plummy, spicy flavour at a ridiculously low price. **DRINK** 2008–2017.

Price	$15
Region	Hilltops Hunter Valley
Value	●●●●●
Auction	N/A
Score	92 (2006) 93 (2007)

Metala White Label Shiraz Cabernet Sauvignon 2005

Look for this one on special – it can often be had at around the $15 mark. It's full of robust flavour, and on discount offers very firm value.

2005 RELEASE
Maybe it lacks vitality but there's certainly good flavour here. It's riddled with plummy, tarry, currant flavour, chocolaty oak evident but very much as a sideshow. Lovely Langhorne Creek fruitiness is the show here, though there's nice tannin structure too. Big fruity red. **DRINK** 2008–2013.

Price	$19
Region	Langhorne Creek
Value	●●●●●
Auction	★★★
Score	90

Mike Press Shiraz 2006

The 2005 (92 points, $10) of this caused a stampede – it was the bargain shiraz of 2007. The quality of the 2006 shiraz and cabernet will no doubt make them sell out fast too. Simply incredible prices.

2006 RELEASE
Bang on. Musky, perfumed, fruity, plummy, sweet-smelling but dry tasting. This isn't a quaffer, it's a quality cool-climate shiraz. There's tannin here: ripe tannin, chunky and chewy. Quality drinking at a guilt-free price. **DRINK** 2008–2012.

Price	$10
Region	Adelaide Hills
Value	●●●●●
Auction	N/A
Score	88

Mitchelton Parish Shiraz Viognier 2005

About five years ago I attended the launch of the Nagambie Lakes wine region where it announced that its mission was to 'own' Rhône Valley varieties in Australia – think shiraz, viognier, marsanne, roussanne and company. My view is that the Nagambie region is a fantastic place to grow grapes, but that it has not made progress in this aim.

2005 RELEASE
Attractive wine. It slinks across your tongue with the smoothness of a cat burglar, dry tannins the only break to the seductive display. Blackberries and black cherries, kirsch and chalk (drink it, you'll see what I mean), the more I tasted it the more it impressed. This is the best balanced red wine I have seen from Mitchelton for some considerable time. **DRINK** 2009–2017.

Price	$30
Region	Nagambie Lakes
Value	♦♦♦
Auction	★★★
Score	93

Mitchelton Print Shiraz 2003 & 2004

The oak regime for this wine is now far more sensible than it once was – for a good while it was hard to see the fruits for the trees. It is a more impressive wine now, and will age better.

2003 RELEASE
Tight, spicy, savoury wine – though it is still profoundly intense. Coconut-like oak is evident, but as a vague perfume rather than as a dominant force. Blackberries, leather and plums, all locked in a tight fist of tannin. Lovely syrupy texture. **DRINK** 2011–2027.

2004 RELEASE
Much like the 2003 but for greater generosity through the mid-palate. This is a really good wine. Balance! Deep blackberry and plum-like flavour. Long fruit-driven length. Appropriate levels of chocolaty oak and regional influences of eucalypt and cloves. Congrats to the team. **DRINK** 2011–2018.

Price	$50
Region	Nagambie Lakes
Value	♦♦♦
Auction	★★★
Score	92 (2003) 94 (2004)

Mitolo Reiver Shiraz 2005

Reiver is Mitolo's Barossa shiraz and it's normally the one I'm slightly less impressed by; not this year.

2005 RELEASE
Gorgeous black shiraz. Full of inky, slinky, berried fruit flavour, boosted here by flavours of roast meats, smoke, coal and cedar. It's a very ripe wine but a well structured one, with supple tannins keeping the rage of flavour in balance. **DRINK** 2011–2019.

PREVIOUS
2001 Great mid-palate; lacks finish. 2003–2007. 88 pts.
2002 Ripeness, length, mouth-filling flavour. 2008–2015. 93 pts.
2003 Solid, ripe, punchy flavour. 2004–2009. 90 pts.
2004 Sweet, warm, long and ripe. 2006–2011. 91 pts.

Price	$56
Region	Barossa
Value	♦♦♦♦
Auction	★★★
Score	96

Mitolo Savitar Shiraz 2005

2005 RELEASE
This, to coin a phrase, is the inside thigh of wine. Bugger the Handsome Prince – pour a drop of this on Sleeping Beauty's mouth and she'd wake up in a flash and demand a Big Red glass full. It's a persistent, plummy, provocative wine that finishes chalky, loamy and firm, despite its smooth, velvety ride. It needs time to build complexity, but all of its inky, oozing fruit and smoky oak is bound to build into something. For pure hedonism: drink it now. For its full glory: drink it in ten or more years. **DRINK** 2013–2020.

PREVIOUS
2003 Great wine from a tough vintage. 2008–2014. 94 pts.
2004 Super-ripe but super-composed. 2006–2012. 94 pts.

Price	$73
Region	McLaren Vale
Value	♦♦♦♦
Auction	★★★
Score	96

Mollydooker Goosebumps Sparkling Shiraz 2006

Most sparkling reds are (in today's terms) moderate in alcohol, but very sweet. Mollydooker always do things differently, and so they have with this: it is very high in alcohol (sixteen per cent) but low in sugar. It means that it's rich but dry, and remarkably refreshing.

2006 RELEASE
It tastes a lot like a mix of apple and plum sauce – probably why it drinks so well with roast turkey. It's got the fresh tanginess of apple and the dark lusciousness of plum, dry chocolate-like flavours oozing over the top. Despite its oomph, it has an elegance and a distinct more-ishness. **DRINK** 2008–2012.

Price	$50
Region	Padthaway, Langhorne Creek
Value	♦♦♦♦
Auction	N/A
Score	93

Mollydooker The Boxer Shiraz 2006

I tasted most of the Mollydooker range and this was the best value: I didn't like The Scooter Merlot, and the Blue-Eyed Boy Shiraz and Carnival of Love Shiraz were solid but not worthy of their price tag.

2006 RELEASE
This was released in the second half of 2007 and is getting better as it rests in the bottle. It's blisteringly high-octane stuff, big in alcohol and sweet, chocolaty, smoky, raisiny fruit flavour. Clearly you have to enjoy its blistering style. But if you do – this is right on the money, for not much money. **DRINK** 2008–2011.

Price	$23
Region	McLaren Vale, Padthaway, Langhorne Creek
Value	♦♦♦♦♦
Auction	N/A
Score	91

Moondah Brook Shiraz 2005

They pull grapes from a range of different West Australian wine regions to make this wine, and it invariably comes up a treat. They've hit the mark again here.

2005 RELEASE
Super value. Heaps of chunky, plummy flavour, one slurp of it and you have yourself a mouthful of gutsy red wine. As it leaves your mouth a run of minerally, toasty flavours are left over – just to emphasise its class. Shop around and get a good price on it – and then make hay.
DRINK 2008–2012.

Price	$18
Region	Western Australia
Value	♦♦♦♦♦
Auction	★★★
Score	89

Mount Langi Ghiran Cliff Edge Shiraz 2004 & 2005

2004 RELEASE
Intriguing mix of brooding, tarry, spicy fruit weight and leaner, more herbal characters, the mix suggesting that some of the grapes managed to get very ripe, while others didn't quite make it. I suspect that this is partly why I've had different reactions to it on the three occasions I've drunk it. **DRINK** 2008–2012.

2005 RELEASE
It's a whole new world of shiraz, spicy to its gills and full of cherry-plummed heart. Sophistication beats loud. And tannin – none of the powdery stuff here, this is fine, mature, firm and convincing. I'm a huge wrap for this. Spectacular cool-climate shiraz. **DRINK** 2011–2018.

Price	$27
Region	**Grampians**
Value	♦ ♦ ♦ ♦
Auction	★ ★ ★ ★
Score	89 (2004)
	95 (2005)

Mount Langi Ghiran Langi Shiraz 2005

At the risk of channelling the late Murray Tyrrell, there would be a strong argument to suggest that this is the best Langi shiraz ever.

2005 RELEASE
This is the duck's guts. It is a fan-bloody-tastic wine. It's firm, enclosed, calculated in what it'll let you see for now, but the suggestions of kirsch, blueberry, dark cherry, cedarwood, sandalwood, graphite and strong black pepper are gloriously positioned, powered, and presented to your palate. It needs seven to ten years in the cellar, and will probably live for thirty. It is the wine Langi had to have. **DRINK** 2015–2025.

Price	$55
Region	**Grampians**
Value	♦ ♦ ♦ ♦
Auction	N/A
Score	98

Mount Majura Shiraz 2006

Mount Majura has produced a number of interesting wines over the past five years, the shiraz invariably the stand-out. I don't like all the wines, but when I do like one, it is invariably outstanding value.

Price	$25
Region	Canberra District
Value	♦♦♦♦♦
Auction	★★★
Score	94

2006 RELEASE
If you've ever enjoyed a glass of Craiglee shiraz – or indeed a wine from the heart of France's Rhône Valley – you should hunt out this wine. It crackles with dark, peppery spice, its cushion of plums and dark cherries flavours both succulent and pure, but second in appeal to the minerally, spicy crackle of it. I love this wine's dry, chocolaty tannins too – indeed, I love this wine. **DRINK** 2009–2015.

PREVIOUS
2002 Violetty, bacony, cherried and spicy. 2005–2014. 92 pts.
2003 Salty, baked, plummy but hard. 2007–2010. 85 pts.
2004 Taut, deep, needs time. 2010–2016. 93 pts.
2005 Frisky, plummy, peppery and balanced. 2007–2017. 94 pts.

Mount Pleasant Maurice O'Shea Shiraz 2005

Maurice O'Shea didn't plant the first vines at Mount Pleasant but he was the one who gave it the name, set up the winery, made the first wine and turned it into a legend. And it is a legend; as indeed is he.

Price	$65
Region	Hunter Valley
Value	♦♦
Auction	★★★
Score	94

2005 RELEASE
Strong, tannic and thick with oak – but it manages the style terrifically. This is an excellent release. Its plummy, earthy fruit flavour ripples with tannin and sandy, minerally character; its length long and sure. When it's mature, it will be seriously good. **DRINK** 2012–2021.

PREVIOUS
1994 Gamey, leathery, earthy. 2001–2009. 91 pts.
1996 Leather, game, nutty oak. 2004–2010. 90 pts.
1997 Light, leathery, fading. 2002–2007. 86 pts.
1998 Warm, coffeed, oak-driven but good. 2007–2015. 93 pts.
1999 Very earthy, very leathery, very gamey. 2006–2012. 89 pts.
2000 Great fruit, mediocre oak flavour. 2008–2018. 93 pts.
2003 Cedar, blueberry, plums, rose; excellent. 2013–2025. 94 pts.
2004 Unbalanced and over-oaked. 2008–2013. 87 pts.

Mount Pleasant Old Paddock & Old Hill Shiraz 2003

The 2003 Hunter vintage was hot but very good for reds; the 2004 vintage tougher but still good; the 2005 vintage a pearler. Indeed the 2005 OP & OH shiraz is a likely future winner of the Red Wine of the Year Award – it is a stunning Hunter red.

2003 RELEASE
There's a lot of nice fruit but also a lot of malty, coffeed, caramel-like oak, and to my way of thinking it spoils the show. The fruit itself tastes of cherry-plums, salt, cheese and coffee, and while it should all taste a lot better in three to five years, I doubt that it will ever come into proper balance. **DRINK** 2010–2015.

Price	$50
Region	Hunter Valley
Value	♦ ♦
Auction	★ ★ ★
Score	89

Mount Pleasant Philip Shiraz 2005

Every now and then Philip rips out a regionally distinctive ripper. This release is bigger on flavour than usual.

2005 RELEASE
I love this wine. I'm going to raid my piggy bank and buy as much of it as I can scrounge together. It's tense and tannic and in need of five years in the cellar, but it's also full of the flavours of thick cherry-plums, salt, autumn leaves, blueberries and earth. It's a wine that gives 'savouriness' a good name. I tasted this in among a range of far more expensive reds, all served with their identities masked, and it shone. It's also, for the first time, available under a screwcap seal. **DRINK** 2009–2017.

Price	$16
Region	Hunter Valley
Value	♦ ♦ ♦ ♦ ♦
Auction	★ ★ ★
Score	93

Mount Pleasant Rosehill Shiraz 2003

A single vineyard wine that's an absolute monte for the cellar; I might not love the oak flavours here but that's just my personal taste. The wine is good, and it will taste terrific in eight or so years.

2003 RELEASE
Full of glossy, vanillin, cedary oak but packed with hearty plum-like flavour too, the Hunter's trademark earthy, dark cherry notes singing freely here. The longer it sat in the glass, the more it seduced. This is a juicy, regional, lengthy wine that will reward the patient handsomely. **DRINK** 2012–2022.

Price	$32
Region	Hunter Valley
Value	♦ ♦ ♦ ♦ ♦
Auction	★ ★ ★
Score	94

Mountadam Shiraz 2006

Somewhere around the start of this century Mountadam seemed to lose its way. The wines also became too expensive. It's great to see Mountadam back on form – this wine went within a whisker of winning the Big Red 'Widely Available' Bargain of the Year. (I've tasted Mountadam's Cabernet Merlot 2006 and it's a good drink, but not quite up to the standard of the shiraz.)

Price	$18
Region	Barossa
Value	♦♦♦♦♦
Auction	N/A
Score	90

2006 RELEASE
It's worth buying multiple bottles of this. It tastes of liquid milk chocolate and jubes and licorice, and has just enough earthy, peppery spiciness to make it appeal to both savoury-seekers and sweet-toothers (not that it's sugary, it's just full of sweet, ripe, juicy shiraz flavour). A creamy smooth, juicy red. **DRINK** 2008–2010.

Mountadam Shiraz Viognier 2006

The Barossa Valley is generally too warm to make successful shiraz viognier blends – with notable exceptions – but the Eden Valley is a different matter. This is a sound release.

Price	$24
Region	Eden Valley
Value	♦♦♦♦
Auction	N/A
Score	90

2006 RELEASE
Juicy as all get up. This is a lighter expression of Eden Valley shiraz but that said, it does not lack power through the finish – it's not weighty, but it is lengthy. It's spicy too. And slightly bitter. And so tense in the mouth that you just know that a good lie down will do it the world of good. In short, it's not the wine's size that matters, it's the way you use it – cellar this for two or three years, and it will satisfy. **DRINK** 2010–2014.

Mr Riggs The Gaffer Shiraz 2006

This is named after John 'Gaffer' Riggs, a South Aussie farmer between 1814 and 1902. Ben Riggs (the Mr Riggs of the label) is his great, great, great grandson.

Price	$22
Region	McLaren Vale
Value	♦♦♦♦♦
Auction	★★★
Score	92

2006 RELEASE
There's a syrupiness to this wine that really sets the seduction rolling. It tastes like an exotic mix of aniseed, raspberry, toast and burnt sugar, and while there's a touch of alcohol warmth it wears it proudly and well. It's all about dark, highly slurpable fruit. **DRINK** 2008–2012.

Ngeringa Syrah 2005

Syrah and shiraz are the same grape, the 'syrah' word used as a statement on the style of the wine more than anything else. Some call syrah a more European expression of shiraz. Others, more simply, that syrah is more about nuance than power.

2005 RELEASE
Exquisite. It tastes as much like a pinot noir as a shiraz, a point you'll appreciate when you listen to the flavour profile: it tastes of dried herbs, beetroot, pepper, dark cherries and kirsch. That said, there's a chocolaty, cedary hit too, and the wine does not lack impact. It's also noticeably persistent. If I wanted to be critical, I would note the wine's slight eucalypt character, something that's almost inevitable in Australian reds, but which doesn't have a place in a Euro-style wine like this. That noted, this wine is quite superb. **DRINK** 2012–2020.

Price	$40
Region	Adelaide Hills
Value	●●●●●
Auction	N/A
Score	95

Noon Reserve Shiraz 2006

Drew Noon was at the forefront of the 'cult' wine boom of the late 1990s, pushed forward by the very high ratings of American critic Robert Parker. Truth is that Drew Noon and his wines are highly authentic in what they do – there's nothing faddish here.

2006 RELEASE
The best Noon shiraz for some time. It's seamless, loaded with sweet, ripe, dark fruit flavour, super supple in its texture and long, glycerol and warm on the finish. It tastes of blueberries and blackberries and sundry summer berries, its grainy, sawdusty oak far in the background. Yes, there's a portiness to this wine, but it's integral to its shtick. **DRINK** 2008–2016.

Price	$25 (Cellar Door)
Region	Langhorne Creek
Value	●●●●●
Auction	★★★★
Score	95

PREVIOUS
2001 Warm licorice and leather flavour. 2004–2011. 89 pts.
2002 Big, deep, hearty and soft. 2007–2015. 92 pts.
2003 Stuffed with pure, pristine fruit. 2005–2012. 91 pts.
2004 Big, rich, generous and tannic. 2005–2011. 92 pts.
2005 Hot alcohol; potent fruit. 2006–2010. 87 pts.

Nugan Estate Parish Vineyard Shiraz 2005

Is all this talk of spicy, cool-climate shiraz and medium-weight flavour not really your bag? Then this wine is for you. It's South Aussie shiraz: bold, pure and beautiful.

2005 RELEASE
This is really good clobber. There's a helluva lot of meat on its bones too. It's dark, plush, dense and satisfying, the power of its plummy, blackberried, coffeed fruit flavour as good as many wines at twice the price. Its tannin profile is fruity and sure, it's persistence of flavour unquestioned. It's a bloody boomer actually. You have to enjoy a nice clip of American oak to enjoy it – but then, most people do.
DRINK 2008–2014.

Price	$22
Region	McLaren Vale
Value	♦♦♦♦♦
Auction	N/A
Score	94

Oliver's Taranga Vineyards HJ Reserve Shiraz 2005

2005 RELEASE
There's a lot about this that reminds me of 1999 Penfolds Grange (just to be a name-dropper). It's got similar intensity, similar tannin, similar flavour, and should cellar similarly well. It tastes of leather, coffee, blackberry and malt, its meaty, peppery complexity giving it a kick along. It's quite beautiful. **DRINK** 2010–2020.

Price	$45
Region	McLaren Vale
Value	♦♦♦♦♦
Auction	N/A
Score	96

Oliver's Taranga Vineyards Shiraz 2005

Oliver's Taranga is a family owned and run operation of outstanding quality. The Oliver family has farmed in the McLaren Vale area since 1839, though it's only since 1994 that they've made wine. Corrina Rayment is the winemaking star of the family, and (blessedly) they only make red wines under the Oliver's label.

2005 RELEASE
Wow! This had me going from the first sip. This is rich, viscous, chocolaty and impressive, its dark fruitiness pure and big and wonderful. If you like your reds big, you have to try this – it's a flamin' beauty. It's not just big though, it's structured, controlled, complex – full of personality. Outstanding wine. **DRINK** 2008–2020.

Price	$28
Region	McLaren Vale
Value	♦♦♦♦♦
Auction	N/A
Score	95

Paringa Estate 'Estate' Shiraz 2005

2005 RELEASE
It's a medium-weight wine but there's enough oomph here to really get things singing. This is a wine to pour into big glasses and give a good swirl, so that you can properly enjoy its heady perfumes. Think forest berries, mint, pepper, soy and dark cherries. Add a clip of perfectly judged French oak. Swallow now, and notice the fine run of tannin – lingering longer than you expected. This is a winning drop of the elegant, savoury kind. **DRINK** 2012–2019.

Price	$45
Region	Mornington Peninsula
Value	♦♦♦
Auction	N/A
Score	92

Paringa Estate Peninsula Shiraz 2005

Mornington is thought of as a marginal climate for shiraz, though Paringa's Lindsay McCall has a long record of making good wines from it. I suspect that he's as good in the vineyard as he is in the winery.

2005 RELEASE
This is a good juicy drink but at twenty-five bucks there's plenty better to the found. It tastes of cherry-plum and mild spice and has lots of tangy acidity, the fresh medium-weight fruitiness of it the total extent of its appeal. **DRINK** 2008–2012.

Price	$25
Region	Mornington Peninsula
Value	♦♦♦
Auction	N/A
Score	87

Paringa Estate Reserve Shiraz 2005

It's an incredible price for a Mornington Peninsula shiraz, but if anyone can ask it, Paringa Estate can. The consistent high standard of this estate is phenomenal.

2005 RELEASE
Easy to be a big fan of this. It's lusciously perfumed, struck with flavour and then brilliant through the finish – the complete wine. Those flavours are in the dark cherry, rose petal and various shades of pepper spectrum, while the tannins are so gritty and fine that they seem bespoke tailored. Classy. **DRINK** 2012–2022.

Price	$80
Region	Mornington Peninsula
Value	♦♦♦
Auction	N/A
Score	94

Paxton Vineyards AAA Shiraz Grenache 2006

Paxton is not only one of the largest growers of wine grapes in McLaren Vale, but also one of the most progressive. They run a number of their vineyards along biodynamic principles, and in recent years have lifted their wine quality markedly.

2006 RELEASE
This has got the lot: flavour of meat, chocolate, minerals and crushed blackberries, the main ticket being the richness of McLaren Vale red grapes – rather than excessive oak. Elements of it taste like dry licorice, and it lingers tastily, and lengthily, in your mouth long after you've swallowed it. A beauty. **DRINK** 2008–2014.

Price	$22
Region	McLaren Vale
Value	♦♦♦♦♦
Auction	N/A
Score	92

Paxton Vineyards Jones Block Shiraz 2004

Wine reviewers cost you money by (hopefully) getting you excited over lots of wines you never knew about, and inevitably trading you up on occasion. You have to live a little. But with wines like this, we bring it home and save you money. That's my argument, and I'm sticking with it.

2004 RELEASE
It's a good wine but I don't like it as much as the far cheaper AAA. It's got lots of fruit grunt but no great brightness or length, the energy of it bound up entirely in the mid-palate. Blackberry jam, tar and toast, the finish somewhat disappointing. **DRINK** 2008–2013.

Price	$37
Region	McLaren Vale
Value	♦♦♦
Auction	N/A
Score	86

Penfolds Bin 28 Shiraz 2005

I've had a lot of experience drinking Bin 28 Shiraz and it rarely disappoints; now it is back in top form.

2005 RELEASE
Son of a gun – much like the 2004, except better. I've tasted a pre-sample of the 2006 and it's a ripper too. Penfolds is on a roll here. Musk-shot plums, rolling ripe tannin, whispers of vanillin oak and long, blackberried, fleshy length. Super wine. **DRINK** 2014–2022.

Price	$32
Region	South Australia
Value	♦♦♦♦
Auction	★★★★★
Score	92

PREVIOUS
1995 Lovely, medium-weight drinking. 2007–2013. 88 pts.
1996 Meaty, cherried, nutty and delicious. 2010–2020. 94 pts.
1997 Simple but good drinking. 2006–2014. 88 pts.
1998 Fantastic. Bold and generous. 2012–2030. 94 pts.
1999 Fresh, clean, fruity and fine. 2010–2022. 93 pts.
2000 Surprisingly good. Choc-mint deliciousness. 2007–2012. 89 pts.
2001 Drink it young. 2007–2011. 87 pts.
2002 Minerally, plummy, minty and controlled. 2012–2022. 92 pts.
2003 Savoury, sandy and muscular. 2009–2013. 87 pts.
2004 Fresh, musky, plummy. 2013–2020. 92 pts.

Penfolds Coonawarra Bin 128 Shiraz 2006

Penfolds has pumped up the tyres of this one. It's been looking like a slouch for a few years, but the simultaneous release of the 2004 and 2005 jumped the quality back up, and the 2006 is a beauty. Unusually for Penfolds, this is wholly matured in French oaks (only a third of it new), and grown in one region.

2006 RELEASE
Totally gorgeous. Massively floral, musky, perfumed, welcoming, scented – it's just yum. Tannins frame it all perfectly – there are masses of them underlying it all, but they're fruity and integrated and essentially unobtrusive to the smooth flow of it. Lots of cherried, plummy flavour. Medium weight. **DRINK** 2011–2021.

Price	$33
Region	Coonawarra
Value	♦♦♦♦♦
Auction	★★★
Score	92
Past greats	1986, 1991

PREVIOUS
1996 Structure plus. Spicy, strawberried, savoury. 2008–2017. 92 pts.
1997 Game, menthol, lots of pepper. 2009–2014. 86 pts.
1998 Peppery, strawberried, lovely. 2009–2019. 91 pts.
1999 Balanced, structured, complex. 2011–2020. 93 pts.
2000 Gamey, plummy, minty. 2007–2012. 84 pts.
2001 Cherried, peppery, light but attractive. 2006–2012. 90 pts.
2002 Juicy, sweet-bitter, spicy. 2007–2016. 92 pts.
2003 Over-oaked, minty, spicy. 2006–2012. 87 pts.
2004 Pretty, pink, smoky. 2008–2017. 92 pts.
2005 Fresh, delicious, plummy. 2007–2018. 93 pts.

Penfolds Grange Shiraz 2003

Made each year since 1951; it will always be the flag bearer of quality Australian wine.

2003 RELEASE
Great result for the vintage. Has hot, brandied, salty characters but lots of fleshy, pippy fruit through its core, and enough fruit attachment to the tannins to bear it well. This is a ripping result. There's an odd bitterness on the finish, thanks to the high heat stress of the vintage. A sneak preview 2004 and 2005 showed both to be great Granges. **DRINK** 2015–2025.

PREVIOUS
1990 Phenomenally long, strong, impressive wine. 2015–2030. 95 pts.
1991 Beautifully mature. 2008–2016. 93 pts.
1992 Simple, leathery, drinking now. 2007–2012. 89 pts.
1993 Leafy, different, structured and long. 2010–2022. 84 pts.
1994 Big, sweet, structured and welcoming. 2011–2025. 95 pts.
1995 Good dark fruit; unpleasant oak. 2006–2014. 88 pts.
1996 Perfect Grange. Structure, class, power. 2012–2035. 98 pts.
1997 Leathery, blackberried; lacks endurance. 2005–2012. 87 pts.
1998 Wall of sound. Great. 2012–2026. 97 pts.
1999 Perfect poise, perfect weight. 2010–2027. 96 pts.
2000 Green, leathery, bitter and roasted. 2007–2012. 87 pts.
2001 Supple tannin, substantial flavour. 2010–2020. 94 pts.
2002 Gorgeous curves of plush fruit. 2018–2037. 96 pts.

Price	$550
Region	Barossa
Value	♦♦
Auction	★★★★
Score	93

Penfolds Koonunga Hill Shiraz 2005

Koonunga Hill was once a shiraz–cabernet only (first vintage was 1976) and, importantly, it was the entry to Penfolds red wine drinking. It meant that every experience of a Penfolds red was likely to be a positive one. It would be great to return to those days.

2005 RELEASE
A good wine. Indeed it's well worth taking a crack at. It tastes of cherry-plums, dried herbs, vanillin, spices and chocolate, its ability to satisfy punching above its medium weight. Lovely ripeness. **DRINK** 2014–2022.

Price	$14.95
Region	South Australia
Value	♦♦♦♦
Auction	★★★
Score	87

Penfolds Koonunga Hill Shiraz Cabernet 2005

This is the original Koonunga Hill and it's still the one to seek out.

2005 RELEASE
The best for years – maybe even since the 1999. It's plummy, raw and still finding its feet, but it has a lovely rush of savoury, sandy, loamy character, mixed with rich, ripe, cherry-plummed goodness. It smells good, and it tastes good. Awesome finish. Really good structure for a wine at this price. Made my heart smile when I tasted this.
DRINK 2008–2013.

Price	$14.95
Region	South Australia
Value	♦♦♦♦
Auction	★★★★★
Score	90

PREVIOUS
1995 Medium weight but drinking well. 1999–2009. 87 pts.
1996 Leathery, porty, toffeed. 2000–2008. 88 pts.
1997 Packs a convincing, if odd, punch. 2002–2011. 88 pts.
1998 Ripe herbs, currants and game. Drying. 2003–2012. 90 pts.
1999 Structured, curranty, well defined. 2004–2011. 89 pts.
2000 Gamey, tannic, herbal. 2004–2008. 84 pts.
2001 Sweet mint, toffee and game. Mature. 2004–2008. 86 pts.
2002 Easy-going blackcurrant and herbs. 2006–2011. 87 pts.
2003 Baked, tannic, tarry. 2006–2008. 86 pts.
2004 Simple, minty, curranty. 2007–2010. 87 pts.

Penfolds RWT Barossa Shiraz 2005

It's only been around since the 1997 vintage but it's become the French-oaked superstar of the Penfolds range. A French-oaked RWT-styled cabernet is now on the drawing board. From a quality perspective (only), recent vintages of RWT shiraz are starting to look like Grange killers.

2005 RELEASE
Beautiful integration of sensuous oak and bold blue fruit flavour. Seductive, but not at all tarty. Plums, toast, violets, blueberry, musk. Flows effortlessly through the finish. Will live for a very long time. (A sneak preview of 2006 was a perfect storm of fruit and tannin. Tastes fantastic.)
DRINK 2015–2025.

Price	$160
Region	Barossa
Value	♦♦♦
Auction	★★★
Score	97

PREVIOUS
1997 Salty, cedary, gamey. 2008–2013. 87 pts.
1998 Big oak, big fruit. 2011–2021. 92 pts.
1999 Minty, elegant, beautiful. 2010–2020. 93 pts.
2000 Salty, leathery, creamy. 2006–2011. 84 pts.
2001 Salty, plummy, minty. 2010–2016. 92 pts.
2002 Voluminous, chocolaty, blueberried, big. 2015–2030. 94 pts.
2003 Thick blackberried flavour, gritty tannin. 2009–2015. 92 pts.
2004 Poised, balanced, powerful. 2018–2035. 96 pts.

Penfolds St Henri Shiraz 2004

The interesting thing is that when St Henri was first released in the 1950s, it was the same price as Grange. Now there's a $400 (plus) price gap. It's the result as much of fashion and fortune as of quality; I regularly prefer St Henri.

Price	$90
Region	South Australia
Value	♦♦♦
Auction	★★★★
Score	96

2004 RELEASE
Super violety. Lovely. Lifted, pure, sweet but not jammy. Gorgeous really. Will be a long term stunner. Excellent tannin, without being excessive. Gorgeous purity of fruit flavour. Perfume to die for; smelling it is like sticking your head in a florist's shop. Going to be an absolute beauty. **DRINK** 2017–2035.

PREVIOUS
1994 Sweet and jammy, but good. 2009–2023. 93 pts.
1995 Drinking well. Leathery and briary. 2007–2017. 88 pts.
1996 Poised, balanced, effortless class. 2010–2027. 96 pts.
1997 Porty and simple. 2009–2017. 87 pts.
1998 Bold and fruity. Needs time. 2014–2030. 93 pts.
1999 Minty, tannic, leathery, classic. 2014–2028. 94 pts.
2000 Dilute, oystery, plummy. 2009–2014. 86 pts.
2001 Tarry, tannic, impressive. 2010–2019. 93 pts.
2002 Rich, exuberant and complex. 2017–2030. 94 pts.
2003 Eucalypt, blackberry, bit simple. 2011–2022. 90 pts.

Penfolds Thomas Hyland Shiraz 2005

When this wine was introduced a few years ago, it effectively pushed Koonunga Hill lower in the Penfolds pecking order. It was one of the least intelligent moves in Penfolds' marketing history.

Price	$20
Region	South Australia
Value	♦♦
Auction	★
Score	84

2005 RELEASE
The wine is OK but no better than Koonunga Hill, and a long way from the quality of the Bin range. It tastes of mulberry and dilute cherries, spicy oak keeping it all neat and tidy. The length is reasonable, the palate savoury and succulent. **DRINK** 2008–2011.

Penley Estate Hyland Shiraz 2005

The range of Penley red wines has expanded greatly in recent years, but Hyland shiraz is still the one I reach for most commonly. Always does very well in the price/quality equation.

2005 RELEASE
Remarkably sophisticated for the price. Blooming with vibrant plummy flavour and cut with flavours of cloves, cedar and blueberries, the play of oak and fruit a joy to hold in your mouth. Simply, a lovely drink.
DRINK 2008–2012.

Price	$19
Region	Coonawarra
Value	●●●●●
Auction	★★
Score	90

Penny's Hill Red Dot Shiraz Viognier 2006

Penny's Hill makes a range of very good reds, all in the full-bodied, full-flavoured style. This relatively inexpensive shiraz viognier is a real find.

2006 RELEASE
Now we're talking! This is the real deal at a very reasonable price. It's chocked with warm, spicy, savoury flavour and bursts of liquorice and red raspberry-like flavour. The drinkability factor is high. I tell you what, I could go this! The more I drink of it the more I like it – always a good sign. It's a big, warm wine, but there's enough spice to keep it interesting. **DRINK** 2008–2011.

Price	$14
Region	Fleurieu Peninsula
Value	●●●●●
Auction	N/A
Score	90

Pepperjack Shiraz 2006

The best thing about these Pepperjack reds is that they're widely distributed, and so shouldn't be hard to find. They're almost always good, but I'm particularly taken by these 2006s.

2006 RELEASE
For delivery of ripe, dark, satisfying red wine flavour, it's hard to pass this by. It's a soft, cuddly, welcoming red wine, rich with blackberry and chocolate-like flavour and then warm and creamy through the finish. I think the technical term is 'winter warmer'. This hits the spot just right.
DRINK 2008–2015.

Price	$25
Region	Barossa
Value	●●●●
Auction	★★
Score	91

Pepperjack Shiraz Viognier 2006

One of the issues with shiraz viognier blends is not simply whether or not the two combine well, but whether both the shiraz and viognier components are of similar quality. As one winemaker noted, 'There's no use putting crappy quality viognier in good quality shiraz'.

Price	$25
Region	Barossa
Value	♦ ♦ ♦
Auction	N/A
Score	87

2006 RELEASE
A pretty good drink but something about it just doesn't work for me. I suspect it's the viognier; the wine seems to lack both oomph and finish and the viognier is sticking out to the point that it smells more like a white wine than a red wine. It's a pity, because overall the wine is decent.
DRINK 2009–2013.

Petaluma Shiraz 2005

Petaluma shiraz has been a good wine since its inception in 1998 but it's rarely reached great heights. For my money, this is about the best so far.

Price	$35
Region	Adelaide Hills
Value	♦ ♦ ♦ ♦ ♦
Auction	★ ★ ★ ★
Score	93

2005 RELEASE
Maybe it's a bit oak-dominant and heavy-footed but there's a classiness here that makes it worth the money. It feels satiny in the mouth, its flavours of sour cherries, dark cherries, chocolate, bacon and blackberry jam richly concentrated and surely structured. It's a good drink now but it has been built for a decent cellaring life.
DRINK 2010–2018.

PREVIOUS
2000 Nicely balanced; rich sweet flavour. 2005–2009. 90 pts.
2001 Creamy oak, sweet fruit, balance. 2005–2011. 92 pts.
2002 Herbal. Cherried, persistent. 2007–2014. 91 pts.
2003 Lots of flavour, but short. 2006–2012. 88 pts.
2004 Packed with sweet, blackberried flavour. 2011–2018. 92 pts.

Peter Lehmann Futures Shiraz 2005

When Peter Lehmann set out to help pull the Barossa from its then doldrums – back in the early 1980s – he made a wine called The Future Shiraz, made for family and friends only. It was the inspiration for this new wine in the range.

2005 RELEASE
They mature this wine entirely in French oak, and it sure does give the wine a touch of class. The fruit flavours themselves, though, are essence of Barossa: aniseed, coal, blackberry nip and milk chocolate. The more I drank of it the more I swear I started to taste a violety, rose-like flavour – but who really cares? It's a powerful, refined Barossan red of the highest quality. **DRINK** 2012–2020.

Price	$29.95
Region	Barossa
Value	●●●●●
Auction	★★★★
Score	94

Peter Lehmann Shiraz 2005

This is regularly one of the best red buys of the year, though this seems strangely below par.

2005 RELEASE
There's a reasonable amount of flavour and grip here but I'm left wanting more. It tastes raspberried and plummy and there's a touch of toasty oak – all good stuff – but it lacks an extra degree of punch. There are better wines around the same price (even within the Lehmann range). **DRINK** 2008–2012.

Price	$19
Region	Barossa
Value	●●●●●
Auction	N/A
Score	86

Pirathon by Kalleske Shiraz 2005

The Kalleske family have been grapegrowers in the Barossa Valley for five generations. Their vineyard is grown organically, parts of it biodynamically.

2005 RELEASE
This tastes like a wine of double the price. It's tight, tannic, almost ferrous in both its structure and flavour, shafts of ironstone keeping exuberant, high-octane, dark fruit flavour in sturdy check. It's a warm, generous, tasty package, and the flavour lingers brilliantly. **DRINK** 2008–2012.

Price	$24
Region	Barossa
Value	●●●●●
Auction	N/A
Score	92

Plantagenet Lioness Shiraz Viognier 2005

Plantagenet was the first winery in the Great Southern wine region of Western Australia and thirty years on it's not only got a bit of size to it, but also a hefty reputation. Shiraz should be one of its stars.

2005 RELEASE
We're looking at a classy wine here, though for a spicy, savoury, elegant style there's a rip of alcohol coming through the finish, which seems at odds with the wine's intentions. Tight cherry-like flavour, ferrous tannins, notes of iodine and shale and a warm, meaty finish. Very good, though perhaps not quite good enough. **DRINK** 2011–2018.

Price	$25
Region	Great Southern
Value	♦♦
Auction	N/A
Score	90

Plantagenet Omrah Shiraz 2005

Omrah has become one of Australian wine's ever-reliables. No dent in the reputation here.

2005 RELEASE
This is a sweet red wine with a firmness to its tannin; a contradiction perhaps but it works. It tastes, I swear, like liquorice swimming in a pool of raspberry juice, the entire impact of it about sweet fruit, more sweet fruit, and then some more sweet fruit. Oak is essentially nowhere to be seen. Personally I think it is a 100 per cent winner. **DRINK** 2008–2012.

Price	$17
Region	Great Southern
Value	♦♦♦♦♦
Auction	N/A
Score	89

Polleters Moonambel Shiraz 2005

When I was living in Melbourne I used to travel to the Pyrenees quite often. It's one of those regions it feels great to drive into, the flat grazing lands suddenly rising towards hillside vineyards. Magic region.

2005 RELEASE
Straightforward shiraz but a seriously satisfying drink. Flavours of plums, mint and coffee-cream, the easy, warm power of it very easy to enjoy. **DRINK** 2009–2017.

Price	$25
Region	Pyrenees
Value	♦♦♦♦
Auction	N/A
Score	90

Port Phillip Estate Tete De Cuvee Rimage Syrah 2005

The run of warmer years is doing wonders for shiraz on the Peninsula.

2005 RELEASE
Wow-wee. What a wine. Taut, lengthy, flushed with black spice, fresh meat, stalks, dark cherries and smoke. There's a lot going on! Lots of tannin, spice, interest and daring.
DRINK 2012–2023.

Price	$40
Region	Mornington Peninsula
Value	♦♦♦♦
Auction	★★
Score	95

Pyrette Shiraz 2005

This is made by renowned Bindi winemaker Michael Dhillon. It's the only wine he makes that isn't from his home vineyard, hence the different name.

2005 RELEASE
It seems at odds with itself. On the one hand it's big, sweet, vanillin and loaded with eucalypt-like flavour, the archetypal Central Victorian shiraz. In other ways though it's cool, meaty and spicy, as if a style is being applied to what the vineyard would rather say. It's still a good wine; but not a harmonious one. **DRINK** 2009–2014.

Price	$40
Region	Heathcote
Value	♦♦
Auction	N/A
Score	89

Ravensworth Shiraz Viognier 2006

The Canberra district wine region is fiercely continental – which means it's an inland region that's characterised by both cold nights and warm days. Water is scarce in the region, and there is significant threat of spring frost. It's tough going, but the results can be superb.

2006 RELEASE
Vigorous, juicy, quality wine, full of galloping flavour. It races through the mouth and sucks you back for more (I swear officer, it was the wine's fault!). Lots of spice, lots of aniseed-like flavour, flashes of lavender and vanilla and racy, lacy tannins. A complete wine, and a lovely one.
DRINK 2008–2013.

Price	$27
Region	Canberra District
Value	♦♦♦♦♦
Auction	N/A
Score	92

Red Knot Shiraz 2006

This brand comes out of the excellent Shingleback wines operation in McLaren Vale, and has hit the ground sprinting over the past few years. I'd argue that any of the red wines produced under the Red Knot label so far have been excellent value drinking.

2006 RELEASE
I guess you'd call it sweet and jammy but it drinks like a deadset charm. This is a full-bodied, sweet-fruited red crammed with flavours of blackberry jam, burnt sugar and orange rind. This has a tiny touch of grenache blended in, and it's helped it be ablaze with sweet fruity perfume. What a beautifully balanced bargain. (Can you please do me a favour and decant it for 20 minutes before you start glugging?) **DRINK** 2008–2011.

Price	$14.95
Region	McLaren Vale
Value	♦♦♦♦♦
Auction	N/A
Score	89

Reilly's Barking Mad Shiraz 2006

Little-known Clare Valley winery Reilly's planted its first vines in 1993, and has been hard at it ever since. I've come across a number of its wines over the years, but this is the first to make me really take note.

2006 RELEASE
They have to be barking mad to stuff this amount of flavour into a wine of this price! This is dense and plummy, smacked with coffeed oak and then sweet and aniseed-like through the finish. A little bit rough but a whole lot ready. **DRINK** 2008–2011.

Price	$13
Region	Clare Valley
Value	♦♦♦♦♦
Auction	N/A
Score	89

Reynella Basket Pressed Shiraz 2005

The 2005 vintage was excellent in McLaren Vale, particularly for shiraz. If any producer is set to capitalise on good shiraz conditions it's Hardys; they are the cornerstone of the McLaren Vale region.

2005 RELEASE
A big wine but firm and controlled, the plummy, chocolaty, glycerol fruitiness of it kept securely in place by grainy, chalky, superfine tannins. A very impressive, high quality wine. It's weighty in its flavour too, though not overly so. And the longer it's opened, the more persistent it seems, and the classier its structure. Hardys should be proud of this one. Big on flavour, and big on quality.
DRINK 2008–2013.

Price	$50
Region	McLaren Vale
Value	♦♦♦♦
Auction	★★★
Score	95

Richard Hamilton Gumprs' Shiraz 2006

It's a label that has bounced around in prominence over the past ten years but the quality–price equation is almost always far in the consumer's favour. This 2006 is a cracker.

2006 RELEASE
Bargain alert! Rarely is such serious, tannic structure combined with such ripe, easy-going, medium-weight fruit – at such a bargain price. This is great red wine drinking, full of style and balance and good honest flavour. I'd give you a list of those flavours – but I got so carried away drinking this, I forgot to write them down.
DRINK 2008–2013.

Price	$17.95
Region	McLaren Vale
Value	♦♦♦♦♦
Auction	★★
Score	92

Rockbare Shiraz 2006

Winemaker Tim Burvill started up this label with the 2002 vintage, following a stint making wine at various posts in (the former) Southcorp wine empire. The shiraz has been consistently good. A quick search online should help you find it at prices around the $16–17 mark.

2006 RELEASE
It's a hefty drink for a wine at this price. It's full of warm, dark blackberries-shot-with-licorice flavour, chocolaty oak swimming in among it all. Talk about a mouthful of flavour; this is full on. If you want subtle, do not knock on this wine's door. If you want awesome red wine power, come to mumma ... **DRINK** 2008–2012.

Price	$19
Region	McLaren Vale
Value	♦♦♦♦♦
Auction	★★
Score	92

Rockford Basket Press Shiraz 2005

In the eyes of many folks Rockford is the doyen of Barossa shiraz. It is also arguably the strongest performer on the Australian auction market, particularly when it comes to peak vintages. Problem is, it's essentially only available via the cellar door, and then only at certain times of year.

2005 RELEASE
Like the 2004 it's a brooding wine, dark and chocolaty and yet, importantly, vibrant and controlled too. Its vanillin oak is a touch obvious now, but it's not heavy or overdone and should sink into the wine easily and seamlessly over time. There's an earthiness here – really. There's a plummy cakeyness. Drinking it is incredibly evocative of the Barossa. **DRINK** 2008–2012.

PREVIOUS
- **1995** Green, savoury, reasonable drinking. 2001–2008. 86 pts.
- **1996** Concentrated blackberry and raspberry. Beautiful. 2008–2015. 95 pts.
- **1997** Clumsy, minty, medium-weight. 2004–2010. 85 pts.
- **1998** Fat with dark berried flavour. Luscious. 2008–2014. 94 pts.
- **1999** Elegant power. Top class. 2009–2015. 94 pts.
- **2000** Smoky, funky, earthy and blackberried. Drying. 2005–2011. 88 pts.
- **2001** Earth, dried herbs and blackberry. Lovely. 2007–2013. 91 pts.
- **2002** Porty and overdone, but intense. 2012–2019. 91 pts.
- **2003** Big, sweet and fruit-forward. 2007–2011. 91 pts.
- **2004** Beautiful smell, beautiful taste, beautiful finish. 2012–2019. 96 pts.

Price	$48 (Cellar Door)
Region	Barossa
Value	♦♦♦♦♦
Auction	★★★★★
Score	95

Rolf Binder Bulls Blood Shiraz Mourvedre 2005

I love Rolf Binder's answer to how old the mourvedre vines are that go into this wine. 'The bloke who lives across the road (from the vineyard) is ninety, and the vines have been there all his life – that's old enough for me.'

2005 RELEASE
'Fully committed' red wine. Dense, lush and unconditional, so much so that it seems thick with flavour: like bulls blood, no less. It tastes like a slippery smooth version of plum cake, though there are also clips of both dried herbs and attractive French oak; there's more new French oak in this release than is customary, partly because it's such a good vintage. Great structure here too. **DRINK** 2008–2014.

Price	$45
Region	Barossa
Value	♦♦♦♦
Auction	★★★
Score	92

Rolf Binder Hanisch Shiraz 2005

This is the top-of-the-line wine from Rolf Binder, matured in 100 per cent new oak, about eighty per cent of it American. The vines that produce this wine were planted in 1972; Rolf Binder remembers the day they were planted, and as a boy he used to water them.

2005 RELEASE
Great wines soak up the oak they've been matured in – no matter how strong or new they are – taking those flavours and making them their own. This wine has done just that. It's a warm, dense wine, raisiny, blueberried, plummy and cedary, its depth of sweet, spicy flavour impossible to ignore. Its tannins are a gnarly fist through the finish, in need of time to soften. It's quite huge, and quite special. **DRINK** 2012–2022.

Price	$95
Region	Barossa
Value	♦♦♦♦
Auction	★★★
Score	95

Rosemount Diamond Label Shiraz 2006

There was a time when this was the role model of affordable red wine; then it all went grape bunch-shaped. Slowly, slowly, things are on the improve. This is a blend of grapes from many regions.

2006 RELEASE
Impressive wine. The flavours are sweet and red-berried and there's quite a bit tannin reining it all in. It's both fresh and satisfying. Best of all, it rings clear and fruity through the finish, with barely any oak influence at all. A good quality red. Succulence and structure. I prefer the 2005 but this is good. **DRINK** 2008–2011.

Price	$15
Region	Australia
Value	♦♦♦♦
Auction	N/A
Score	87

Rosemount Show Reserve Shiraz 2004

One of the key things to look for in assessing a wine's 'cellarability' is its tannin structure. There are many reasons for this but the simplest is that tannin is a natural preservative. The tannin structure of this wine is exemplary.

2004 RELEASE
It's not a profound wine but it's back to its respectable self. It's a simple display of blackberry jam, coffeed vanillin oak, tips of raspberry and bitter chocolate – it's a teeth-stainer, that's for sure – the texture soft and the finish firm and well-mannered. It may not be an exciting wine, but there's not a hair out of place. **DRINK** 2008–2014.

Price	$24
Region	McLaren Vale
Value	♦♦♦♦
Auction	★★
Score	91

Rutherglen Estates 'Red' 2006

It may not be a name you're familiar with but it's one of Rutherglen's biggest producers now, courtesy of a large-scale, meticulously-tended vineyard that's just about to reach maturity. The quality and value of the wine is testament to the vineyard resources this company has. This is a blend of shiraz and that old Rutherglen warhorse, durif.

Price	$12.95
Region	Rutherglen
Value	♦♦♦♦♦
Auction	N/A
Score	87

2006 RELEASE
Take a look at the price! This is brilliant value. It's a dark, gutsy, beefy wine, full of raspberry, iodine and beef-stock flavour and soundly fruity through the finish. It has no pretensions other than to provide good, gutsy red wine flavour at a good, honest price. Can't help but admire it.
DRINK 2008–2011.

S.C. Pannell Shiraz 2005

There's a lot of talk about high alcohols in Aussie reds right now, and how they tend to grab your throat and scorch it as the wine passes by. It's not the most pleasant feeling. Steve Pannell's wines don't do that, but in all his new top-priced wines the obviousness of the alcohol was distracting.

Price	$65
Region	McLaren Vale
Value	♦♦
Auction	N/A
Score	93

2005 RELEASE
Strong, tough, brutish shiraz; rich with warm, blackberried, spicy flavour and then long, sweet and pure through the finish. Quite a wine. Great persistence. Sandy, gravelly and gritty. **DRINK** 2009–2014.

St Hallett Blackwell Shiraz 2005 & 2006

If I wanted a big red wine to serve at a corporate lunch, I'd be begging to serve this. It's what people think of when they think of Barossan shiraz: thickly flavoured, smoothly delivered.

2005 RELEASE
If you like Barossa shiraz, you will like this. It's like a coalface of blackberry fruit flavour, the texture of it so smooth you've got two options: guzzle it, or ski down it. Coffee-cream, toast, rich, saturated plums – the flavours are all here. **DRINK** 2008–2014.

2006 RELEASE
Much like the 2005 except gruntier and better structured. Rich dark fruit, coffee, meat and vanilla, the tide of tannin pulling right through a brightly flavoured palate. This has a long future ahead of it. **DRINK** 2011–2019.

Price	$29.95
Region	Barossa
Value	♦♦♦♦♦
Auction	★★★
Score	93 (2005)
	93 (2006)

St Hallett Old Block Shiraz 2004 & 2005

This is made off vines aged between sixty and 100 years. Shiraz vines like this are largely unique to Australia, hence their rarity is necessarily built into the price.

2004 RELEASE
Full of old, coffeed, chocolaty fruit and already showing the signs of leathery development. It's a rich, smooth, easy-to-drink wine, and it would go down a treat over a steak right now – but it's not a long termer.
DRINK 2009–2015.

2005 RELEASE
This is excellent. The punctuation of tannin through the boldness of its juicy, bright, dense fruit allows the wine to speak its quality clearly. Not a monster, but a rich, chocolaty, balanced wine of excellent structure.
DRINK 2013–2022.

Price	$70
Region	Barossa
Value	♦♦♦
Auction	★★★★
Score	91 (2004)
	94 (2005)

Saltram Mamre Brook Shiraz 2005

The quality of Mamre Brook shiraz leaps about from year to year, unusual for a big company winery. When it's good, it does the sumptuous Barossan shiraz style as well as anyone.

Price	$25
Region	Barossa
Value	♦♦♦♦♦
Auction	★★★
Score	93

2005 RELEASE
This is a good one. Its dark-centred, chocolaty fruit flavours melt in your mouth, helped along by creamy, coffeed, super-smooth oak. It's so rich and slippery it tastes glycerol, its high alcohol noticeable but thoroughly at ease with the overall big-hearted style of the wine. I kept drinking it and kept loving it. It's got richness and smoothness galore. Just don't expect subtlety. **DRINK** 2008–2015.

Saltram No. 1 Shiraz 2004

I know that I'm supposed to be impressed with this but I'm not. I also know that a lot of wine drinkers will love it. Sometimes you just have to make a stand on what you believe in. This to me is an over-oaked concoction largely devoid of charm. Unfortunately it's made by Nigel Dolan, inarguably one of the nation's best winemakers.

Price	$68
Region	Barossa
Value	♦♦
Auction	★★★
Score	89

2004 RELEASE
Coffeed, syrupy, citrusy, leathery, almost smelling of tinned corn. The palate is the same: lifeless, if bold and soft and hefty, its syrupy oak weighing the glory of the fruit down. The grapes that went into this were undoubtedly good quality; but overzealous oak leaves me cold. Medium-length. Tasted better on day two, and longer through the finish, but the charm factor was still low. **DRINK** 2009–2016.

PREVIOUS
1999 Muscular, chunky, substantial. 2010–2016. 93 pts.
2000 Stylish, lighter, leathery. 2004–2008. 89 pts.
2001 Structured, perfumed, medium-weight. 2005–2012. 92 pts.
2002 Leathery, tarry, substantial. 2006–2014. 92 pts.
2003 Needs decanting. Beautifully bold. 2007–2015. 93 pts.

Scarpantoni School Block Shiraz Cabernet 2004

Scarpantoni are a self-contained wine operation in McLaren Vale – they grow their own grapes, make the wine, bottle and label it themselves, do their own PR, the whole shebang. I admire them greatly. Helps keep the prices reasonable too.

2004 RELEASE
Rough and ready but the hit of flavour is excellent and there's a lot of chewy tannin through the finish. Tarry, blackberried flavour, a touch of dusty saltiness and very low oak. **DRINK** 2010–2016.

Price	$15
Region	McLaren Vale
Value	♦ ♦ ♦
Auction	N/A
Score	85

Scotchmans Hill Cornelius Syrah 2005

When folks talk of high alcohol reds they're usually referring to the wines of the Barossa, McLaren Vale and Clare Valley regions. Fact is – amazingly – there are an increasing number from regions like Geelong, the Yarra Valley and Margaret River, all supposedly 'cool climate' regions. This wine is fifteen per cent alcohol.

2005 RELEASE
Despite its high alcohol it smells like a mix of herb and tomato bushes, strange considering that there are also porty, overripe smells too. Taste it and you get more of the same, though in a far more delicious context. It sure is an interesting wine. It's quite persistent through the finish and will age well – though those under-ripe, herbal, stalky characters will always be evident. **DRINK** 2010–2016.

Price	$45
Region	Geelong
Value	♦ ♦
Auction	N/A
Score	89

Seppelt Benno Shiraz 2005

Seppelt has expanded its regional range of shiraz-based wines in recent years. It's part of an impressive move to highlight the strengths and difference of various Central Victorian regions.

2005 RELEASE
The first time I tasted this I thought the label had come of age. It tasted tannic but ballooned with inky dark fruit, the array of flavour tremendously impressive: violets, smoke, eucalypt, fresh leather and blackberries. The second time though, its creamy oak seemed a little too heavily applied, and worst of all the mid-palate seemed to lack a notch of grunt, especially considering the wine's overall, warm, saturated style. My notes concluded 'almost excellent'.
DRINK 2011–2022.

Price	$55
Region	Bendigo
Value	♦ ♦
Auction	★ ★
Score	91

Seppelt Chalambar Shiraz 2006

It's been a red drinker's favourite for years, but this 2006 is one out of the box.

2006 RELEASE
Seppelt releases this wine on 1 April but it's not a wine for fools – it's a wine for very switched on wine folks. This 2006 is also one of the smoothest, plummiest wines of the year, its rich chocolaty flavour so soft and yummy that it feels like velvet on your tongue. It's a beautifully satisfying wine. **DRINK** 2008–2016.

PREVIOUS
2000 Earthy and chocolaty. 2003–2009. 90 pts.
2001 Smooth, fruity, persistent. 2004–2013. 92 pts.
2002 Elegant, easy complexity. 2006–2014. 93 pts.
2003 Power and balance. 2006–2016. 95 pts.
2004 Firm, savoury, floral. 2007–2028. 90 pts.
2005 Meaty, gravelly, minty. 2010–2017. 90 pts.

Price	$26
Region	Grampians
Value	♦♦♦♦♦
Auction	★★★
Score	94

Seppelt Mount Ida Shiraz 2005

The Mount Ida vineyard was once a winery and brand all of its own. After a complicated set of corporate manoeuvres it's now under the Seppelt banner, where it will likely experience its best days.

2005 RELEASE
You'd pick this as a Heathcote wine from a mile off. It reeks of the region's trademark eucalyptus and sandalwood, the following mouthful of inky, strong, plummy fruit confirming the bet. Cloves, cedary oak, fresh acidity and a peppery aftertaste – there's a lot here to sink your chops into. Serve this on a cold evening and you'll have the table swooning. **DRINK** 2009–2016.

Price	$50
Region	Heathcote
Value	♦♦♦
Auction	★★★
Score	92

Seppelt St Peters Shiraz 2005

One of the greats of Australian wine, and finally receiving the recognition it deserves. The vines that produce this wine were mostly planted in the 1960s.

2005 RELEASE
It's becoming a spicier, drier, less obvious style – which is saying something, because it's never been a plush crowd-pleaser. This release is floral, plummy, peppery and pure, its husky undercarriage of cured meat, fennel and cedar giving it a rare sophistication. Love the finesse of this, even if it does have a slightly sappy, herbal streak. What it needs is eight or so years in a cool, dark place. **DRINK** 2013–2022.

PREVIOUS
1996 Rustic but powerful; beautiful length. 2007–2013. 94 pts.
1997 Powerful but balanced. 2007–2015. 93 pts.
1998 Exuberant oak, solid fruit, drying finish. 2005–2012. 92 pts.
1999 Dry, gamey, perfumed and leathery. 2006–2014. 90 pts.
2000 Gamey, lighter, dry. 2006–2010. 88 pts.
2001 Elegant but plush. 2007–2015. 94 pts.
2002 Powerful and complete. 2009–2018. 96 pts.
2003 Peppery, fruity, long. 2011–2019. 95 pts.
2004 Exquisitely blueberried wine. 2012–2021. 95 pts.

Price	$60
Region	Grampians
Value	♦♦♦♦
Auction	★★★★
Score	93

Seppelt Silverband Shiraz 2005

For some time Seppelt has had great wines in the $15 and under bracket and in the $25 bracket – and then the range leapt to over $50. The new Silverband range fills in the gap.

2005 RELEASE
You have to like tannin, that's for sure. There's so much of it here that it seems chalky, minerally, gravelly even – it makes you wonder whether the wine is a bit out of whack. From there it's a complex wine with flavours ranging through eucalypt, mulberry, black pepper, violets and toast. It's only a smidge above medium weight – as many of the best wines are. I like the wine, and I even like the tannins, but at the price I'm not sure. **DRINK** 2009–2017.

Price	$35
Region	Bendigo
Value	♦♦
Auction	N/A
Score	90

Seppelt Silverband Sparkling Shiraz NV

Seppelt has long been the reigning champion of Australian sparkling shiraz, its prime movers the bargain Seppelt Original and super premium Seppelt Show Sparkling – a gap of nearly $50 between them. This new Silverband sparkler fills that gap.

NV RELEASE
I had high hopes for this but it's not quite up to the mark – especially not at $35. It tastes like simple cherry-cola and licorice, its leather-developed flavours the only real sign of complexity. Worse, the finish has a dried herb character bordering on bitterness. Look, it quaffs really well, but it's not a 'fine wine'. **DRINK** 2008–2010.

Price	$35
Region	Grampians
Value	♦♦
Auction	N/A
Score	88

Seppelt Victoria Shiraz 2005

Seppelt has a long history but it's really been a leading light of Australian wine over the past five or so years. The Victoria shiraz is a drinker's bonus.

2005 RELEASE
I first tasted this among a large group of far more expensive shiraz wines, and it more than held its own – it's a bit of a giant killer. You have to like the cool-climate Victorian shiraz style, which means flavours in the pepper, cherry, blackberry and leather spectrum – rather than the plum jam spectrum of warmer climates. There's a nice amount of savoury tannin here too, making me think it will go OK in the cellar over the medium term. **DRINK** 2008–2013.

Price	$18.95
Region	Victoria
Value	♦♦♦♦♦
Auction	★★★
Score	90

Setanta Cuchulain Shiraz 2005

I've seen this on sale for $25 but to be honest the listed price of $32 is fair. Setanta is a name to watch.

2005 RELEASE
This is a high quality wine not because it's the most intense wine in the pack; power is important in the assessment of wine, but it is not the only thing. This wine mixes powerful flavours with elegance, length, structure and complexity, making it the complete package. Five spice, polished dark cherries, licorice, classy French oak and lots of lifted fruit fragrance. There are brandied, cakey flavours too, like drinking the inside of a Christmas mince tart. It is all quite beguiling. **DRINK** 2008–2018.

Price	$32
Region	Adelaide Hills
Value	♦♦♦♦♦
Auction	★★★
Score	94

Shaw & Smith Shiraz 2005 & 2006

There was a time when the Adelaide Hills was seen as too cool for shiraz. Time, drought and more appropriate vineyard sites have changed all that.

2005 RELEASE
Perfumed and delicate but bold too, its spicy, floral, blackberried grunt ably framed by chunky tannins. It all works seamlessly together, notes of black cherries, salami and black pepper delivered on a very smooth ride.
DRINK 2012–2021.

2006 RELEASE
This is the epitome of elegance and class, its spicy, meaty, cherried flavour firmly set by superfine tannins and presented within a context of intoxicating aromatics. Totally gorgeous. Complex and beguiling. **DRINK** 2012–2021.

PREVIOUS
2002 Bright, peppery and pure. 2005–2012. 92 pts.
2003 Gamey, spicy, awkward. 2006–2010. 87 pts.
2004 Rose, cherries, spice, length. 2010–2017. 94 pts.

Price	$39
Region	Adelaide Hills
Value	●●●●●
Auction	★★★
Score	95 (2005) 96 (2006)

Stanton & Killeen Shiraz Durif 2005

Chris Killeen succumbed to cancer in June 2007, a great loss to the Australian wine industry.

2005 RELEASE
It's a bit funky and gamey but there is a lovely push of sweet, raspberried, jubey flavour here, its sweet softness very easy to tuck into. Not much tannin and not much acid – perfect for guzzling. **DRINK** 2008–2009.

Price	$18
Region	Rutherglen
Value	●●●
Auction	★★
Score	86

Starvedog Lane Shiraz Viognier 2005

This has been slaying them on the wine show circuit. It's not hard to see why – you don't get this class at this price very often.

2005 RELEASE
The idea of blending viognier with shiraz is that it softens the wine and increases its perfume – a great goal in anyone's books. When it's done well though, the integrity of the shiraz is maintained, without the viognier dominating. Here it has been done very well. It's a tight, focused, spicy wine, cherry-plummed flavour kissed only lightly by toasty oak. The really impressive thing is the tight control of it. **DRINK** 2011–2018.

Price	$24
Region	Adelaide Hills
Value	♦♦♦♦♦
Auction	★★
Score	94

Stella Bella Shiraz 2006

The 2006 vintage was desperately cool in Margaret River, making life quite good for white wines, but extremely difficult for reds. They've done well to make this as good as it is.

2006 RELEASE
It tastes like the wine of a far cooler climate than Margaret River, but it's testament to the extreme winemaking abilities of Janice McDonald – and to the people who grow her grapes. This is peppery, cherried, nutty, medium-weight but solid, its firm tannins in remarkable balance. **DRINK** 2008–2013.

Price	$24
Region	Margaret River
Value	♦♦♦
Auction	★★
Score	89

Tahbilk Reserve Shiraz 2002

Tahbilk has long been a master of the food-friendly, savoury style of regional shiraz. Its value to Australian wine is greater than ever.

2002 RELEASE
There's a trace of regional eucalypt here but it's otherwise a gorgeously savoury, complex, interesting wine. It deserves to be cellared. A frame of cedary oak encloses plummy, spicy, earthy flavour, the concentration of it significant but not in any way over done. More length than power. **DRINK** 2011–2025.

Price	$60
Region	Nagambie Lakes
Value	♦♦♦♦
Auction	★★★
Score	96

Tarrington Artemisia Shiraz 2006

2006 RELEASE
This has been polarising opinions around the traps. Some reckon it's green and ugly, others reckon it's ethereal and exotic ... I've even heard a rival winemaker call it 'superb'. The spread of opinions is caused by the simple fact that it's 'different' (but noice and unusual). It tastes rubbery, smoky, rich and blueberried, the wine itself seeming to swing between bitter, twiggy, unripe flavours and rich, toasty, fruity ripeness. To my taste it pulls the style off, though I can understand the detractors. You have to give this wine a glass or two before making up your mind – a credit in itself. **DRINK** 2011–2016.

Price	$36
Region	Henty
Value	♦♦♦♦
Auction	N/A
Score	93

Taylors Eighty Acres Shiraz Viognier 2005

This new range of wines from Clare heavyweight Taylors is bang on the money from the get-go. Adam Eggins, head winemaker at Taylors, is one of the stars of Australian winemaking.

2005 RELEASE
Spiffy wine. Flooded with sweet fruit flavour, the texture of it luscious, smooth, ripe and bright. Just a great value wine. Flavours of plums, coconut, eucalypt and violets. Nice, easy-going tannin structure too. **DRINK** 2008–2013.

Price	$16.95
Region	Clare Valley
Value	♦♦♦♦♦
Auction	N/A
Score	89

Taylors Jaraman Shiraz 2005

Taylors is a Clare Valley wine company but a few years ago they decided to source grapes from other regions too and to launch the result under the 'Jaraman' name. There have been some good results, but in general the wine has failed to excite.

2005 RELEASE
Full of ugly, malty, overbearing oak. There's no doubt good, rich, chocolaty fruit underneath it all, and the texture is as smooth as a coffee cream, but why so much unattractive oak has been applied to this wine is a mystery. It could have been a contender. **DRINK** 2008–2013.

Price	$29.95
Region	Clare Valley McLaren Vale
Value	♦♦
Auction	★★
Score	87

Taylors St Andrews Shiraz 2003

Taylors' flagship shiraz has had its grand moment but I generally find it disappointing. The 2003 edition is a particularly uninspiring offering.

2003 RELEASE
It mostly tastes like chocolate, malt, mint and raspberry jam, but there's an unpleasant bitterness to the aftertaste and a generally jumbled feeling to the tannins. Otherwise it's juicy and fruity and flavoursome. **DRINK** 2008–2013.

Price	$60
Region	Clare Valley
Value	♦♦
Auction	★★
Score	87

Temple Bruer Preservative Free Shiraz Malbec 2007

Temple Bruer was a beacon of organics in the Australian wine industry well before it became trendy. They have had, and still have, an important place in Australian winegrowing history.

2007 RELEASE
It's a decent red wine. It tastes of blackcurrant and mint and is fresh and honest, not a hair out of place. That said, there's a hollowness to the mid-palate and its tannins are too fierce. Possible that I tasted it too soon after it was bottled. If you need a preservative-free wine, this is the best I've yet tasted. **DRINK** 2008.

Price	$18
Region	Langhorne Creek
Value	♦♦♦
Auction	N/A
Score	85

The Story Shiraz 2005 & 2006

Rory Lane calls himself an 'urban winemaker'. He buys grapes and makes them into wine (more or less in his garage) in Melbourne.

2005 RELEASE
Wow. It is very tannic, but the mix of flavours suits the style perfectly – we're talking leather, cherries, tar and fresh, boisterous blueberries. It's a wine that needs food to tone down the tannin, but the length of flavour stamps it with class. **DRINK** 2008–2015.

2006 RELEASE
Another beauty. Lots of silken, boysenberried, raspberried fruit flavour, knocked to higher realms by flavours of earth and pepper. This was a bushfire year in the Grampians region, but there is no sign of smoke taint. Lovely. **DRINK** 2008–2012.

Price	$19
Region	Grampians
Value	♦♦♦♦♦
Auction	N/A
Score	92 (2005) 90 (2006)

The Story Westgate Vineyard Shiraz 2006

A few years ago Australian wine started copping flack over its lack of regional identity. Hundreds of 'single vineyard' wines have since been launched – before long, it will be a criticism that is impossible to make.

2006 RELEASE
Deliciously smooth, polished, complete wine. Give it an hour in the decanter to show its best – then it's a glorious medium-weight ride of cherry-plummed flavour, its background leathery-earthiness paying good homage to its region. Nice length, nice tannin and excellent balance. It is not a blockbuster, but it's super stylish. **DRINK** 2010–2018.

Price	$40
Region	Grampians
Value	♦♦♦
Auction	N/A
Score	93

Tollana Bin TR16 Shiraz 2006

This label has been shunned and bastardised over the years, especially sad because it has a loyal following. The quality of this release, however, is good.

2006 RELEASE
Quite a big wine for a Tollana shiraz, though to some extent it's the tannin that gives the wine its size; there's a lot of very fine tannin here. Strong flavours of eucalypt, plums, blackberry and cloves fill the mouth with flavour, the finish then clean and well balanced. I'll say one thing for sure: you can cellar this with confidence. **DRINK** 2010–2016.

Price	$18
Region	South Eastern Australia
Value	♦♦♦♦♦
Auction	★★★
Score	92

Toolangi Estate Shiraz 2005

This wine was made by exceptionally talented winemaker Tom Carson at Yering Station. He's massaged some really good shiraz grapes into a really interesting shiraz wine.

2005 RELEASE
You have to be of a certain bent to enjoy this – but if you are, you're in for a helluva ride. It's medium-bodied but rushes powerfully through the mouth, dark cherries and chocolate combining with violets and cedarwood to create quite an impression. It finishes bitter and twiggy, which is mostly where individual differences will determine whether you like it. Its tannin profile is both expansive and perfectly formed. It's not a bruiser; it's elegant and lovely. **DRINK** 2011–2016.

Price	$35
Region	Yarra Valley
Value	♦♦♦♦
Auction	N/A
Score	94

Toolangi Shiraz 2005

Toolangi is a quality-focused Yarra Valley producer who until now has been known for its chardonnay and pinot noir. This latest round of shiraz releases might re-arrange the pecking order.

2005 RELEASE
A lovely rendition of a cool-climate shiraz. Peppery, sappy, a touch stalky and ripped with spice, the fruit cherried, medium-bodied and very easy to enjoy. The thing I like here is the bright juiciness of it, the gentle smokiness, the way the tannins have melted into the wine. There's a sense of sophistication to this wine. **DRINK** 2008–2013.

Price	$23
Region	Yarra Valley
Value	♦ ♦ ♦ ♦
Auction	N/A
Score	89

Torbreck Run Rig Shiraz 2005

Torbreck Run Rig Shiraz is one of the enduring darlings of American wine critic Robert Parker; his successor, Jay Miller, seems to be a big fan too. It's not hard to see why.

2005 RELEASE
Beautiful wine but its warm alcohol does poke out on the finish; a small criticism, but this is a $200 plus wine. Now for the positives: it smells like a blaze of crushed fennel, smoke, blackberry, jet fuel and oysters, the riot of it then chanted out through a palate saturated with flavour. It's a mass of brandied, smoky, licoricey, jammy flavour, the depth and intensity of it almost impossible to convey; you simply have to taste it, to believe it. Drinking it is a hell of an experience. **DRINK** 2008–2020.

Price	$225
Region	Barossa
Value	♦ ♦ ♦
Auction	★ ★ ★ ★
Score	95

PREVIOUS
1995 Gamey, smoky, irresistible. 2008–2012. 90 pts.
1996 Soft, nutty, leathery and beguiling. 2010–2016. 95 pts.
1997 Leathery, smoky, maturing steadily. 2008–2013. 89 pts.
1998 Grunty fruit power, substantial tannins. 2012–2024. 96 pts.
1999 Gamey, meaty, spicy, abbreviated finish. 2010–2015. 89 pts.
2000 Not made.
2001 Gamey, sweet, long. 2009–2017. 93 pts.
2002 Complex, complete, profound. 2013–2027. 97 pts.
2003 Muscular, sweet; transcends the vintage. 2011–2019. 94 pts.
2004 Super-intense, but elegant. 2011–2020. 95 pts.

Torbreck The Gask Shiraz 2006

Torbreck makes them big, bold, sweet and sustained, a style you either love or loathe. The drinkability of these wines though, is phenomenal; you have to be in the mood, but when you are, they go down in a wave of seduction. This is the second release of The Gask.

2006 RELEASE
It might be soft, cuddly, rich and sumptuous, but there are also layers of complex flavour, all licorice, blackberry, ground coffee, smoke and sweet dark jam. There's no doubt that the fruitiness of it tastes sweet – almost like dark, muscovado sugar – but also little doubt that it's a drop-dead sexy drink. **DRINK** 2008–2017.

Price	$75
Region	Eden Valley
Value	♦♦♦
Auction	N/A
Score	95

Torbreck The Struie Shiraz 2005

The Torbreck wine I buy for myself is The Struie; no doubt price plays a part but it's the best vale Torbreck wine by a long shot. It delivers big time.

2005 RELEASE
Emphatically good. Soft and rich and amazingly inviting, flavours of burnt sugar, raspberry, aniseed and earth munching deliciously on all my tastebuds. I love drinking this. It's a Torbreck wine first and a regional wine second, but there's room for that; there surely is. **DRINK** 2008–2017.

PREVIOUS
2001 Juicy, spicy, good. 2004–2008. 90 pts.
2002 Spicy, chocolaty, flavoursome. 2007–2013. 91 pts.
2003 Fleshy, floral, primed with flavour. 2006–2011. 92 pts.
2004 Hedonist's dream. Outstandingly delicious. 2007–2013. 94 pts.

Price	$48
Region	Barossa Eden Valley
Value	♦♦♦♦
Auction	★★★
Score	94

Torzi Matthews Frost Dodger Shiraz 2005

The Torzi Matthews wines have fast become highly anticipated. No wonder when they keep putting out wines like this.

2005 RELEASE
You get a whole lot of joy for your cash here. Tremendously fragrant, fruity, dark and ripe, at every turn you get fragrance and flavour to the max. Choc-cherries, smoke, mint, cedarwood, raspberries and more – it gives you the full floor routine. Hedonistic, and highly enjoyable.
DRINK 2008–2013.

PREVIOUS
2002 Sweet, savoury, rich and spicy. 2005–2012. 95 pts.
2003 Deep, silken, ripe and rich. 2006–2012. 92 pts.
2004 Rich, slick, inky and bright. 2006–2013. 93 pts.

Price	$30
Region	Eden Valley
Value	♦♦♦♦♦
Auction	N/A
Score	94

Torzi Matthews Schist Rock Shiraz 2006 & 2007

Domenic Torzi makes this wine as if it's destined for a far higher price: open fermenters, whole berry bunches, wild yeast and mostly French oak. Bravo!

2006 RELEASE
Flavoursome, stylish, regional, bristling with fresh dark fruit and then long and impressive through the finish. Super-rich flavours. **DRINK** 2008–2013.

2007 RELEASE
The only problem is that within weeks of this guide being released this wine will be sold out, so get in quick. It's as smooth as a big-lipped kiss, as satisfying as a pay rise, as full and fruity as a blackberry pie. Curranty, soft, long and stylish, its tannins, fruit complexity and oak full of 'wow' factor.
DRINK 2008–2014.

Price	$17
Region	Eden Valley
Value	♦♦♦♦♦
Auction	N/A
Score	92 (2006)
	94 (2007)

Turkey Flat Shiraz 2005

This is a much tamer wine than it was a few years back – and if it weren't broke back then, some wonder why they've tried to fix it. It now seems to be made in a style reminiscent of Penfolds St Henri – low in oak, clean of fruit flavour, and built to impress as a ten-year-old rather than as a two-year-old. Time will tell.

Price	$40
Region	Barossa
Value	♦♦♦
Auction	★★★
Score	90

2005 RELEASE
It tastes of plums, prunes, raisins and cola – all of which is highly enjoyable – but it seems to lack focus and tannin. It's certainly generous of flavour, and soft of texture.
DRINK 2008–2018.

PREVIOUS
2000 Plummy, cherried, smooth. 2006–2013. 91 pts.
2001 Rich, dark, beautiful. 2006–2011. 92 pts.
2002 Syrupy, herbal, ripe. 2005–2013. 93 pts.
2003 Warm, tannic, licoricey. 2006–2011. 88 pts.
2004 Pure, concentrated, smooth. 2006–2017. 94 pts.

Turkey Flat Sparkling Shiraz NV

Barossa neighbours Charles Melton and Rockford have been long-time exponents of sparkling red, but Turkey Flat are relative newcomers. Of course, they've been making rich black shiraz since the early 1990s, and have access to vines about a century older than that – they're perfectly placed to make a goodun'.

Price	$40
Region	Barossa
Value	♦♦♦♦
Auction	N/A
Score	94

NV RELEASE
You could bite into this! It's dense, black, chocolaty and richly flavoured, the smooth, spreading flavour of it very easy to fall for. It tastes of Christmas cake, plums and chocolate, the combination resulting in a big fat ball of dark-coloured fun. **DRINK** 2008–2013.

Tyrrell's Four Acres Shiraz 2007

This is a cellar-door only wine, due for release in mid-2008. Get onto Tyrrell's and see if you can get yourself some – it's very limited, and very good.

2007 RELEASE
This is a single-vineyard wine to die for. The 2007 is a particularly strong version of it too. It's still only medium weight, but the flavours are brilliant. Violets, boysenberry, French-polished cedar, rich, ripe plums and red earth. If I could buy the whole production, I would. I like it that much. **DRINK** 2009–2025.

Price	$35 (Cellar Door)
Region	Hunter Valley
Value	♦♦♦♦♦
Auction	★★★
Score	96

Tyrrell's Reserve Stevens Vineyard Shiraz 2005

There was a time not long ago when Hunter Valley reds were out of favour. That's fast turning around, kicked along by a string of very good red vintages. Hunter reds are more medium weight – or lighter in intensity – than South Australian reds, but less weight does not mean less quality.

2005 RELEASE
A good Hunter red is not unlike a good Italian chianti. There's a nutty savouriness that I often fine totally adorable – though here too we have pulpy plums and racy, cherried acidity. A lovely regional distinctive wine. **DRINK** 2010–2017.

Price	$29
Region	Hunter Valley
Value	♦♦♦♦
Auction	★★★
Score	93

Tyrrell's Rufus Stone Shiraz 2005

Five years ago I always grabbed the Heathcote version; now I prefer the McLaren Vale version.

2005 MCLAREN VALE
Full of cuddly flavour, exactly as it should be. Opulent, settled and (thankfully) dark fruit flavours mix lusciously with milky, chocolaty oak. It's a wine good enough to eat. Minty, mentholy characters are a minor distraction and while it finishes warm, it's very satisfying. **DRINK** 2008–2012.

2005 HEATHCOTE
This is a noisy red, too high in alcohol. It does though have chunky, chocolaty, plummy flavour laid on and lots of eucalyptus notes too. Maybe I'm just having a wine-wanker moment. **DRINK** 2008–2010.

Price	$22
Region	McLaren Vale / Heathcote
Value	♦♦♦♦
Auction	★★★
Score	90 (MV) / 85 (H)

Tyrrell's Vat 9 Shiraz 2005 & 2006

These Vat 9 shiraz wines were aged in very large (new) oak barrels – so that the beauty of the grape flavour is not overcome with sweet oak.

2005 RELEASE
An elegant, medium-weight expression of Australian shiraz. I'm a big fan of wines like this. It's full of cherried, earthy, spicy (but not peppery) character, with moderate but fine tannins and a slightly salty, raw finish. **DRINK** 2009–2017.

2006 RELEASE
The great thing is the smell. It's richly scented, like dipping your head into a vat of musky, smoky cherries. Intoxicating! The palate is slippery and spicy and lovely, its cherry-plummed heart riddled with trademark Hunter earthiness. **DRINK** 2012–2018.

Price	$45
Region	Hunter Valley
Value	♦♦♦♦
Auction	★★★
Score	92 (2005)
	94 (2006)

Ulithorne Flamma Sparkling Shiraz Disgorged 2007

I have to confess that this wine makes it into this book mainly for its packaging. It's amazingly well done, completely befitting of the wine's style. If they can get the contents of the bottle right, this is a superstar wine in the making.

2007 RELEASE
It smells like dark Christmas cake and earthy, gamey complexity – the gameyness most definitely a love it or hate it factor. I didn't like it. It tastes the same as it smells – quite lovely – but finishes hard and gamey, its length of flavour corrupted by a leathery, metallic bite. Almost really good, but no cigar unfortunately. **DRINK** 2008–2011.

Price	$29
Region	McLaren Vale
Value	♦♦
Auction	N/A
Score	84

Ulithorne Frux Frugis Shiraz 2005

When I first saw the name of this wine a few years ago I thought it was a joke. I promptly put my laughing gear away when I tasted the wine and it was excellent. Apparently frux frugis means 'fruit of the earth' – fitting for a single-vineyard wine grown pesticide-free.

2005 RELEASE
Big, firm bugger. Liqueurous too. There's a lot about this wine that tastes of liquid chocolate poured over fresh-picked blueberries, the chewy, tannic, pulpy grape skins floating in among the inky thickness of it. That said, it's also crisp with acidity and fresh to the point of rawness – this has a whopping future ahead of it. Bolts of Grange-like tannin. **DRINK** 2013–2025.

Price	$42
Region	McLaren Vale
Value	♦♦♦♦
Auction	★★
Score	94

Valhalla Wines Shiraz 2005

New Rutherglen outfit – you don't get to write that too many times these days – with environmental sustainability high on their agenda. This wine is a lovely start.

2005 RELEASE
It doesn't have a great deal of length but it's a lovely show while it lasts. Indeed, classy. Full of iodine and blackberry-like flavour, there are subtle tips of orange peel, raspberry and malt, the combination bright, exuberant and super attractive. A joy to drink. **DRINK** 2008–2012.

Price	$25
Region	Rutherglen
Value	♦♦♦
Auction	N/A
Score	89

Vasse Felix Shiraz 2005

It pushes the boundaries at fifteen per cent alcohol but the wine shows no signs of excessive heat – indeed the opposite. It tastes balanced and charming.

2005 RELEASE
Classy shiraz in anyone's language. Clean, solid, structured and enticing. Violet-like fragrance leads to layered flavours of blackberry, leather, malt, menthol, toast and ink, a ripple of ripe tannin running from the mid-palate onwards. It's a substantial wine. **DRINK** 2010–2018.

PREVIOUS
1999 Gamey, leathery, plummy. 2002–2008. 88 pts.
2000 Leaf and plum flavours. Robust. 2006–2012. 91 pts.
2001 Beautiful wine. Plummy, satiny, sustained. 2007–2012. 93 pts.
2002 Pure, interesting, structured. 2004–2010. 91 pts.
2003 Blocky, but heartily flavoured. 2006–2011. 89 pts.
2004 Sweet, flavoursome, easy drinking. 2007–2013. 90 pts.

Price	$35
Region	Margaret River
Value	♦♦♦♦
Auction	★★★
Score	93

Victorian Alps Dividing Range Shiraz Cabernet 2006

It's a new range from the Victorian Alps winery and it is excellent value. There's a cabernet merlot in the range too (2006 vintage, 85 points), which is good, though this shiraz cabernet just edges it. Very good red-wine drinking.

2006 RELEASE
Good amount of mulberried, briary flavour and nice texture too; its creamy, chocolaty mouthfeel putting all the wine's features in the best possible light. The more I drank, the more I liked – always an excellent sign. **DRINK** 2008–2010.

Price	$9.95
Region	South Eastern Australia
Value	♦♦♦♦♦
Auction	N/A
Score	87

Vinea Marson Syrah 2006

There's a growing trend among the cooler regions of Victoria to name their shiraz wines as syrah; as indeed there is in New Zealand. It certainly does roll off the tongue nicely.

2006 RELEASE
Stylish, restrained, loaded with exotic spice and nutty, savoury influence and long and chewy through the finish. More about structure and savouriness than sweet fruit; a point of distinct difference to most of its Heathcote neighbours. This needs to be decanted. The quality is high. I'd be raving except that I like Vinea Marson's nebbiolo and sangiovese even more. **DRINK** 2011–2017.

Price	$39
Region	Heathcote
Value	♦♦♦♦
Auction	N/A
Score	93

Voyager Estate Shiraz 2006

Margaret River shiraz is generally in the cooler, spicier style – it tastes more Victorian than South Australian. Voyager Estate is one of the few Western Australian estates to consistently make good shiraz.

2006 RELEASE
Voyager has pulled a rabbit out of a hat with this wine – 2006 was basically a disaster for reds in Margaret River, and while this wine lacks oomph, it does not lack either charm or class. Indeed, it smells sensational, all violety and peppery, like a punnet of fresh wild berries. It tastes pretty good too: cherries, boysenberries, lots of black pepper and a minerally, stalky finish. It's a lighter wine, but I love the cut and polish of it. **DRINK** 2008–2012.

PREVIOUS
2001 Gamey, spicy, leathered; lacks something. 2004–2006. 89 pts.
2002 Dry, gamey, cherried, bitter. 2004–2009. 86 pts.
2003 Smooth, structured, fruit-driven. 2005–2010. 92 pts.
2004 Dried cherries, meats, cedar, spice; complex. 2006–2013. 93 pts.
2005 Chocolaty, cedary, cherried; very fine. 2008–2015. 92 pts.

Price	$29.50
Region	Margaret River
Value	♦♦♦♦
Auction	★★★
Score	91

Wanderer Shiraz 2006

The Yarra Valley is bustling with young winemakers taking a shot at quality – usually by making very small volumes of wine. Winemaker Andrew Marks only produces 100 dozen of this shiraz.

2006 RELEASE
It tastes a bit odd at first, so slosh it into a jug and give it some air before you start drinking. It then becomes savoury-sweet, full of boysenberry, dark cherry and kirsch-like flavour, with quite a bit of funky, gamey character included in the mix. It's a wild one – but the longer you sit with a glass of it, the more attractive it seems. Beautifully weighted with tannins that are slick, ripe and sensual. Interesting. **DRINK** 2009–2014.

Price	$32
Region	Yarra Valley
Value	♦♦♦
Auction	N/A
Score	89

Wanted Man Shiraz 2006

I love the label design on this bottle. It has a graphic of Ned Kelly standing front and square, pistols drawn, feet firmly apart. It fits the wine perfectly.

2006 RELEASE
It's like it's been custom-made for *The Big Red Wine Book*. It's all about frank flavour but not at the expense of tannin structure; it's all about giving red-wine drinkers something smooth and bold and delicious. Check for flavours and note blackberry, aniseed, eucalypt and cloves. But I suspect you won't have time for that – you'll be too busy hooking into it. This is worth lashing out for. **DRINK** 2008–2016.

Price	$30
Region	Heathcote
Value	♦♦♦♦
Auction	N/A
Score	93

Warburn Estate Premium Reserve Shiraz 2006

I bought a single bottle of this and the cabernet merlot for $7.50, something of a mockery of the words 'premium reserve'. There are moves afoot to eradicate such ludicrous labelling from the Australian wine industry.

2006 RELEASE
It tastes like a ten buck wine – but a very good one. It smells and tastes like sweet blackberry jam and the tannins have a tough, chewy nature about them, the weight of it medium-to-full and the colour inky and dense. It's almost rough, but the fruit wins the day, making it satisfying and impressive. At the price, really, they don't come much better – this is worthy of serious consideration. **DRINK** 2008–2010.

Price	$9.50
Region	Barossa
Value	♦♦♦♦♦
Auction	N/A
Score	87

Warburn Estate Stephendale Shiraz 2006

This is made from Barossa shiraz grapes. When you look at the quality, and at the price, you can't help but shake your head and ask: how did they do that? The value is freaky. Must have been the grape glut.

2006 RELEASE
Drink it young and drink it well. There's not a lot of structure here but the flavour is spot on, all blueberry and blackberry and chocolate. It's just a lovely smooth ride of flavour. **DRINK** 2008–2009.

Price	$11.50
Region	Barossa
Value	◆◆◆◆
Auction	★★★
Score	87

Warrabilla Reserve Shiraz 2006

Winemaker Andrew Sutherland Smith reckons that he's a balanced bloke; he has a chip on both his shoulders. His family once part-owned All Saints Estate, and ever since he left he's had a point to prove.

2006 RELEASE
Super rich, super big, super sweet and super lovely. It tastes of caramel, blackberry jubes, iodine, smoke and tar, its sixteen per cent alcohol taken wholly in its stride. A top example of the monster red style. **DRINK** 2008–2012.

Price	$22
Region	Rutherglen
Value	◆◆◆◆◆
Auction	★★★
Score	92

Water Wheel Memsie 2006

This is a blend of shiraz, cabernet sauvignon and malbec, though the overwhelming bulk of it is shiraz. It's aged in second- and third-use American oak, and it tastes exactly right.

2006 RELEASE
You can't go wrong here. It's sweet and warm, full of juicy, blackberried flavour and smooth enough to keep it casually slipping down. No alarms, no bumps, no surprises: just a good, honest fix of red wine flavour. You little beauty. **DRINK** 2008–2009.

Price	$12
Region	Bendigo
Value	◆◆◆◆◆
Auction	N/A
Score	87

Water Wheel Shiraz 2006

Recent releases have been a little too alcoholic for my tastes (and this 2006, puzzlingly, is an enormous 15.5 per cent), but this one does taste very good.

2006 RELEASE
Easy to rate this highly. It's a seductive package, rich with dark, sweet, brandied berry fruit flavours, plain and glorious. There's custardy vanillin oak, but it seems to add smoothness as much as flavour. This is all about dark, heady, warm fruit. A great red for winter. Very pure and very dark. **DRINK** 2008–2012.

Price	$18
Region	Bendigo
Value	♦♦♦♦♦
Auction	★★★
Score	92

West Cape Howe Two Steps Shiraz Viognier 2005

There's a theory that shiraz that has a naturally spicy element blends best with viognier – and it's wine like this that help promote that theory.

2005 RELEASE
Talk about generosity of flavour! It's a smooth, dark ride of spicy, syrupy fun, the flavours coming at you in waves. Squishy-ripe, dripping-rich blackberries, fennel, old wood flavour and then grainy, unobtrusive tannins to lead it out. One of the best shiraz viognier blends in the country on this showing. **DRINK** 2008–2012.

Price	$25
Region	Great Southern
Value	♦♦♦♦
Auction	N/A
Score	92

Wirra Wirra Catapult Shiraz Viognier 2006

They're mostly selling this through the Wirra Wirra cellar door, and through restaurant wine lists. It might then, be a bit hard to find, but grab a drink of this if you can.

2006 RELEASE
I'm tempted to call this wine fabulous fun but it's better than that. No wonder Wirra Wirra has become known as such a red wine star. Rich, soft, commanding fruit flavour, the mix of bright, floral aromatics beautifully accented by tight tannin and alluring flavours of smoky, sawdusty oak. The fruit is bold and plummy – this is a complete red wine drinking package. **DRINK** 2008–2012.

Price	$20 (Cellar Door)
Region	McLaren Vale
Value	♦♦♦♦♦
Auction	N/A
Score	92

Wirra Wirra RSW Shiraz 2005

Robert Strangeways Wigley (RSW) played cricket for South Australia in the late 1800s, and also started up the Wirra Wirra winery. The wine that commemorates him is hardly a forward defensive shot – it's a six all the way.

Price	$60
Region	McLaren Vale
Value	♦♦♦♦♦
Auction	N/A
Score	95

2005 RELEASE
Talk about rich! This is a cake of blackberried chocolate melted down and poured into a bottle, the oozy, smooth, groovy flavour of it layering your tongue with chocolate and blackberry and the classiest cedary, creamy oak. Tannin-wise it's remarkable, a flurry of chewy velvet rippling through the wine's syrupy softness.
DRINK 2013–2022.

Wirra Wirra Woodhenge Shiraz 2006

Samantha Connew is the chief winemaker at Wirra Wirra and she's among the best in the world at what she does. She's improved the Wirra reds immeasurably over the past few years.

Price	$35
Region	McLaren Vale
Value	♦♦♦♦
Auction	★★★
Score	94

2006 RELEASE
Do you like thick, syrupy, smooth-as-silk red wine? Do you like it riddled with sweet, dark, ripe fruit flavours, overlaid with a light tap of savoury French oak? Do you like red wine that impresses from the first pour, and keeps purring at you all the way to the end of the bottle? Thought you might. This wine does all that, with ease. **DRINK** 2008–2012.

Wolf Blass Gold Label Shiraz 2005

Price	$24
Region	Barossa
Value	♦♦
Auction	N/A
Score	85

2005 RELEASE
Spotlessly clean and fruity but dull and gangly to the taste – it's a decent wine, just not at the price. Black olives, toast, blackberry jam and chocolate flavours. Clumpy, powdery, slightly green tannins. A poor result from this vintage. **DRINK** 2008–2011.

Woodstock Shiraz 2005

I saw this recently for $17, which is fabulous buying. This is the kind of wine people who love Rufus Stone Shiraz should seriously consider.

2005 RELEASE
It tastes great at first but it's even better than you immediately think. It hits you with a wave of musky, vanillin, plummy, chocolaty (and slightly acidic) flavour, and for a few minutes you think that's it. But the more you drink of it the more you notice its fresh, juicy, tannic finish. The way it stretches out long through the aftertaste. The way its structure is carved in a nebbiolo-like way – a very good thing. **DRINK** 2009–2016.

Price	$20
Region	McLaren Vale
Value	♦♦♦♦♦
Auction	N/A
Score	91

Woop Woop Shiraz 2006

The idea for this wine label first took shape among three mates turning sausages as they stood around the BBQ. Funny, it's a good wine for just that setting.

2006 RELEASE
This isn't the best wine in the book by a long stretch, but once I gave it a bit of air I was impressed, simply, with the bang for the buck it offers. Hey, I'm a simple bloke at heart. It tastes like mashed blackberries and tar, the hit of flavour substantial. Don't be put off by the score; this is good value. **DRINK** 2008–2012.

Price	$12.95
Region	South Eastern Australia
Value	♦♦♦♦
Auction	N/A
Score	85

Wynns Coonawarra Estate Michael Shiraz 2005

Michael has changed its face considerably in recent times – from a heavy Barossa wannabe to a lighter, more ethereal style. I like the change, and I particularly like this 2005.

2005 RELEASE
Full of gorgeous, sweet, perfumed fruit. Soft, plummy, violety and seductive, though its musky, chewy, spicy tannin will ensure that its cellaring life is a long one. The mid-palate silkiness here is quite something. The longer it sits in the glass the louder its raspberried, plummy heart sings. **DRINK** 2012–2021.

PREVIOUS
2003 Perfumed, elegant, medium-bodied. 2007–2016. 93 pts.
2004 Light fruit, lots of tannin; challenging. 2017–2028. 92 pts.

Price	$75
Region	Coonawarra
Value	♦♦♦♦
Auction	★★★★
Score	95

Wynns Coonawarra Estate White Label Shiraz 2006

It might be one of Australia's most beloved red wines, but recent years haven't been its best. I was thrilled when I tasted this; it demands to be bought again.

Price	$19
Region	Coonawarra
Value	●●●●●
Auction	★★★★
Score	91

2006 RELEASE
Back in action. Depth, power, flavour, silken texture – what more could you want? Flavours of dark olives, plums, red berries and toast, the flavour lingering and the value high. It's not rocket science, it's just a bloody good red wine.
DRINK 2007–2013.

PREVIOUS
2001 Warm and plummy. 2003–2005. 86 pts.
2002 Soft, plump, plummy wine. 2004–2007. 90 pts.
2003 Light- to medium-weight. Ripe. 2005–2007. 86 pts.
2004 Lacking. Cherry-cola flavours; light-ish. 2006–2007. 86 pts.
2005 Complexity returns. Pepper, plums, cherries. 2006–2010. 89 pts.

Yalumba Hand-picked Shiraz & Viognier 2005

This wine has come a long way since the first release seven or eight years ago. Back then it had almost fifteen per cent viognier; this 2005 has only four per cent. It tastes better than ever.

Price	$29.95
Region	Barossa
Value	●●●
Auction	★★★
Score	93

2005 RELEASE
Yummo. Terrifically savoury–sweet, sophisticated, smooth and supple. The damn thing even looks vibrant, and its fresh flavours of blackberry, cherry, sandalwood and earth make the wine seem lively in your mouth. If you're planning on serving this at dinner – would you mind if I dropped in? Please? **DRINK** 2008–2016.

Yalumba Octavius Shiraz 2004

When this was first made it was matured in oak that had itself been aged for eight years, prior to being coopered into barrels. It's always been an American (bordering on ugly) oak-driven style, and largely not to my taste. The 2004 is the first vintage to use a small amount of French oak, and hallelujah for that.

Price	$99.95
Region	Barossa
Value	♦♦
Auction	★★★
Score	95

2004 RELEASE
For the first time ever, this smells and tastes fabulously modern. It's fresh and elegant, but does not lack an inch of power. Lots of long filigreed tannin, lots of liqueur-like fruit, coffeed oak and a delicious sense of sweet–savouriness. Crackerjack Barossa red wine: juicy, smooth, deep and brilliant. DRINK 2012–2022.

Yalumba Shiraz & Viognier 2005

Yalumba was one of the first to start using a dab of the 'white' grape viognier in its everyday drinking reds, though for a few years it was only mentioned on the back label. It was a huge success, and since viognier made it to the front label, sales have jumped further.

Price	$19.95
Region	Barossa
Value	♦♦♦♦
Auction	N/A
Score	87

2005 RELEASE
Quite a dark, malty style, very much in the toasty, dark-fruited Barossa tradition. Real good winter drinking here. It's a lifted, fragrant wine – courtesy of the viognier influence – but the heart of it is all about Barossa shiraz: leathery, coffeed, blackberried and dark. DRINK 2008–2012.

Yalumba Y Series Shiraz Viognier 2006

Yalumba winemaker Louisa Rose reckons 'Winemaking for us is about making wines that you think might drink well when you've got a glass of wine in one hand and food in the other. We're not comfortable with the Yalumba name being on a bottle of wine unless it's highly drinkable.'

Price	$12.95
Region	South Australia
Value	♦♦♦♦♦
Auction	N/A
Score	90

2006 RELEASE
This is pretty much an unoaked red wine, and for cool, spicy drinkability it takes some beating. It lays a strong claim to being the best wine in its price range. It tastes of cherries, blueberries and tobacco, and rushes up out of the glass with a blaze of sweet, spicy perfume. Mega value. DRINK 2008–2010.

Yering Station Shiraz Viognier 2006

A pioneer in the push to affordable, cool-climate shiraz viognier. This is on the money again.

2006 RELEASE
The flavours are all about sweet, savoury fruit but the wine's main game is its texture, which is syrupy soft and, simply, seriously seductive. It means that the wine works on three levels: as a savoury food wine, as a drink worthy of contemplation, and as a simple act of vinous seduction. All good in my books. **DRINK** 2008–2012.

PREVIOUS
- **2001** Fleshy, chocolaty, superfine. 2004–2009. 89 pts.
- **2002** Peppery, smooth, elegant. 2005–2011. 93 pts.
- **2003** Fleshy, smooth, spicy. 2006–2011. 92 pts.
- **2004** Dry and savoury. 2006–2010. 90 pts.
- **2005** Medium-weight, cherry-plummy, sweet-spicy. 2008–2013. 90 pts.

Price	$24
Region	**Yarra Valley**
Value	♦♦♦♦♦
Auction	★★★
Score	**92**

PINOT NOIR

Pinot noir is the most controversial of wine grapes. A lot of people can't stand the stuff; others drink almost nothing else. The reason is that it's generally a lighter, more delicate style of wine, its charm more for the way it smells and then lingers on your tongue than for the weight of flavour in the middle of your mouth. It's the wine style you are either besotted by, or can't be bothered with. As recently as five years ago there was a great deal of Australian pinot noir that was overpriced and under-performing; now it is arguably the opposite way around. Pinot lovers, make hay!

TOP TEN OF THE YEAR
1. Punch Close Planted Pinot Noir 2005
2. Ata Rangi Pinot Noir 2006
3. PHI Lusatia Park Vineyard Pinot Noir 2006
4. Ashton Hills Reserve Pinot Noir 2006
5. Kooyong Haven Pinot Noir 2005
6. By Farr Sangreal Pinot Noir 2005
7. Giant Steps Sexton Pinot Noir 2006
8. William Downie Pinot Noir 2006
9. Savaterre Pinot Noir 2005
10. Bannockburn Serre Pinot Noir 2005

Adam's Rib The Red 2006

Technically this isn't a pinot noir – or it is, but with a significant difference. It's a blend of eighty per cent pinot noir with twenty per cent shiraz, inspired in some way by the great old Maurice O'Shea wines of the 1930s and 1940s. It works beautifully.

2006 RELEASE
It is quite clear that more folks should be making this blend – it could easily become both as uniquely Australian, and successful, as cabernet-shiraz blends. This wine is full of grunty, grainy, grapey tannin and dark, polished, kirsch-like cherry flavours, its cedary French oak admirably tucked into the wine's fruit flavour. It's a long, structured, serious wine. **DRINK** 2009–2016.

Price	$35
Region	Beechworth
Value	♦♦♦♦♦
Auction	N/A
Score	93

Ashton Hills Estate Pinot Noir 2006

Ashton Hills's Stephen George is one of Australian wine's quietest, but most successful, achievers. His wines do the talking.

2006 RELEASE
It slips down so easily that the bottle almost should carry a health warning. It tastes of sour cherries, sap, dried herbs and burning cedarwood, and its drinkability rating is enormous. It's got enough tannin to see it improve in the cellar over the medium term. Juicy aftertaste!
DRINK 2008–2014.

PREVIOUS
2001 Perfumed and fruity. 2004–2008. 92 pts.
2002 Ashen and herbal, but good. 2006–2011. 93 pts.
2003 Bright and complex. 2006–2012. 93 pts.
2004 Meaty and substantial, yet varietal. 2008–2012. 92 pts.
2005 Classy, lengthy, impressive. 2010–2014. 94 pts.

Price	$37.50
Region	Adelaide Hills
Value	♦♦♦
Auction	N/A
Score	92

Ashton Hills Reserve Pinot Noir 2006

A lot of wineries reckon they only release a 'reserve' wine when quality warrants it – and then release one every year. Ashton Hills is true to its word – its reserve releases are the exception rather than the rule.

Price	$50
Region	Adelaide Hills
Value	♦ ♦ ♦ ♦
Auction	N/A
Score	96

2006 RELEASE
I love this wine. It's a deep, varietally pure pinot noir, rich with cedar, sandalwood, sour cherry, smoke and sap flavours. There are lifted floral fragrances, but the way it spreads out through the finish is the sure sign of its class. Its tannins are meaty, peppery, smoky and intoxicating. This wine will be far more complex with age. **DRINK** 2011–2018.

PREVIOUS
2004 Fine, complex, great depth. 2008–2014. 94 pts.
2005 Long, perfumed, voluminous. 2010–2016. 95 pts.

Ata Rangi Crimson Pinot Noir 2006

The buzz over New Zealand pinot noir usually focuses on the Central Otago region, but personally I'm more of a Martinborough man. This is the 'second' wine of this famous pinot noir producer.

Price	$37
Region	Martinborough, NZ
Value	♦ ♦ ♦
Auction	N/A
Score	92

2006 RELEASE
Smell this. It's intoxicating in its array of forest berries, smoke, cedarwood, tobacco and, no doubt, other yummy scents – I had to stop smelling and get down to drinking, because my mouth was watering so much. Magically, it tastes as good as it smells, its silken texture wandering deliciously across your tongue. A beauty.
DRINK 2008–2014.

Ata Rangi Pinot Noir 2006

Ata Rangi has been toiling with grapevines since 1980, placing it firmly as a pioneer of modern New Zealand wine. It's not one of the pretenders; it's the real deal.

2006 RELEASE
This wine proves just how great New Zealand pinot noir can be. It's lush and dense and yet it never tastes like anything other than high quality pinot noir – sometimes pinot as powerful as this can taste a bit non-descript, or simply like a 'dry red'. No such flaws exist here. It tastes of tobacco, cherry-plums, spice and cedar, its flashy purple-crimson colour glistening in the glass. The stamp of authority: a long, long aftertaste. **DRINK** 2012–2020.

Price	$80
Region	Martinborough, NZ
Value	♦ ♦ ♦
Auction	★ ★ ★ ★
Score	96

Bannockburn Pinot Noir 2005

Bannockburn has had the odd hiccup over the past few years but new-ish winemaker Michael Glover has things back on track. The wines from the 2006 vintage onwards will mark a new era for this famous Australian wine name.

2005 RELEASE
This is the Bannockburn we know and love. Composed, juicy, structured and steady through the mouth, the full, sour-cherried fruit flavour laced with grapey tannin. Gorgeously varietal. Bannockburn has always carried sappy, stalky, dried herb edges – it's a trademark of its pinot – but those flavours are not as obvious here as they have been in the past – a good thing. **DRINK** 2010–2014.

Price	$65
Region	Geelong
Value	♦ ♦ ♦
Auction	★ ★ ★
Score	92

Bannockburn Serre Pinot Noir 2005

The Serre vineyard was planted in 1984 by former winemaker Gary Farr. The vines on this vineyard are planted a lot closer together than is customary in Australian vineyards; it usually produces Bannockburn's best pinot noir.

2005 RELEASE
It doesn't look much. It's light in colour, lacks brightness, smells like garden mulch and at no time does it seem concentrated, even after you're moved onto the second glass. What it does have though, is structure, complexity, length of flavour and the kind of mouth perfume – it feels like you smell it as it moves through your mouth – that is very easy to find beguiling. In the end the bottle I opened went like the clappers – I want some more! Ripe tannins bite through the finish. **DRINK** 2011–2018.

Price	$110
Region	Geelong
Value	♦ ♦ ♦
Auction	★ ★ ★
Score	95

Bass Phillip 'The 21' Pinot Noir 2006

If you were to track the development of quality pinot noir in Australia, an awful lot of the most interesting paths would lead back to Phillip Jones, the man behind Bass Phillip. This wine marks his twenty-one vintages of pinot noir growing.

2006 RELEASE
It smells good, tastes great, and then finishes with a smoky, toasty aftertaste. If those smoky nuances stay well behaved, then we have an exquisite wine on our hands, with lots of dry tannin and flavour and pretty floral aromatics. The problem is that such smokiness has a habit of becoming more obvious, and unpleasant, the longer the wine sits in the bottle; only time will tell. **DRINK** 2008–2010.

Price	$80
Region	Gippsland
Value	♦ ♦ ♦ ♦
Auction	★ ★ ★
Score	89

Bay of Fires Tigress Pinot Noir 2006

The Bay of Fires wines fly under the radar a tad but they are uniformly excellent. The sparkling is a beauty. So too is this pinot noir.

2006 RELEASE
Just about everything you could ask for in a young pinot noir. It's a fascinating mix of undergrowth, red roses, bright cherries, deli meats and cedarwood, its creamy oak giving the wine a silken smoothness rather than overt flavour. Bravo. This has got me swooning. **DRINK** 2008–2015.

Price	$30
Region	Tasmania
Value	♦♦♦♦♦
Auction	★★★
Score	93

By Farr Pinot Noir 2005

Pinot noir is Gary Farr's specialty. He flies close to the wind, producing both spectacular wines and wines that leave you puzzled. Always, his wines are worthy of consideration.

2005 RELEASE
Awkward wine. The fruit and oak and acid seem to pull in different directions, a shame because the individual components are good. Sour cherries, sap and smoky oak. Might just need to rest in the bottle for a year or two. **DRINK** 2010–2015.

PREVIOUS
1999 Beefy, fresh, good. 2006–2010. 91 pts.
2000 Powerful and persistent. 2006–2011. 92 pts.
2001 Baked and clumsy. 2005–2009. 88 pts.
2002 Bitter, beetrooty, fresh. 2006–2012. 89 pts.
2003 Sappy and leathery. 2005–2009. 87 pts.
2004 Fresh, long, structured. 2009–2015. 95 pts.

Price	$55
Region	Geelong
Value	♦♦♦♦
Auction	★★★
Score	89

By Farr Sangreal Pinot Noir 2005

This is Farr's deluxe pinot noir. It's worth the dosh.

2005 RELEASE
Fabulous pinot noir. Dramatically long through the finish, the true sign of elite pinot. Cherries, stalks, hay, dried herbs, cedarwood and smoke – though to be honest, it's all seamless. Quite a sour fruit profile. But in all, just really good. **DRINK** 2012–2020.

Price	$60
Region	Geelong
Value	♦♦♦♦
Auction	★★★
Score	96

Carrick Pinot Noir 2006

In all the hype over the expected quality of Central Otago pinot noir, Carrick is one of the few to consistently put runs on the board.

2006 RELEASE
Brooding, intense, meaty, peppery, slippery through the mouth and bold with fruit flavour. Big pinot, but big on quality too. Quartz-like tannin jagging through the finish. Sweet, smoky aftertaste. DRINK 2008–2014.

Price	$50
Region	Central Otago, NZ
Value	♦♦♦
Auction	★★★
Score	93

Chatto Pinot Noir 2005

The year 2005 was excellent for Tasmanian pinot noir.

2005 RELEASE
Burly, beefy, meaty pinot noir. Chewy even. Something of a take-no-prisoners style, and yet it never tastes like anything other than varietal pinot noir; this is not a 'dry red' style in any way. Cherries, smoke, pepper and dried meats. This is a pinot that could stand up to a super-deluxe hamburger. DRINK 2009–2013.

Price	$40
Region	Tasmania
Value	♦♦♦
Auction	★★
Score	88

Clos Pierre Reserve Pinot Noir 2005

The pinots in this range are invariably the ones to look out for – though from this vintage the 'standard' release is as good as the more expensive version.

2005 RELEASE
It slips into 'dry red' territory but if you approach it in that vein, it's a nice drink. Structured tannin, lots of acidity, flavours of smoke and cherries and a reasonably long finish. Needs at least an hour in the decanter prior to drinking. DRINK 2008–2013.

Price	$30
Region	Yarra Valley
Value	♦♦
Auction	N/A
Score	88

Coldstream Hills Amphitheatre Pinot Noir 2006

Coldstream Hills might be owned by a corporate giant (Foster's), but it's still got street cred. Its oldest vineyards are over twenty years old, their steep slopes renowned for growing top-quality grapes.

Price	$80
Region	Yarra Valley
Value	♦♦
Auction	N/A
Score	92

2006 RELEASE
Sheesh, this is a brute of a pinot. It's smothered in sweet, smoky, slippery-smooth oak, the feel of it on your tongue like licking at chocolate-coated glass. It's big on cherry-plummed fruit and either needs a couple of hours in the decanter or, preferably, seven or eight years' rest in a dark, cool place. **DRINK** 2013–2019.

Coldstream Hills Pinot Noir 2007

Coldstream Hills was one of the main players in the Australian push towards quality pinot noir being released at reasonable prices. I believe, however, that this wine is now headed for near-exclusive distribution through the restaurant and export trade, rather than through domestic wine shops. If you see some though – grab it.

Price	$29
Region	Yarra Valley
Value	♦♦♦♦♦
Auction	★★★
Score	93

2007 RELEASE
What a lovely release this is. It's got grunt but it's got elegance too, the cherry-plummed hit of flavour contained beautifully by firm, lengthy tannins. Coldstream Hills will not release a 'reserve' pinot noir from the 2007 vintage, and this 'standard' release is all the better for it. Super wine. **DRINK** 2008–2014.

Coldstream Hills Reserve Pinot Noir 2006

Coldstream reserve pinot has a history of being a muscular, oak-assertive style. It has an impressive cellarability if not an outstanding one. I often prefer the 'standard' pinot noir.

Price	$50
Region	Yarra Valley
Value	♦♦
Auction	★★★
Score	92

2006 RELEASE
This is at the robust, firm, muscular end of pinot noir, big on blueberried, dark-cherried fruit flavour and bursting with glossy, grainy, cedary oak. For all that it seems shy on the nose, and tasted much better 24 hours after I first opened the bottle. I suspect that it will seem far more impressive as a mature wine than as a young wine. **DRINK** 2011–2017.

Curly Flat Pinot Noir 2004 & 2005

Curly Flat is a meticulously managed vineyard currently converting its vines to biodynamic farming practices.

2004 RELEASE
Easily the best Curly Flat pinot noir to date. It's steely, perfumed, powered by medium-weight cherry-plummed flavour and gorgeously cuddled in cedary oak. It has balance, varietal integrity, structure and power.
DRINK 2012–2018.

2005 RELEASE
The jury is out on this. It's all tense and bound in on itself, its fruit flavour and tannin scrunched up close – it's hard to get a good look at its face. This can mean that it's got a big future ahead of it. There are signs of malty, cedary oak and bright, cherried ripeness, the mix of flavours, sweet acids and tannins nicely balanced. **DRINK** 2013–2019.

Price	$46
Region	Macedon Ranges
Value	♦♦♦♦
Auction	★★★★
Score	95 (2004) 94 (2005)

Curly Flat Williams Crossing Pinot Noir 2005

Winemaker Phillip Moraghan makes all his wine as if it's destined for the $45 plus range, and then classifies it later. It means that everything gets the Rolls Royce (or Boeing superliner) treatment. No wonder the $20 range is so damned good. This wine took top honours at the 2007 Macedon Ranges Wine Show, beating off a raft of higher priced rivals.

2005 RELEASE
I think it's called having your cake and eating it too. You can quaff this now, or keep it for a few years; either way it will be delicious. It's bursting with floral fragrance – but it's not just pretty, there's substance here too. Sap, cherries, stalks and chewy tannin. The price is frivolous, the flavour serious. I'm in. **DRINK** 2008–2012.

Price	$20
Region	Macedon Ranges
Value	♦♦♦♦♦
Auction	★★★
Score	92

Dalwhinnie Moonambel Pinot Noir 2005

The Pyrenees is hardly regarded as a pinot noir region, but Dalwhinnie's vineyards are planted at altitude, helping keep them cool. The estate can produce good pinot noir.

2005 RELEASE
The texture is the thing. It's a silken, balanced, slippery wine, the smooth flow of it carrying flavours of dark cherries, pine-needles and spicy sandalwood. Structure, texture and flavour are all good, but the pine-like, minty character is distracting. **DRINK** 2008–2013.

Price	$38
Region	Pyrenees
Value	♦♦
Auction	★★
Score	87

De Bortoli Estate Grown Pinot Noir 2006

It wasn't all that long ago that De Bortoli pinot noir was routinely disappointing. Now it's a leader in its field. No producer signifies the dynamic nature of Australian wine better than De Bortoli Yarra Valley.

2006 RELEASE
Plush, ripe, luxurious – if you love pinot noir, you have to get yourself some of this. It tastes of cherries and stalks and ribald, cedary oak, the sheer sheen of it 100 per cent class. Great, ferrous, muscular tannin structure too, the mark of the highest quality pinot noir. This is a boomer, and at a very nifty price (for the quality, and the variety). **DRINK** 2009–2015.

Price	$38
Region	Yarra Valley
Value	♦♦♦♦♦
Auction	★★★
Score	94

De Bortoli Gulf Station Pinot Noir 2006

The great thing about De Bortoli's pinot surge is that it extends all the way down the range. No one misses out, at all price levels.

2006 RELEASE
Quality pinot noir at a price like this was unheard of ten years ago in Australia – watch out world. This is fragrant, spicy, vibrant and juicy, the aftertaste terrifically sour-sweet. There's grip, focus, detail of both flavour and aroma – all the kinds of things you expect in higher priced wines. Hats off. **DRINK** 2008–2012.

Price	$18
Region	Yarra Valley
Value	♦♦♦♦♦
Auction	★★★
Score	92

De Bortoli Windy Peak Pinot Noir 2007

The recommended price for this wine is $12, but I walked into a shop and bought it for $9.95, a remarkable price for a pinot noir.

2007 RELEASE
There's quite a deal of smoky flavour here. That said, the wine carries these flavours well, with a mix of bright cherries and chocolate flavour (almost like Turkish delight) and lots of juicy acidity. The tannins are bold for a wine of this price, but necessary to keep the wine intact. I would not cellar this; those smoky flavours will come to dominate. For now, it's lovely drinking. **DRINK** 2008.

Price	$12
Region	Victoria
Value	♦♦♦
Auction	N/A
Score	85

Eldridge Estate Clonal Blend Pinot Noir 2006

David Lloyd has planted a number of different pinot noir 'clones' (different types of pinot noir) on his property. He picks each separately and keeps them apart in the winery, producing a range of different pinot noirs from each vintage. Some he bottles individually, others he blends. This is the blend.

2006 RELEASE
Delightfully fragrant and strawberried, the sweet lift of it a joy to stick anywhere near your nose. There's a slightly heavy sense of syrupy, polished oak sitting atop that luscious fruitiness, but time should meld the two together. Fresh acidity, a healthy crack of tannin, and a good, crisp, lingering finish. It needs extra bottle time, but it is very good. **DRINK** 2010–2016.

Price	$60
Region	Mornington Peninsula
Value	♦♦♦
Auction	N/A
Score	92

Eldridge Pinot Noir 2006

There was a time when Mornington Peninsula pinot meant Stoniers, Main Ridge and Paringa. Those producers are still performing very well, but there's a whole new range of outstanding pinot makers, Eldridge very much one of them.

2006 RELEASE
Super wine. Depth, class, impact and structure – this is one for the cellar, for sure. Lots of sour, cherried tannin and bursts of citrusy acidity, all of it dancing about a core of delicious, controlled, substantial flavour. Cedary, sophisticated oak completes the picture. Wonderful. **DRINK** 2011–2016.

Price	$48
Region	Mornington Peninsula
Value	♦♦♦♦
Auction	★★★
Score	94

Epis Pinot Noir 2006

Noted ex-footballer Alex Epis is well on the way to becoming more famous for wine than sport. Judging by the wines he has produced over the past five years he is a great grapegrower.

2006 RELEASE
There's great joy to be had here. It's a profound pinot noir. It's taut and undergrowthy, complex and satiny, and if you manage to keep it in your glass long enough you'll find yourself noticing more and more in it. Cedar, wood smoke, eucalypt, dark cherries, herbs ... it's got it going on. On past experience it's also fair to say that Epis pinot noir does age, and does age well. **DRINK** 2012–2017.

PREVIOUS
2000 Tight, complex, impressive. 2006–2009. 91 pts.
2001 Tight, plummy, spicy. 2007–2012. 92 pts.
2003 Born to age. 2008–2014. 92 pts.
2004 Soft, pretty, long. 2009–2014. 95 pts.
2005 Depth and elegance. 2008–2014. 95 pts.

Price	$60
Region	Macedon Ranges
Value	♦♦♦♦
Auction	★★★★
Score	94

Escarpment Pinot Noir 2006

The 2005 was one of my wines of last year (94 points) and so I was desperate to get my mitts on this. It's made by Larry McKenna, one of the stars of New Zealand pinot noir (even though he's an expat Aussie).

2006 RELEASE
Heavy for a pinot noir but, hey, when the quality is as good as this, it can be whatever it wants to be. Dark, saturated cherry flavours are infused with Asian spice and sap, notes of pepper and dried meat popping in among the wine's sizeable structure. Rather impeccable, really. **DRINK** 2011–2017.

Price	$48
Region	Martinborough, NZ
Value	♦♦♦♦
Auction	★★★★
Score	94

Frogmore Creek Reserve Pinot Noir 2005

This organically grown wine is made by the doyen of Tasmanian pinot noir, Andrew Hood. The standard Frogmore Creek pinot noir is excellent; this takes it a gentle step up.

2005 RELEASE
A wine of taut, savoury control. It tastes of earth and stewed rhubarb, undergrowth, cranberries and sour cherries. There's a sappy bitterness on the finish, but it's in harmony with the wine. This is a subtle, complex, structured pinot noir that should amply reward the patient. **DRINK** 2011–2017.

Price	$60
Region	Tasmania
Value	♦♦♦♦
Auction	N/A
Score	94

Giant Steps Sexton Pinot Noir 2006

Giant Steps pinot noir has been getting steadily better over the past few years, and can now count itself in the upper tier of the Yarra Valley hierarchy. This wine is from owner Phil Sexton's home vineyard.

2006 RELEASE
There's nothing lollied or sweet here. This is a serious pinot noir, and I like it a lot. It has a rigid sense of architecture, with dry flavours of cherry and sap and cedar kept straight and linear by firm, decisive tannins. Accordingly, the bulk of the flavour reaches out through the finish. **DRINK** 2012–2017.

Price	$34.95
Region	Yarra Valley
Value	♦♦♦♦♦
Auction	N/A
Score	95

Grosset Pinot Noir 2006

Jeffrey Grosset might be renowned for his single vineyard rieslings but his reds can be stellar (as indeed can his chardonnay – wash my mouth out!).

2006 RELEASE
This is a long, taut, minerally pinot noir, the emphasis more on structure than on fruit-driven pleasure. That said, there are attractive beetroot and cherry notes, the aftertaste (in a good way) like chewing on autumn leaves. Classy wine. **DRINK**: 2012–2017.

Price	$65
Region	Adelaide Hills
Value	♦♦♦
Auction	★★★
Score	93

Hillcrest Reserve Pinot Noir 2006

Hillcrest has been reborn over the past handful of years under the obsessive care of David and Tanya Bryant. The vineyards though, are thirty-seven years old. They are run organically, and are among the lowest yielding in the Yarra, meaning that the wines do not lack power.

2006 RELEASE
This will need a fair number of years to show its best. It's a smoky, meaty, substantial pinot noir, sculpted with tannin and cut with sappy, tangy, natural acids. There's a lot of dark cherried fruit flavour and a lot of stalky character too; in time these will mellow out and turn into something complex, and enchanting. **DRINK** 2012–2018.

Price	$75
Region	Yarra Valley
Value	♦ ♦ ♦
Auction	N/A
Score	94

Hoddles Creek Pinot Noir 2006

This has held the title as the best value pinot noir in the land for the past few years. It's made by gun winemaker Franco D'Anna.

2006 RELEASE
A delicious combination of sweet, ripe, fruity flavour with savoury, edgy, fine-grained tannin. One for drinking now or one for the cellar – this pinot will go a treat both ways. Flavours of dark cherry, strawberry, mint and cedar-spice. It's as good as many pinot noir at twice the price. **DRINK** 2008–2016.

Price	$17.95
Region	Yarra Valley
Value	♦ ♦ ♦
Auction	N/A
Score	93

Innocent Bystander Pinot Noir 2006

Innocent Bystander is the everyday drinking range of the Yarra Valley's Giant Steps winery – arguably the hottest cellar door in the valley at the moment, and well worth a visit.

2006 RELEASE
Pinot noir is a rage in the market at the moment and this wine is a graphic example of why. Yes, it's only light- to medium-bodied, but it's perfumed and structured and long, and drinks well both casually and contemplatively (it's my word, and I'm sticking with it). Sour cherries and undergrowth, elegance and finesse. Yummo.
DRINK 2008–2014.

Price	$19.95
Region	Yarra Valley
Value	♦ ♦ ♦ ♦ ♦
Auction	★ ★ ★
Score	91

Kooyong Haven Pinot Noir 2005

Kooyong makes three single vineyard pinot noirs; they're all good, but the Haven is the doyen. Word is getting around, and it is beginning to sell out very, very fast. The 2005 Kooyong Ferrous Pinot Noir is outstanding too.

2005 RELEASE
Something about this wine makes me want to put on my best Nigella voice and mention how deeply, deeply satisfying it is. It is profound pinot noir. It's luxurious, rich, sophisticated and strong, its muscular tannin almost completely overwhelmed by deep, varietal fruit complexity. A deeply flavoured wine, yet a buoyant wine. This wine is at the vanguard of extreme quality Australian pinot noir.
DRINK 2009–2016.

Price	$60
Region	Mornington Peninsula
Value	♦♦♦♦♦
Auction	★★★★★
Score	96

Kooyong Meres Pinot Noir 2005

When Kooyong started out I had my doubts; now I have no doubts at all. This is a superstar producer of very fine pinot noir.

2005 RELEASE
This seemed light and muted when I first tasted it but with extra time in the bottle, it has blossomed. It is now magnificently fragrant, sour, smoky, undergrowthy, ripped with herb-infused cherries and long through the finish. The colour is light, the effect is not. There's a blaze of tannin and a milky texture (not flavour) that manages to carry quite a deal of acid with ease. Fabulous wine.
DRINK 2009–2017.

Price	$58
Region	Mornington Peninsula
Value	♦♦♦♦♦
Auction	★★★
Score	94

Kooyong Pinot Noir 2006

In the rush for the single vineyard wines the 'standard' Kooyong pinot noir can become a bit lost. It shouldn't.

2006 RELEASE
Kooyong pinot noirs are never flabby; they always have structure. This is a particularly fine-boned example. Rose-like, strawberried, sour–sweet fruit curls around sturdy limbs of tannin, lines of acidity keeping it both fresh and refreshing. The oak is smoky and spicy, the tannins cut with flavours of minerals. A rather gorgeous pinot noir. **DRINK** 2009–2016.

Price	$40
Region	Mornington Peninsula
Value	♦♦♦♦♦
Auction	★★★
Score	94

Lillydale Estate Pinot Noir 2006

It almost seemed like the forgotten estate for a few years there, until the 2005 chardonnay threw a great deal of attention its way. Looks like the estate's quality as a whole is on the rise.

2006 RELEASE
Glossy texture, a nice mix of sappy/stemmy flavour and pure, well-ripened fruitiness, enough tannin to keep it well behaved and an overall feeling of balance. It's not heavy, but it's not light. It's good. **DRINK** 2010–2015.

Price	$26
Region	Yarra Valley
Value	♦♦♦
Auction	N/A
Score	91

Matua Valley Pinot Noir 2006

Pinot noir is such a finicky variety that it's usually (though not always) left to small producers. Matua Valley is owned by Foster's, and it's not a great advertisement for big company pinot noir.

2006 RELEASE
It tastes and smells like pinot noir and comes complete with the refreshing acidity you would expect, but the flavours themselves are dilute and lifeless. Martinborough pinot at this price should be better. Smoke, sour cherries, dried herbs. All good; just not enough. **DRINK** 2008–2011.

Price	$25
Region	Martinborough, NZ
Value	♦♦
Auction	N/A
Score	85

Maude Pinot Noir 2006

Dan and Sarah-Kate Dineen were winemaking stars in the Hunter Valley until a few years ago – when they hitched up and left for the beautiful Central Otago in New Zealand. This wine is a blend of four sub-regions of Central Otago.

2006 RELEASE
Pretty, perfumed, exotic – damn it, it's got me falling head over heels. It actually tastes like a mix of Turkish delight, cranberry juice and Campari – and before you turn off let me quickly note that it's a super combination of sweet delicacy and background herbal complexity. I love it. It's also got a deceptively muscular tannin structure tucked away beneath the surface. **DRINK** 2008–2013.

Price	$38
Region	Central Otago, NZ
Value	♦♦♦♦
Auction	N/A
Score	92

Mayer Pinot Noir 2006

Timo Mayer is one of a growing band of young gun winemakers hell-bent on revolutionising the Yarra Valley. He describes this wine as 'way off centre'.

2006 RELEASE
An unusual pinot noir, yet a beautiful one. It carries a lovely, sweet, Turkish delight-like flavour, the charm of which keeps you diving back at the glass for more. There's a lot going on here. Flavours of tree sap, fennel, smoke and dried herbs, the odd note of undergrowth rising and falling as the seduction powers on. Its tannin structure is impeccable. This wine almost seems feathery and light-bodied, and yet it does not lack pinot noir impact. Fascinating. **DRINK** 2008–2018.

Price	$50
Region	Yarra Valley
Value	♦♦♦♦
Auction	N/A
Score	94

Mount Langi Ghiran Bradach Vineyard Pinot Noir 2006

New release wine from a revitalised Mount Langi Ghiran. Winemaker Dan Buckle looks set to kick a lot of goals in coming years.

2006 RELEASE
I didn't even know that pinot noir was grown in the Grampians. And yet here we have a lovely pinot noir, suitable for drinking now or in the medium term. It's just so bright with flavour. Ripe, generous, smoky, cherried, lengthy – in short, it's a lip-smacking wine. **DRINK** 2008–2014.

Price	$28
Region	Grampians
Value	♦♦♦♦
Auction	N/A
Score	92

Ngeringa J.E. Pinot Noir 2005

A new biodynamic producer in the Adelaide Hills. Feeling is that a new star has been born here.

2005 RELEASE
Spectacular first-up release. It smells fascinating – like dried clay, like sour–sweet cherries, like wood sap and dried meats and black pepper. It tastes just as good, and just as interesting – indeed, it pushes all the buttons of the ardent pinot lover. There's a deal of classy oak here too, and noticeably, mouth-watering acid, but every indication is that both will slink further into the wine as time goes on. Definitely classify this under 'outrageous quality' in the pinot files. **DRINK** 2008–2017.

Price	$25
Region	Adelaide Hills
Value	♦♦♦♦♦
Auction	N/A
Score	95

O'Leary Walker Pinot Noir 2006

O'Leary Walker is a name to remember when looking for excellent quality at excellent prices. Riesling and shiraz are usually their stars; this is their best pinot noir yet. I've seen this discounted to $16.

2006 RELEASE
This is one of the best value pinot noirs of the year. It tastes of strawberry, sour cherries, raspberries and bright, fleshy plums – the punch and carry of it super impressive for the price. The oak input is toasty and appropriate, and it keeps your interest right to the bottom of the bottle – which appears far too fast. **DRINK** 2008–2012.

Price	$18.50
Region	Adelaide Hills
Value	♦♦♦♦♦
Auction	N/A
Score	90

Over The Shoulder Pinot Noir 2006

This is made by outstanding winemaker Dave Bicknell at Oakridge in the Yarra Valley. I prefer it to the higher priced Oakridge pinot noir.

2006 RELEASE
This is good. It carries a lovely cloak of polished, smoky, cedary oak, the class of it giving a lovely sheen to the pure, plummy, slightly sour fruit flavour that make up the heart of the wine. There's quite a bit of attractive, woody tannin here, suggesting that it will hold and develop well over the next few years. A quaffing pinot with cellaring potential; excellent value. **DRINK** 2008–2011.

Price	$18
Region	Yarra Valley
Value	♦♦♦♦
Auction	N/A
Score	88

Pfeiffer Sparkling Pinot Noir 2004

Jen Pfeiffer is the next generation of Pfeiffer winemakers and she's a talent. This wine is good, if overpriced, and it's one of a range of good drinking reds.

2004 RELEASE
It's fresh, fruity, undergrowthy, full of soft, stewed cherry flavour and while bitter and nutty on the finish, it holds its line well, and manages to satisfy. Good sparkling reds are a dying breed; and this is good. **DRINK** 2008–2011.

Price	$29.95
Region	Rutherglen
Value	♦♦♦
Auction	N/A
Score	86

PHI Lusatia Park Vineyard Pinot Noir 2006

This is a joint venture between Stephen Shelmerdine and De Bortoli. The grapes are grown off a twenty-year-old hillside vineyard in red basalt soils. The grapes are hand-picked, hand sorted, and fermented using wild yeasts. The aim is 'elegance and finesse with texture and structure'.

Price	$54
Region	Yarra Valley
Value	♦♦♦♦♦
Auction	N/A
Score	96

2006 RELEASE
There was much hoo-ha over the inaugural 2005 release of PHI, but after several attempts I had to concede that the wine just wasn't for me. This year is different. This is a big, bony, statuesque pinot noir, heftily perfumed, beautifully ripened, and authoritative in all respects. This is headed for Grand Cru status in Australian wine. **DRINK** 2012–2022.

Philip Shaw No. 8 Pinot Noir 2006

The Philip Shaw vineyard at Orange in New South Wales reaches to as high as 900 m above sea level, making for cool grape growing conditions. This pinot noir spends a year in French oak, all of it new or one year old.

Price	$40
Region	Orange
Value	♦♦
Auction	N/A
Score	90

2006 RELEASE
The Orange region rarely springs to mind when thoughts turn to pinot noir, but this is a lovely wine. For starters, it tastes like pinot noir, with sour cherry and sap flooding the palate, sawdusty, cedary, creamy oak then offering substantial support. It rings clear and bright through the finish – if it weren't so expensive, it would be worth hunting out. **DRINK** 2008–2013.

Picardy Tete de Cuvée Pinot Noir 2005

Picardy's 'standard' pinot noir from 2005 was excellent, and sold out fast. This reserve release is as good, but not necessarily better. Made in tiny quantities; expect it to be scarce.

Price	$40
Region	Pemberton
Value	♦♦♦♦
Auction	N/A
Score	93

2005 RELEASE
Big, serious pinot noir. Not the kind of wine to take lightly. Ribbed with tannin, fleshed with sour berried fruit, smoky and cedary through the finish and then spicy and fruity as an aftertaste. For all that, the nose is still muted, and needs time to evolve. Impressive. **DRINK** 2011–2018.

Punch Close Planted Pinot Noir 2005

Pruned and picked by hand from vines grown very close together. Fermented naturally. Neither fined nor filtered. This is hand-crafted, hard work winemaking with absolute quality the only master.

2005 RELEASE
Stratospheric pinot noir. As good as a super duper French pinot noir. Structured, ethereal, weighty, varietal, charming – it's one with the lot. There's no need to rant and rave; the wine says it all. Great pinot. **DRINK** 2008–2020.

Price	$80
Region	Yarra Valley
Value	♦♦♦♦
Auction	N/A
Score	97

Punch Lance's Vineyard Pinot Noir 2005

Punch is the new endeavour of the Lance family, formerly of Diamond Valley Vineyards. In an odd deal they've retained ownership and access to the best vineyards of Diamond Valley Vineyards – the brand was the main asset sold. As they say in the classics, 'the land is the brand'; I reckon the Lance's did well out of this deal.

2005 RELEASE
Layered and delicious at once. This is a pretty, perfumed, alluring wine, alive with flavours of ripe cherries, smoke, box hedge and sap. The line of acidity running along the wine's spine is daring and direct, the length of flavour through the finish pristine and persistent. Resistance to its seduction is useless. **DRINK** 2008–2015.

Price	$50
Region	Yarra Valley
Value	♦♦♦♦
Auction	N/A
Score	93

Punt Road Yarra Valley Pinot Noir 2006

Ten years ago pinot of this quality cost $35 to $40. Times have changed. Punt Road has been one of the leaders in this change.

2006 RELEASE
It needs another twelve months in the bottle to settle down and work a bit more softness into its tannin, but this is a high quality drop. It's full of juicy, cherried flavour ably supported by smoky, cedary oak, and it rings clean and true through the finish. **DRINK** 2009–2014.

Price	$25
Region	Yarra Valley
Value	♦♦♦♦
Auction	N/A
Score	91

Riposte The Sabre Pinot Noir 2006

Tim Knappstein is something of a living legend of Australian wine. Riposte is his latest venture.

2006 RELEASE
Back when Tim Knappstein was renowned for his Lenswood pinot noir he regularly put out a robust, dry-red style of wine that gathered a lot of attention. Some of the wines were very good, but it was a different (and lesser) era in Australian pinot noir. Riposte is in that same style: robust, meaty, chunky and substantial, the flavours themselves varietal but the structure and presence of it decidedly on the 'big' side. That said, there's a lot about this wine that reminds me of a decent nebbiolo, and if you think along those lines you find a lot to admire. **DRINK** 2010–2015.

Price	$26
Region	**Adelaide Hills**
Value	♦♦♦♦
Auction	N/A
Score	90

Savaterre Pinot Noir 2005

Savaterre was only planted a decade ago but it has already established itself as one of the nation's best pinot noir producers. It's a high altitude vineyard overlooking the Victorian Alps, near Beechworth.

2005 RELEASE
Not at all sweet. Indeed it's quite bitter and daring on the finish, and has a sense of dry chocolate there even as a line of minerals crackles through the taut, dry frame of tannin. It's tight, ripe, savoury, and stalky too, and needs at least a couple of hours in the decanter to start showing its wares. It's a wine of personality. A wine that won't come to you – you need to go to it. I do not question its quality.
DRINK 2012–2019.

PREVIOUS
2002 Substantial complexity and flavour. 2008–2014. 95 pts.
2003 Dry, tannic, smoky. 2005–2007. 87 pts.
2004 Structured, powerful, complex. 2010–2016. 94 pts.

Price	$70
Region	**Beechworth**
Value	♦♦♦♦
Auction	★★★★
Score	95

Scotchmans Hill Swan Bay Pinot Noir 2007

I have a long history of buying Scotchmans Hill wines, mainly because it's on the stretch of Victorian coast I've spent a lot of time on. The quality of the wines has sloshed about a bit, but they're in good form now.

2007 RELEASE
Looking for a quaffing pinot noir? This is an excellent one. It's varietal and tangy, spicy on the finish and nicely weighted. There's even a meaty minerality here – it's the kind of class you don't expect to see at less than twenty bucks. This is even better than the (very good) 2006.
DRINK 2008–2012.

Price	$19
Region	Geelong
Value	●●●●●
Auction	N/A
Score	90

Shadowfax Pinot Noir 2004

You don't see too many 'multi-regional' blends of pinot noir, mostly because it's a grape variety that attracts purists, and purists like to (attempt to) capture the essence of their land in the flavour of their wine. The grapes for this wine come from the Victorian areas of Geelong, the Cardinia Ranges and the Yarra Valley.

2004 RELEASE
No doubt about the quality of this. It's earthy and different, loaded with sour, savoury cherry flavours and even spruced with peppery, almost meaty, complexities. Its tannins are supple but substantial and it finishes juicy and satisfying. It should age very well. **DRINK** 2009–2013.

Price	$30
Region	Victoria
Value	●●●●
Auction	N/A
Score	92

Stefano Lubiana Primavera Pinot Noir 2006

Steve Lubiana is one of the leading lights of both Tasmanian and mainland Australian wine. His hillside vineyard near Hobart has really hit its straps over the past few years.

2006 RELEASE
Right in the groove. Deliciously fragrant and fruity, all strawberry and boysenberry and sap, creamy oak helping it slip down a treat. There's juicy acidity and dry, easy-going tannins, and there's just enough of the undergrowth character pinot lovers look for to elevate it above the ruck. More for drinking than cellaring, this is certainly a wine to seek out. **DRINK** 2008–2012.

Price	$28
Region	Tasmania
Value	●●●●●
Auction	★★★
Score	92

Stoney Rise Pinot Noir 2006

Joe Holyman used to make wines under this label from grapes grown in South Australia. Since buying a vineyard in his native Tasmania though, the ante has been upped significantly – this wine took out the top trophy at the 2008 Tasmanian Wine Show.

2006 RELEASE
Beautiful drink. Flush with ripe, bright, succulent fruit flavour and underscored with more funky, earthy, foresty influences. It is simply a terrific drinking pinot noir. It's easy to see why the judges were seduced; it's got yumminess written all over it. **DRINK** 2008–2012.

Price	$25
Region	Tasmania
Value	♦♦♦♦♦
Auction	N/A
Score	94

Stonier Pinot Noir 2006

This was once the shining light of affordable pinot noir – not sure if it's me, the expansion of this market, or the wine, but it doesn't quite have the appeal it once had. This despite a general enthusiasm for the label and winery itself.

2006 RELEASE
It just seems a bit simple. Light- to medium-weight flavour, mostly in the sweet strawberry and red cherry spectrum. There's oak too, creamy to the point of vanillin, the mouth-feel of it good but the effect of it loose and frivolous. This is for early consumption. And it is enjoyable. But didn't Stonier pinot noir used to be better than this? It seems a step off the pace. **DRINK** 2008–2010.

Price	$23
Region	Mornington Peninsula
Value	♦♦♦
Auction	★★
Score	87

Stonier Reserve Pinot Noir 2005

The thing about Stonier's reserve pinot noir is that it always feels really good in your mouth; it's always satiny and seductive.

2005 RELEASE
When I first tasted this I wasn't so impressed, but subsequent bottles have really started to sing. It's flush with sour, minerally, cherried fruit and it punches long through the finish – it even does a fair rendition of the fabled 'peacock's tail' of quality pinot. Spice, musky oak, fragrant plum – these flavours appear as the wine unfolds in your glass. Served in good glassware, this would bring the house down at a dinner party. **DRINK** 2008–2014.

Price	$45
Region	Mornington Peninsula
Value	♦♦♦
Auction	★★★
Score	94

Stonier Windmill Vineyard Pinot Noir 2005

Part of a growing trend among Australian wineries to produce 'single vineyard' (or even specific parts of a vineyard) wines. It's all to do with giving Australian wine a greater sense of place – a good thing.

2005 RELEASE
Grab a bunch of dried herbs and stick them in your mouth, then take a swig of cranberry juice. You're now close to tasting this wine. It's very dusty and very herbal, its sweet, elegant fruitiness almost secondary to those sappy, herbal flavours. It's confronting, and certainly not to everyone's taste. Herbal flavours in pinot noir can be very attractive; they have gone too far here. It should age successfully. **DRINK** 2012–2017.

Price $60
Region Mornington Peninsula
Value ♦♦
Auction ★★
Score 89

Ten Minutes by Tractor Pinot Noir 2006

It wasn't all that long ago that Australian pinot noir often tasted a lot like shiraz; which apart from anything else, defeated the purpose. Those days are thankfully gone, perfectly illustrated by a complex, insistent wine like this.

2006 RELEASE
Robust and powerful for a pinot noir; though still true to the variety. This is seedy, grainy, structured and meaty, its perfumed, cherried heart needing at least another six months rest in the bottle to start mellowing and unfolding. The finish is fruity and sappy, having admirably shrugged off the richness of the cedary oak somewhere along the way. It's a nice drop. **DRINK** 2009–2014.

Price $36
Region Mornington Peninsula
Value ♦♦♦
Auction ★★★
Score 91

T'Gallant Juliet Pinot Noir 2006

T'Gallant is now well and truly part of the Foster's wine empire. Shortly after Foster's took over, the quaffing Juliet range was launched, complete with delightfully decorated love-heart style front label. Against the odds, the wine is pretty good.

2006 RELEASE
It's a mix of sweet, sour and savoury flavours, and while it's by no means profound, it's satisfyingly persistent and admirably clean and fresh. If you're drinking this in winter, good-o. If you're drinking it in summer, it will need to be gently chilled. **DRINK** 2008–2009.

Price $18
Region Mornington Peninsula
Value ♦♦♦
Auction N/A
Score 86

William Downie Pinot Noir 2006

William Downie is the real deal: devoted to pinot noir only. The wines don't need the pomp; they speak for themselves.

2006 RELEASE
Downie pinot noir is all about structure. It's built to age. It often takes an hour or so to start singing in the glass, and (don't you hate this?) the last glass you pour from the bottle is the one that makes you go: WOW! It's refined drinking, with flavour of wood sap, dark cherry, spice and earth, the tannins themselves leaving a flinty, minerally, curious taste in your mouth. It's contemplative wine, for a certain mood. Drink it now-ish, or hold onto it for five years plus. **DRINK** 2009–2017.

Price	$45
Region	Yarra Valley
Value	●●●●●
Auction	N/A
Score	95

Wolf Blass Gold Label Pinot Noir 2005

A lot of the Wolf Blass red range lacks punch – until you get to the Gold Label series, which turns out the odd pearler. This pinot noir unfortunately isn't one of them.

2005 RELEASE
I guess it's a decent introduction to pinot noir – it's fragrant, semi-sweet in its fruit flavours, spicy and complex. Its succulent acidity also makes it a refreshing drink. That said, for me it lacks texture and true ripeness, the existence of both tomato-leaf and mandarin flavours in the wine distracting and largely unpleasant. **DRINK** 2008–2011.

Price	$24
Region	Adelaide Hills
Value	●●
Auction	N/A
Score	85

Yering Station Pinot Noir 2006

If you want consistency, go to Yering Station. The wines are elegant and refined, and there is never a dud among them, at any level. Or so it can easily seem.

2006 RELEASE
Classic pinot noir. Extremely varietal. Bursts of floral, undergrowthy, cherried scent, lots of tangy, medium-bodied flavour, good length and a sense of resonance once you've finished the bottle – you remember it, and want to go back and buy more. Nice (understated) oak handling too. **DRINK** 2008–2012.

Price	$24
Region	Yarra Valley
Value	●●●●
Auction	★★★
Score	91

CABERNET
+ blends

Cabernet sauvignon used to dominate Australian red wine but over the past fifteen years attention has drifted to the sexier shiraz and, more recently, pinot noir. It's unfair on cabernet but often good news for drinkers, because it means that good quality cabernet is often cheaper than its shiraz equivalent. Cabernet sauvignon is often more chewy and tannic than shiraz, and hence (though not always) better suited to cellaring – especially when it comes from Coonawarra, Margaret River and parts of the Yarra Valley. That said, recent vintages in both the Barossa Valley and McLaren Vale have been very good for cabernet ... indeed, there's lots of good cabernet around.

TOP TEN OF THE YEAR
1. Wynns Coonawarra Estate John Riddoch Cabernet Sauvignon 2005
2. Penfolds Bin 707 Cabernet Sauvignon 2005
3. Petaluma Cabernet Merlot 2005
4. Howard Park Cabernet Sauvignon Merlot 2004
5. Glaetzer Anaperenna Cabernet Sauvignon Shiraz 2006
6. Penfolds Bin 389 Cabernet Shiraz 2005
7. Lindemans St George Cabernet Sauvignon 2005
8. Taltarni Cabernet Sauvignon 2004
9. Voyager Estate Cabernet Merlot 2004
10. Balgownie White Label Cabernet Sauvignon 2005

Alkoomi Cabernet Sauvignon 2005

Alkoomi has cabernet vines on its property that were planted there by Merv and Judy Lange in 1971. Over the years, they've produced some stunning wines.

2005 RELEASE
This will take a lot of years to soften. It's hard and astringent on the finish, despite the mulch-like, curranty, earthy flavours that flesh out the palate. Love the wild, swinging fragrance of it though. **DRINK** 2011–2017.

Price	$20
Region	Frankland River
Value	♦♦
Auction	★★★
Score	85

Angove's Long Row Cabernet Sauvignon 2006

It's not a name that immediately springs to mind, but Angove's is one of Australia's oldest family wine names. It started in the wine business back in 1886.

2006 RELEASE
Super quaffer. Open-faced and generous, its forest berry flavours smooth, simple and satisfying. Excellent complement of chewy tannins. Great value. Contender for Big Red 'Widely Available' Bargain of the Year. I've even seen this around the $7 mark – and extraordinary value at that. **DRINK** 2008–2009.

Price	$9.95
Region	South Australia
Value	♦♦♦♦♦
Auction	N/A
Score	88

Angus The Bull Cabernet Sauvignon 2006

Hamish MacGowan started this label a few years back, the idea being that it would be the perfect steak wine. Every year he has delivered on the promise.

2006 RELEASE
It is a great steak wine! It's chewy and minty and solid, the strength and flavour of it perfectly robust and perfectly suited for matching to seared, charry meat. It's not too concentrated, but it's not insipid either. Bang on for bangers and mash … or whatever you've got grilling. Yum. **DRINK** 2008–2011.

Price	$19
Region	South Eastern Australia
Value	♦♦♦♦♦
Auction	N/A
Score	90

Annie's Lane Cabernet Merlot 2005

The rating here is for the price you will find it discounted to – I've seen it selling for around the $15–$17 mark. At that it's super buying.

2005 RELEASE
It's turned out to be a delicious wine. I tasted it a few times over the course of a few months, and each time it impressed me more, seeming to add both flesh and weight. It's part of the fascination of wine; it's constantly evolving. Now it tastes of pencils, blackcurrant, coffee and cream, its sweet, easy fruitiness lingering on the finish. At the above prices it's a fine buying opportunity.
DRINK 2008–2013.

Price	$20
Region	Clare Valley
Value	●●●●●
Auction	★★★
Score	90

Au Cabernet Sauvignon 2004

Au is the chemical symbol for gold, hence the gold lettering on the label of this bottle. The grapes were grown in Coonawarra, but Granite Belt (Queensland) winemaker Jon Heslop turned them into wine.

2004 RELEASE
You can do a lot worse than this. It's super gluggable. It's soft and harmless, dusty and briary and curranty, the tannin on the finish only evident on close inspection. It has no great pretensions, but it's definitely crowd-pleasing.
DRINK 2008–2010.

Price	$16.50
Region	Coonawarra
Value	●●●
Auction	N/A
Score	85

Baileys of Glenrowan Cabernet Sauvignon 2006

The faster Baileys grafts its cabernet vines over to something more suitable, the better. Some Spanish grape varieties might be the go.

2006 RELEASE
I've tasted a number of Baileys cabernets and they just don't compete with the Coonawarras and Margaret Rivers of this world, even when price is factored in. This 2006 though, is about as good as Baileys cabernet gets. It's fresh, fruity, quite pretty on the nose and satisfyingly flavoursome in the mouth. It's reasonable value, but the shiraz is much better. **DRINK** 2008–2011.

Price	$19
Region	Glenrowan
Value	●●
Auction	★
Score	85

Balgownie White Label Cabernet Sauvignon 2005

You'd almost class Balgownie as one of the old stagers of Aussie red wine now – it was one of the wineries to kick-start the modern era of Victorian wine back in 1969. In recent years winemaker Tobias Ansted has got the cabernet singing.

2005 RELEASE
Just a crackingly good wine. Medium-weight but finely tuned, with cassis-like fruit flavour hanging along a spine of dry, ripe, classical tannins. The odd smidge of mint and earth flavour, but the hallmarks of this wine are balance and structure. My kind of wine. DRINK 2011–2025.

PREVIOUS
2000 Blackberried, leathery, minty. 2006–2010. 91 pts.
2001 Herbal, curranty, medium-bodied. 2006–2011. 88 pts.
2002 Warm, sweet, dusty. 2006–2012. 90 pts.
2003 Curranty, spicy, balanced. 2009–2016. 92 pts.
2004 Lengthy, curranty, structured. 2006–2016. 94 pts.

Price	$31
Region	Bendigo
Value	♦♦♦♦♦
Auction	★★★
Score	95

Balnaves of Coonawarra Cabernet Merlot 2005

Often the forgotten wine in the Balnaves range – not this year.

2005 RELEASE
Yikes, this is a ripper. OK, so you have to be able to handle a bit of tannin (the backbone of all good red wine, I say), but get past that and you're into some seriously good red wine drinking. It's a silk song of kirsch, milk chocolate, savoury toast, crushed herbs and blackcurrant, the tangy, lip-smacking guts of it lingering for a good while after you've swallowed. Will it age? You bet it will. DRINK 2009–2016.

Price	$24
Region	Coonawarra
Value	♦♦♦
Auction	N/A
Score	88

Balnaves of Coonawarra Cabernet Sauvignon 2005

Balnaves are helping put the sexy back into Coonawarra cabernet. This is fabulous red wine drinking.

2005 RELEASE
Big, ripe, bold Coonawarra cabernet. Pure and delicious at all times. There is never a sense though, that it has been overcooked. Tremendous, lengthy, fine-boned tannin structure. Flavours of savoury mince pies, blackcurrant, spice and cedar-smoke, the swish, polished feel of it in your mouth like licking at wine-drenched velvet. Beautiful. **DRINK** 2011–2019.

PREVIOUS
1999 Quintessential Coonawarra cabernet. 2004–2011. 92 pts.
2000 Tannic, oak-strong, opulent; real power. 2007–2014. 92 pts.
2001 Warm, balanced, varietal; nice complexity. 2005–2013. 90 pts.
2002 Perfectly made but lacking ripeness. 2008–2013. 88 pts.
2003 Not made.
2004 Beautifully flavoured, beautifully structured. 2013–2020. 93 pts.

Price	$33
Region	Coonawarra
Value	♦♦♦♦♦
Auction	★★★
Score	94

Balnaves of Coonawarra Reserve The Tally Cabernet Sauvignon 2005

I wasn't sure of this super-premium when it was first released (with the 1998 vintage) but it now comfortably sits in the top ranks of Australian wine.

2005 RELEASE
Ribbons of vanilla, cedarwood, blackcurrant and beef. It's a meal of a wine, but it's not overdone, it's still just a lovely drink. The flavours are pure and lengthy, the tannins long and satiny. It does not, however, wear its heart on its sleeve – it needs quite a bit of coaxing to come out of its shell, so at the least must be decanted for a couple of hours (or better still, cellar it in a cool dark place). **DRINK** 2013–2024.

PREVIOUS
1998 Inky black. Big and long. 2009–2018. 95 pts.
2000 Very ripe but beautifully balanced. 2007–2014. 94 pts.
2001 Could mature into a beauty. 2010–2017. 93 pts.
2004 Massively powerful but structured and elegant. 2012–2020. 95 pts.

Price	$80
Region	Coonawarra
Value	♦♦♦
Auction	★★★
Score	95

Balnaves of Coonawarra The Blend 2005

This is a blend of cabernet sauvignon (fifty-four per cent), merlot (twenty-eight per cent), with the remainder cabernet franc. Balnaves has reached the point where all its wines are good.

2005 RELEASE
This isn't as sweet and ripe as it is some years but it's lost none of its appeal. Dried, almost bitter herbs, lots of currant flavour, a noticeable hit of acidity and a good, satisfying finish. It drinks well in the way that good Italian chianti drinks well; it's refreshing and satisfying at once.
DRINK 2009–2014.

Price	$19
Region	Coonawarra
Value	♦♦♦
Auction	N/A
Score	89

Battle of Bosworth Cabernet Sauvignon 2005

It's a new McLaren Vale outfit but the folks behind it – Joch Bosworth and Louise Hemsley-Smith – have a wealth of experience in the region. All the vineyards are certified organic.

2005 RELEASE
There's nothing being held back here. The wine tastes of sweet, bold blackberry jam and raspberry, but it's been strictly tethered to sappy, almost stalky tannins. The power of flavour through the mid-palate is impressive, though it could use just a touch more length.
DRINK 2008–2013.

Price	$24
Region	McLaren Vale
Value	♦♦♦♦
Auction	★★★
Score	89

Blue Pyrenees Estate Richardson Cabernet Sauvignon 2004

It's probably more famous for its sparkling wines than for its reds, even though it's in the heart of Pyrenees red country (though it is at high altitude). This is a substantial wine.

2004 RELEASE
Extremely smooth wine. It took time to open up but once it did it was a flood of eucalypt and blackcurrant flavour; emphasis on the eucalypt. Fine tannin, powerful fruit, lots of fragrance. It's a fair package. **DRINK** 2011–2018.

Price	$50
Region	Pyrenees
Value	♦♦
Auction	★★
Score	89

Bowen Estate Cabernet Sauvignon 2005

One of my favourite Coonawarra estates, though inexplicably quality seems to have bounced around of late. This is the best Bowen cabernet for a while.

2005 RELEASE
Composed, well-ripened wine, flooded with cassis and dark chocolate-like flavour and then smoky, grapey and strong through the finish. Muscular tannin structure. Aroma, heart, flavour and finish. **DRINK** 2008–2013.

PREVIOUS
2000 Generous and muscular. 2005–2010. 91 pts.
2001 Unbalanced and sweet. 2004–2009. 85 pts.
2002 Lacks substance. 2005–2011. 84 pts.
2003 Ripe and unripe. 2005–2011. 87 pts.
2004 Medium-bodied, medium-length. 2007–2014. 90 pts.

Price	$29
Region	Coonawarra
Value	♦♦♦♦
Auction	★★★
Score	92

Brands of Coonawarra Laira Cabernet Sauvignon 2004

Generally an under-performer and with regards to its merlot, worth avoiding. This 2004 cabernet though is brighter and better.

2004 RELEASE
Simple but attractive. You could open this anytime between now and, say, five years' time, and it would drink well. It tastes of blackcurrant, cedarwood and vanilla and is well equipped with juicy, chewy tannin. Decent wine. **DRINK** 2008–2013.

Price	$19
Region	Coonawarra
Value	♦♦♦♦♦
Auction	★★
Score	89

Cape Mentelle Cabernet Sauvignon 2003

Margaret River may well be considered Australia's 'best cabernet region', though to put it to the test you pay a high price. Cape Mentelle is a very good wine but rarely a great one; it's often a shock to be reminded how much it costs.

2003 RELEASE
It looks awkward as a young wine but it should weld together with extra time in the bottle. It carries quite a bit of both sweet, fruity flavour and green, leafy distractions, the class of the cedary oak doing its best to keep the show on the road. Nervy acidity gets in the way, and while there is a solid power to the wine, it lacks conviction.
DRINK 2009–2016.

PREVIOUS
1999 A flood of currenty, varietal flavour. 2006–2012. 92 pts.
2000 Gamey, smoky, tannic. 2005–2009. 90 pts.
2001 Big, luscious, long. 2010–2025. 95 pts.
2002 Herbal, juicy, beautifully structured. 2010–2018. 91 pts.

Price	$73
Region	Margaret River
Value	●●
Auction	★★★
Score	89

Capel Vale Debut Cabernet Merlot 2005

Capel Vale has gained a bit of attention lately and to be more honest than I perhaps should be – I've been a bit slow to cotton on. This wine is at the lower end of their offering but it's bloody good; I think I've got some further homework to do.

2005 RELEASE
It's a currenty, pruney style of cabernet merlot but, by George, it works! It's even got a bit of chocolaty, gravelly, pencily flavour to it, signs of both interest and quality in my books. Its tannin frame is solid too. Crikey, I'm liking it more and more. (Is it OK, at this stage, to admit that I've been known to swallow a bit of the product?)
DRINK 2008–2012.

Price	$16.95
Region	Western Australia
Value	●●●●
Auction	★★★
Score	87

Carlei Green Vineyards Cabernet Sauvignon 2004

Green Vineyards is the range of wines Sergei Carlei makes from vines grown away from his own estate in the Yarra Valley.

2004 RELEASE
A lot of this wine seems ripe and dense, almost to the point of a blackberried portiness, but then other aspects are cabbage-like and green. It makes for a discordant tune. As it flows through the mouth I enjoy it; as I swallow I'm left with all kinds of questions. **DRINK** 2010–2015.

Price	$29
Region	Central Victoria
Value	♦ ♦ ♦
Auction	★ ★ ★
Score	86

Chapel Hill Cabernet Sauvignon 2004 & 2005

Michael Fragos (ex Tatachilla) has taken over the winemaking reins at Chapel Hill, and has fast picked up the quality.

2004 RELEASE
Smart wine. Full of dark, pencily, blackberried fruit, its tannins integrated and flavoursome. Offers a long, slippery slide of chocolaty flavour through the finish, even though it's the fruit that does the bulk of the talking. **DRINK** 2008–2018.

2005 RELEASE
Just when I thought the value couldn't get any better – along comes this. This is an absolute pearler. Stunningly pure, stunningly rich, silken across the tongue and sophisticated in its flavour profile. Currants, chocolate, lead pencils, blueberries, all of it oozing red wine goodness. **DRINK** 2008–2020.

Price	$25
Region	McLaren Vale
Value	♦ ♦ ♦ ♦ ♦
Auction	★ ★ ★
Score	92 (2004)
	95 (2005)

Charles Melton Cabernet Sauvignon 2005

I'm a longstanding fan of Melton's cabernet: it's not only his best value wine, but also the Melton red that cellars the best. This 2005 is a great example.

2005 RELEASE
A lovely combo of luscious fruit power and elegant structure. It's 100 per cent varietal too. It tastes like a mix of gravel dust and milk chocolate, the core of it all pure cassis and dried herbs. I can't fault it. It reaches long through the finish, its juicy fruit doing all the talking. Lovely, lovely wine. **DRINK** 2011–2019.

Price	$38.50
Region	Barossa Valley
Value	♦ ♦ ♦ ♦
Auction	★ ★ ★
Score	94

Chrismont Cabernet Sauvignon 2004

The King Valley is renowned for its Italian red varieties, but it does well with cabernet sauvignon (and, just quietly, riesling).

2004 RELEASE
It's a different expression of cabernet, for certain. It smells and tastes of sweet tobacco, smoke, mulberry, leather and game, the extra time it has spent in bottle allowing it to gently mellow, and become a mighty easy wine to sit on, and enjoy. It's for one of those quiet Saturday nights spent with your best friend or lover. It's for roast lamb with all the trimmings. **DRINK** 2008–2014.

Price	$26
Region	King Valley
Value	♦♦♦
Auction	N/A
Score	89

Clonakilla Ballinderry Cabernet Sauvignon Merlot Cabernet Franc 2005

The Ballinderry name first appeared as the name of Clonakilla's cabernet blend with the 2004 vintage.

2005 RELEASE
It's begging for roast lamb, this is. It tastes of blackcurrant, violets and earth and has a gorgeous set of powdery, chalky, scented tannins on it – this will make for a great dinner date for years to come. Canberra seems to have had a really strong year for cabernet in 2005. This is a high quality wine. **DRINK** 2008–2015.

Price	$30
Region	Canberra District
Value	♦♦♦♦
Auction	N/A
Score	93

Coldstream Hills Cabernet Sauvignon 2005

Back when the Yarra Valley was being reborn to vines – in the late 1960s – cabernet was one of the leading lights. Pinot noir and chardonnay have since taken over, but the cabernets still have their moments.

2005 RELEASE
Some wines fill you with a sense of joy – for some reason this is one of them. Perhaps it's just that it's so well balanced; sitting with it almost makes you feel calm. It tastes of plums, toast, thyme and malt, its varietal slight edge of herbs never interrupting the flow. Surprisingly rich for a Yarra cabernet – it's worth tucking a few bottles of this away. **DRINK** 2008–2014.

Price	$29
Region	Yarra Valley
Value	♦♦♦♦
Auction	★★★
Score	92

Coldstream Hills Reserve Cabernet Sauvignon 2005

Coldstream Hills reserve cabernet has the ability to be among the nation's best. The 2000 version was a stunner, and this is in the same class.

2005 RELEASE
We have a classic Yarra Valley cabernet on our hands here. It's the perfect combination of grainy, curranty, olive-like intensity matched to slippery, smooth, creamy oak and long, controlled, assertive tannin. It carries the odd flash of tobacco-like complexity; indeed, it combines raw sexiness with persistent elegance in a most refined manner. It's certainly got me going. **DRINK** 2010–2018.

Price	$50
Region	Yarra Valley
Value	♦♦♦♦
Auction	★★★
Score	95

Cullen Diana Madeline Cabernet Merlot 2005

One of the undisputed champions of Australian wine. It's grown on a biodynamically run vineyard in the heart of the Margaret River wine region. This 2005 is the best since the 2001.

2005 RELEASE
A tall, dark, handsome wine. As has become the norm for Cullen cabernet merlot, it's also wrapped in strong arms of tannin; it makes the wine seem statuesque in the mouth. It's perfumed, curranty, bold with cigar-box fragrance and musky, plummy and chocolaty through both the mid-palate and finish. There's the odd high note of eucalyptus. This is a great wine, but it needs years in a cool, dark place to soften and evolve. **DRINK** 2018–2027.

PREVIOUS
1998 Awkward tannins, beautiful fruit flavour. 2009–2018. 92 pts.
1999 Pure, powerful, structured. 2011–2023. 96 pts.
2000 Silken, curranty, tight. 2009–2014. 95 pts.
2001 Strong, rich, tight. 2015–2025. 96 pts.
2002 Awkward, lighter, warm. 2008–2015. 88 pts.
2003 Powerful, elegant, tight. 2011–2018. 93 pts.
2004 Focused, violety, tight. 2013–2024. 93 pts.

Price	$90
Region	Margaret River
Value	♦♦♦
Auction	★★★★★
Score	95

Dalwhinnie Moonambel Cabernet Sauvignon 2005

Australian cabernet in general is vastly under-rated. Dalwhinnie cabernet routinely impresses.

2005 RELEASE
Line and length. Sinewy tannins, defined fruit, succulent acidity and exotic notes of coal, box hedge and blackberry. Vanillin, minty oak keeps the wine smooth and yet robust. This is very fine. **DRINK** 2011–2018.

PREVIOUS
2003 Low alcohol; excellent fruit and tannin. 2005–2014. 90 pts.
2004 Great cabernet. Power plus. 2006–2016. 94 pts.

Price	$45
Region	Pyrenees
Value	♦♦♦♦
Auction	★★★
Score	94

Devil's Lair Cabernet Sauvignon Merlot 2005

Devil's Lair is a large, sprawling vineyard that ranges across hills and dales. It's a beautiful sight, and is beautifully tended – all the vines are hand-pruned, the grapes then hand-picked.

2005 RELEASE
It takes a while to come up in the glass but it's a wine rich with gravelly, eucalypt-shot, currenty flavour, the spread of fruit and oak and tannin reaching right through your mouth – this is super satisfying stuff. There are also flavours of leather, pencils and malt, the aftertaste all gravelly, chocolaty yumminess. This wine delivers. **DRINK** 2013–2019.

PREVIOUS
1999 Minty, gamey, tannic. 2008–2013. 90 pts.
2000 Sweet oak and sweet fruit; effortless quality. 2009–2015. 92 pts.
2001 Gamey, powerful, delicious. 2008–2015. 93 pts.
2002 Elegant, fragrant, riddled with leafy flavour. 2007–2014. 88 pts.
2003 Raw fruit-packed power. 2010–2016. 92 pts.
2004 Precise tannin, ripe fruit, good length. 2011–2017. 90 pts.

Price	$60
Region	Margaret River
Value	♦♦♦
Auction	★★★
Score	93

Dutschke Sami Cabernet Sauvignon 2005

Trust all-round good bloke Wayne Dutschke to pump out a super Barossan cabernet – some reckon the valley doesn't make good cabernet, but it can, and does.

2005 RELEASE
When Wayne Dutschke was first making this he thought it would be part of a blend, but as it sat maturing in oak barrels he tasted it and thought, 'That's too good to be blended, it should be shown in all its glory, on its own'. Or something like that. Wise decision. It's super quality and despite the price tag, still represents super value. Long, full-bodied, succulent cabernet of weight and class.
DRINK 2008–2015.

Price	$30
Region	Barossa
Value	♦♦♦♦
Auction	★★★
Score	93

Edwards Cabernet Sauvignon 2005

I'm not as keen on the 2005 Edwards shiraz (87 points) as I am on this cabernet; I guess you have to expect that in Margaret River. Edwards is a small producer deserving of more attention.

2005 RELEASE
There's a clear herbal streak to this wine but it's still bloody good. It's stylish. It's long, tannic, powerful through the mouth and thick with cassis and chocolate-like flavour. It needs a sleep in the cellar. **DRINK** 2012–2017.

Price	$27
Region	Margaret River
Value	♦♦♦♦
Auction	★★★
Score	92

Elderton 'Friends' Cabernet Sauvignon 2005

It's slowly dawning on me that 2005 was a really good vintage for cabernet in the Barossa. Here's some affordable proof.

2005 RELEASE
A fair amount of the grapes for this wine came from the Barossa Valley's soul mate, the Eden Valley (technically classified as part of the Barossa). Not sure whether it's the power of suggestion but this wine is bright and bouncy with curranty perfume, a red wine hallmark of the Eden Valley. There's also a super-attractive slide of medium-bodied, curranty, chocolaty flavour, and if that's not enough for you there's a bit of vanillin flavour too. Someone once said to me that vanilla is the taste of home; I sure wouldn't mind taking some of this wine home with me. **DRINK** 2008–2010.

Price	$18
Region	Barossa
Value	♦♦♦♦
Auction	★★★
Score	89

Epis The Williams Vineyard Cabernet Merlot 2006

There have been some lovely wines released under this label – and indeed under labels of the past. These cabernet vines are now thirty years old and while this particular release isn't quite to my taste, it's a label that deserves more attention.

2006 RELEASE
The flavours here are attractive – there's a strong hit of eucalyptus (indeed, it's the mainstay of the wine) and a nice dose of blackcurrant, the finish then mentholy and chocolaty. The acidity is good but the tannins collapse through the finish, the core of fruit simply not carrying with any great satisfaction. It needs more oomph, more finish, and arguable less eucalypt. **DRINK** 2011–2016.

Price	$35
Region	Macedon Ranges
Value	♦ ♦ ♦
Auction	★ ★
Score	86

Fox Creek Reserve Cabernet Sauvignon 2005

2005 RELEASE
My only problem with this is that it's maturing reasonably quickly. In all other respects it's a brilliant wine. It's a beautiful mix of blackcurrant, leather and cedarwood flavour, the lot hung majestically off a line of fine, ripe, grapey tannins. This is a wine of elegance, oomph and immense drinkability. I'll be hunting some of this out for myself. **DRINK** 2008–2016.

Price	$36
Region	McLaren Vale
Value	♦ ♦ ♦ ♦
Auction	★ ★ ★
Score	94

Gapsted Cabernet Sauvignon 2005

Gapsted is the premium branded arm of the large Victorian Alps contract winemaking facility based near Myrtleford in Victoria's north-east alpine district. Seems strange that their premium wine contains South Australian grapes – so much for making the most of the home region.

2005 RELEASE
The wine is good. In fact it's very good. It has a juicy appeal that almost stops you in your tracks, the blend of pure, silken, cassis-like fruit and sawdusty, creamy oak as seamless as it is sensational. I love the smell and taste of this wine. Winemaker Michael Cope Williams has done a super job with it. **DRINK** 2008–2016.

Price	$25
Region	South Australia King Valley
Value	♦ ♦ ♦ ♦
Auction	N/A
Score	93

Geoff Merrill Cabernet Sauvignon 2004

McLaren Vale is a better region for shiraz than cabernet – but there are exceptions. Here's one of them.

2004 RELEASE
Great structure, great flavour, great value. Lots of blackberry and olive-like flavour, met by a whack of chewy, appropriately sized, ripe tannins. There's a kind of 'dustiness' to this wine – it's an excellent wine to sit and chew the fat over. **DRINK** 2009–2013.

Price	$25
Region	McLaren Vale
Value	♦♦♦♦♦
Auction	N/A
Score	93

Giant Steps Harry's Monster 2005

This is a blend of forty-eight per cent cabernet sauvignon, forty-seven per cent merlot and then dashes of cabernet franc and petit verdot. It's a true Bordeaux-blend and has all the structure and breadth of flavour you'd expect.

2005 RELEASE
I'm amazed at how long this took to come up in the glass. Given time though, it shows as a firm, expansive red, bold with mulberries and pencil, undergrowth, milk chocolate and the finest, cedary oak. I reckon this needs at least ten years in a cool, dark place. It is a monster – of the most highly structured kind. It's going to live for a very long time. **DRINK** 2013–2023.

Price	$44.95
Region	Yarra Valley
Value	♦♦♦
Auction	N/A
Score	94

Glaetzer Anaperenna Cabernet Sauvignon Shiraz 2006

This wine was, until this year, known as Godolphin. It's one of the emerging superstars of bold, Barossan red wine – it's suddenly one of the leading exponents of the great Australian cabernet shiraz blend.

2006 RELEASE
Ben Glaetzer somehow manages to craft wines of might and elegance at once. They're like iron fists wrapped in silks arranged by Collette Dinnigan. His cabernet shiraz is usually the best example of it, the wine entering your mouth like a mighty flood of blackcurrant and beef stock, but then exiting down your throat in a maze of whispers. It is full of sweet, juicy, persistent flavour, notes of chocolate, mint and blackcurrant oozing to every corner. It is opulence tamed. **DRINK** 2013–2023.

PREVIOUS
2004 Bold and beautiful. 2011–2018. 96 pts.
2005 Needs time. Excellent focus of flavour. 2009–2017. 95 pts.

Price	$55
Region	Barossa
Value	♦♦♦♦
Auction	★★★★
Score	96

Gralyn Unoaked Cabernet Sauvignon 2007

Gralyn is one of Margaret River's top estates, though finding the wines other than via their cellar door is incredibly difficult.

2007 RELEASE
Wild with sweet berried flavour – it makes you wonder why more people don't try for this style. Blackcurrant, mulberry, soft, silky tannins and a slippery-smooth finish. Extraordinarily soft, easy-drinking, sweetish red wine. **DRINK** 2008–2010.

Price	$27
Region	Margaret River
Value	♦♦♦
Auction	N/A
Score	90

Grant Burge Shadrach Cabernet Sauvignon 2004

Barossa cabernet rarely gets a lot of wraps but there have been a number of good releases recently from Saltram, Rockford, Penfolds and others. This is good too, if expensive.

2004 RELEASE
It's just a good red wine. It tastes minty, curranty, juicy and long, and while it may not be highly distinctive or even varietal, it shows all the signs of being an excellent long-term cellaring wine. **DRINK** 2012–2020.

Price	$50
Region	Barossa
Value	♦♦♦
Auction	★★
Score	93

Grosset Gaia Cabernet Sauvignon 2004 & 2005

The windswept Gaia vineyard has been a labour of love for Jeffrey Grosset but to my red-loving heart it's his best wine. This year's composition is seventy per cent cabernet sauvignon, twenty-five per cent cabernet franc and five per cent merlot.

2004 RELEASE
Might sound like a funny thing to say of a red but it's a refreshing, crisp, crunchy wine; it's like it's been plucked from alpine heights. It tastes bracingly clean and pure. It's awash with earthy, dusty, mulberried flavour and comes complete with bold, dark berried cabernet intensity. Supple tannins. Excellent length. **DRINK** 2010–2017.

2005 RELEASE
Pure, clean and stylish. Terrifically structured and presented. It tastes of blackcurrant, cedar, chalk and pencils, and stretches long through the finish. This is the kind of wine the late Len Evans would describe as 'all about line and length'. Exquisite. **DRINK**: 2014–2021.

Price	$53
Region	Clare Valley
Value	♦♦♦♦
Auction	★★★★
Score	93 (2004)
	95 (2005)

Grove Estate The Partners Cabernet Sauvignon 2006

Grove Estate has a beautiful vineyard in the under-appreciated Hilltops region of New South Wales. It's great cabernet country up there – indeed great red country.

2006 RELEASE
Quality. Not all that varietal, but a really good red wine. Malty, sweet, bold and inviting, the rush of fruit offering flavours of tar, blackcurrant and coffeed vanillin. It's all quite heady, and the flavour goes on for a good long time. Supple tannins glide through the finish. Impressive stuff. **DRINK** 2010–2016.

Price	$30
Region	Hilltops
Value	♦♦♦♦
Auction	N/A
Score	92

Hardy's Tintara Cabernet Sauvignon 2005

McLaren Vale cabernet can live for very long periods of time, if rarely rising to great heights. I wouldn't be surprised if this wine held on for a good while too.

2005 RELEASE
It definitely tastes like cabernet. It's dusty, briary, chocolaty and ripped with blackberry-like flavour, a vague saltiness appearing on the finish. The fruit flavours are gently sweetened and attractive, and the tannin structure is above its station. If it wasn't for the saltiness I'd mark it higher. It is a very good wine. **DRINK** 2008–2014.

Price	$18
Region	**McLaren Vale**
Value	♦♦♦♦
Auction	★★★
Score	87

Heartland Cabernet Sauvignon 2006

There's something about Aussie cabernet and roast lamb; it's a marriage made in heaven. I think it might be the minty, earthy flavours cabernet does so well ... though usually I'm too busy eating and drinking to think on it at all.

2006 RELEASE
One of the steals of the year. This is what I love to see in an affordable cabernet: lots of dusty, currranty flavour, a serious darkness to the colour and fruit character, but then a soft drinkability – I'm looking for guiding tannins rather than forceful ones. This wine sums up the style and delivers it spick and span – it's a lovely red. Custom-built for garlic-studded roast lamb. **DRINK** 2008–2014.

Price	$17
Region	**Langhorne Creek** **Limestone Coast**
Value	♦♦♦♦♦
Auction	N/A
Score	92

CABERNET AND BLENDS

Higher Plane Cabernet Sauvignon 2004

There's a small amount of merlot in this wine (eight per cent) and it gives it a lovely mulberried character. It spent two years in French oak prior to release, though only thirty per cent of this oak is new – a very good thing.

2004 RELEASE
Smart winemaking, smart drinking. Complex aromas and complex flavours, but never does it sacrifice straight-out drinkable deliciousness. Pencils, blackcurrant, earth, cedar-smoke, mulberries and a perfumed muskiness. It's finely structured too. I love this. **DRINK** 2008–2016.

Price	$34
Region	Margaret River
Value	♦♦♦♦
Auction	★★
Score	92

Higher Plane South by Southwest Cabernet Merlot 2004

Higher Plane is a respected wine name that has recently been taken over by Juniper Estate. The highly regarded Mark Messenger makes the wines.

2004 RELEASE
Ripper red wine. Lovely mix of savoury, earthy flavours and ripe, strong, blackcurrant, its toasty oak tucked into a very attractive package. Medium-weight, and decidedly delicious. **DRINK** 2008–2012.

Price	$22
Region	Margaret River
Value	♦♦♦♦
Auction	N/A
Score	89

Hoddles Creek Estate Cabernet Sauvignon 2006

Hoddles Creek is renowned for its pinot noir and chardonnay but the cabernet is a tidy wine too – if you can find it.

2006 RELEASE
It just goes to show that style can come cheap – or at least that it can be excellent value. This is an elegant cabernet full of medium-bodied blackcurrant, olive and chocolate flavours, the odd 'cabernet signposts' of dried herbs and dust apparent if you really look hard. I admire wines like this. It's the kind of wine I'd like to be ... if I were, errr, a wine. **DRINK** 2008–2014.

Price	$19
Region	Yarra Valley
Value	♦♦♦♦♦
Auction	N/A
Score	90

Houghton Jack Mann Cabernet Sauvignon 2001

The 2001 Frankland River vintage was the driest on record (at the time). As a result, there is less shiraz and malbec in the blend than usual – this release is ninety-six per cent cabernet sauvignon. By contrast, the 1999 was thirty per cent malbec. This wine spent twenty-four months in new French oak.

2001 RELEASE
Big bodied wine but its tummy is tucked in tight, its significant fruit weight well and truly tightened by monster arms of tannin. Let's be straight though: this wine bristles with flavour, the spectrum of it encompassing licorice, cassis, mint, cedar and (trust me) vanilla custard. It needs a long decanter to get it to relax, or preferably a number of years in the cellar. **DRINK** 2011–2024.

Price	$90
Region	Great Southern
Value	♦♦♦
Auction	★★★
Score	94

PREVIOUS
1994 Firm, bold, syrupy and long. 2004–2014. 96 pts.
1995 Deep, strong, successful. 2006–2011. 94 pts.
1996 Dusty and elegant. 2006–2015. 94 pts.
1998 Classic, elegant cabernet. 2006–2012. 90 pts.
1999 Strong, saturated, tannic. 2009–2022. 95 pts.
2000 Floral, dusty, smooth. 2007–2015. 92 pts.

Howard Park Cabernet Sauvignon Merlot 2004

One of Australia's best reds, and it cellars beautifully. Quality in recent years is as good or better than it has ever been.

2004 RELEASE
Immediately apparent that this is an exceptionally good wine. The palate is a stencil of the nose, the complexity of flavour and aroma including mulberry, gravel, dried herbs and of course thick, satiny blackcurrant. Howard Park's Great Southern vineyard sources have a habit of producing impeccably structured fruit, and this wine is beautifully endowed in this regard. I know it's a lot of money, but it's a classic wine. **DRINK** 2015–2025.

PREVIOUS
1994 Perfect tannin, perfect fruit. 2007–2015. 95 pts.
1995 Pleasant drinking; tastes good, smells odd. 2006–2010. 88 pts.
1996 Good aged cabernet. Elegant and medium-weight. 2008–2013. 91 pts.
1997 Minty, clumsy, lacking. 2006–2010. 85 pts.
1998 Gamey, tannic, leathery. 2006–2011. 88 pts.
1999 Lovely mix of herbs and bold fruit. 2009–2017. 93 pts.
2000 Smoky, currranty, good. 2007–2011. 92 pts.
2001 Superb tannin, superb fruit. 2014–2025. 97 pts.
2002 Lovely mix of oak and fruit; superb winemaking. 2011–2018. 93 pts.
2003 Seductive fruit flavour. 2010–2015. 92 pts.

Price	$75
Region	Great Southern Margaret River
Value	♦♦♦♦
Auction	★★★
Score	96

Howard Park Leston Cabernet Sauvignon 2005

There's a lot of folks reckon Margaret River is Australia's best cabernet region. Coonawarra is currently fighting back, but …

2005 RELEASE
Gorgeous. Clean, elegant, structured, well-flavoured but not massively so – it's a real, gutsy, concentrated red wine, but its easy drinkability is still absolutely intact. Flavours of eucalypt, blackcurrant, gravel and toast, cuddly French oak setting the dial to 'class'. Its tannin structure is perfectly ripe, and perfectly formed. **DRINK** 2013–2019.

PREVIOUS
2001 Super-fine tannin, super-smooth fruit. 2008–2015. 93 pts.
2002 Lean but attractive. 2006–2010. 87 pts.
2003 Structured but accessible. 2006–2011. 90 pts.
2004 Gorgeous cabernet. 2009–2017. 93 pts.

Price	$40
Region	Margaret River
Value	♦♦♦
Auction	★★★
Score	93

Howard Park Mad Fish Premium Red 2005

Mad Fish is a tremendous label and, not surprisingly, it's started to pick up some major wine awards around the globe. If you haven't tried some, do so. This one's a blend of mostly cabernet sauvignon and merlot.

2005 RELEASE
I can't quite believe the quality of this. It's ripped with the classic cabernet flavours of pencils, blackcurrant, cedarwood and dark earth, and it builds to a fair volume of flavour as it works its way through to the back of your throat. I poured myself three glasses just to make sure that this wine really was coming from this bottle (or that's what I told my wife). It's even got a slur of punchy, crunchy, quality tannin. **DRINK** 2010–2016.

Price	$18
Region	Western Australia
Value	♦♦♦♦♦
Auction	★★★
Score	92

Ingoldby Cabernet Sauvignon 2004

A favourite red wine brand that seems to have lost its way in recent times. Nothing wrong with this release though; it's a beauty.

2004 RELEASE
I guess you could call it rustic and old fashioned but really, the most old fashioned thing about it is its value-for-money. This kicks big goals for the price. Dark, currant, loaded with warm blackberry jam flavour but long (even elegant) through the finish. It's not an exciting red but it's a high quality one. At the price, there's a good argument for buying this in volume. **DRINK** 2008–2013.

Price	$18
Region	McLaren Vale
Value	♦♦♦♦♦
Auction	★★★
Score	91

Jacob's Creek Reserve Cabernet Sauvignon 2005

There's a part of me that wants to champion the little guys over the big guys; wines like this make it impossible.

2005 RELEASE
Jolly good wine. Fighting at the top-end of its weight. Dusty and dry with a good lick of chewy tannin, its currant fruit flavour the perfect foil to its dusty, chocolaty cabernet notes. Could do with a year or two in the cellar to help flesh out the mid-palate.
DRINK 2009–2012.

Price	$15.95
Region	South Australia
Value	♦♦♦♦
Auction	★★
Score	88

Jacob's Creek St Hugo Cabernet Sauvignon 2004 & 2005

This was an 'Orlando'-branded wine for years, but the Orlando name is slowly being edged out.

2004 RELEASE
I like the more elegant expression of Coonawarra cabernet and this is certainly heading for that camp – though it doesn't pull it off as successfully as some. This tastes of gumleaf, blackcurrant and spicy, cedary oak, the intensity of it a solid medium weight. Its tannins seem clumsy and not entirely ripe, a no-no in my books. I've tasted this wine three times, and while all three times the quality has been good, I've liked it less each time. **DRINK** 2010–2015.

2005 RELEASE
Rather minty but lovely fruit power and structure, and a noticeably long finish. Blackcurrants, toast, eucalypt and mint flavours, roped together by firm, ripe, rippling tannin. **DRINK** 2013–2020.

Price	$44
Region	Coonawarra
Value	♦ ♦ ♦
Auction	★ ★
Score	89 (2004)
	93 (2005)

Jamieson's Run Cabernet Sauvignon 2004

I tasted all four Jamieson's Run reds for this guide because it's an old favourite – I served the 1994 at my wedding – and these two just made it over the line (I didn't much like the straight shiraz or the straight merlot).

2004 RELEASE
There's a lot to like here. It smells like a real cabernet, all tobacco-leaf and blackcurrant and mint. It tastes it too, adding toasty oak to the show and a spike of raspberried brightness. There's tannin structure, but not too much, just enough to keep the wine firm and solid. To smell and drink it's great; it just lacks a little length. At the right price, it's a good option. **DRINK** 2008–2010.

Price	$19
Region	Coonawarra
Value	♦ ♦ ♦
Auction	★ ★
Score	85

Jamieson's Run Cabernet Shiraz Merlot 2004

It's not hard to find the Jamieson's Run reds selling for $15 or cheaper. For this wine in particular, that's pretty keen value.

2004 RELEASE
It's much like the straight cabernet except lengthier and better; but then, even in France cabernet is usually better as a blend than on its own. This tastes of cocoa, milk chocolate and blackcurrant, its toasty, minty finish in fine form. It's made to be drunk now, but you could tuck this in a cool, dark place for a couple of years and it would go alright. If Jamieson's Run is a favourite label of yours, this is the red in the range to hit on. **DRINK** 2008–2012.

Price	$19
Region	Coonawarra
Value	♦♦♦♦
Auction	★★
Score	88

Kangarilla Road Cabernet Sauvignon 2006

Flavour is never in question with Kangarilla Road – the wines are always high flavour, and usually high alcohol too. The prices are at times extraordinarily low.

2006 RELEASE
It's a big, sweet red, no ifs or buts. Dark, tarry, licoricey and raspberried, the flavour of it strong, the sweet smooth deliciousness of it obvious. Massively easy to drink. **DRINK** 2008–2014.

Price	$17
Region	McLaren Vale
Value	♦♦♦♦♦
Auction	★★★
Score	89

Katnook Estate Founder's Block Cabernet Sauvignon 2005

This would almost never appear at auction but as a drinking wine it offers outstanding value. This is cabernet for cabernet lovers.

2005 RELEASE
Hang on a second. Is this really a $20 red? I swear it tastes like a $30 wine, as much for the aspirations of its tannin structure – this looks like it's been built to age – as for its weight of flavour. This tastes curranty, dusty, minty and peck-kissed by toasty oak, the length of flavour both pure and earnestly structured. It smells good, tastes it, and finishes good. Don't tell Katnook, but I prefer this to its higher priced stablemates. **DRINK** 2008–2014.

Price	$20
Region	Coonawarra
Value	♦♦♦♦♦
Auction	N/A
Score	91

CABERNET AND BLENDS

Lake Breeze Cabernet Sauvignon 2004 & 2005

This is a beautiful wine, as good as many at significantly higher prices.

2004 RELEASE
Snappy red. Delivers a whopping hit of pure, delicious, dark fruit flavour – it tastes of blackcurrant, mint and cedar, and comes complete with a grainy, savoury, enmeshed set of sophisticated tannins. I like this wine more than its big $35 Winemaker's Selection brother.
DRINK 2008–2014.

2005 RELEASE
Right, get in the car and go out and buy yourself some of this. It's beautiful. Full-bodied, syrupy smooth, flush with blackcurrant, pencils and chocolate-like flavour and lip-smackingly intense. I don't mean to sound gushy – but this is a royal flush.
DRINK 2008–2015.

Price	$22
Region	Langhorne Creek
Value	♦♦♦♦♦
Auction	★★★
Score	92 (2004)
	93 (2005)

Langmeil Jackaman's Cabernet 2005

Jackaman's cabernet is grown on a forty-three-year-old vineyard at Lyndoch, in the southern sub-region of the Barossa Valley.

2005 RELEASE
I like this. There are some leafy, tomato-like scents when you first open the bottle, but give it time and rich, succulent, mouth-watering blackberry flavours sally forth, reaching to all corners of your mouth. The thing I like here is the fresh, juicy, dust-flecked appeal of it, despite its strength. Now and as a medium-term wine it will drink beautifully. **DRINK** 2009–2018.

Price	$50
Region	Barossa
Value	♦♦♦
Auction	N/A
Score	92

Leconfield Cabernet Sauvignon 2005

I like to think that wine is all about vines, land and season, but a good winemaker is a very big help. Winemaker Paul Gordon has vastly improved Leconfield's red wine quality over the past few years.

2005 RELEASE
Look at the inky colour of it. It's like cabernet porn; you salivate just looking at it. It's very primary and still quite raw, its currant, concentrated flavour swamped by dry, dusty, elongated tannins. The mid-palate dips a little (in typical cabernet fashion) but the finish is very strong.
DRINK 2009–2015.

Price	$29.95
Region	Coonawarra
Value	♦♦♦
Auction	★★
Score	92

Leeuwin Estate Art Series Cabernet Sauvignon 2004

Leeuwin is renowned for its chardonnay but its cabernet has often been disappointing – despite Margaret River being a grand place to grow cabernet sauvignon.

2004 RELEASE
I can't recall a better Leeuwin cabernet. This is balanced, fresh and lively, its elegant flavours of gravel, blackcurrant, cranberry and dried herbs matched beautifully to ripe tannins and clear, spicy, cedary French oak. It leaves a flavour of dry chocolate in your mouth after you've swallowed too. **DRINK** 2008–2012.

Price	$54
Region	Margaret River
Value	♦♦♦
Auction	★★★
Score	94

Lenton Brae Cabernet Merlot 2006

Lenton Brae isn't one of the bigger names in Margaret River but its semillon sauvignon blanc is among the region's finest, and its reds are steadily increasing in quality. The 2006 vintage – for reds – hasn't helped things.

2006 RELEASE
The 2006 vintage in Margaret River was very cool, making life hard for red wine growers. This wine shows signs of the trouble, though still manages to be a pretty handy drink. It tastes of chalk, dust, gravel, leaf matter and ash, currany fruit keeping it all smooth. Importantly, its tannins are soft and ripe. It's a pleasant drink. **DRINK** 2008–2010.

Price	$22
Region	Margaret River
Value	♦♦♦
Auction	★★
Score	86

Lindemans Pyrus 2004 & 2005

Pyrus won the much prized (and much criticised) Jimmy Watson Trophy for its 1984 vintage red. It's typically a blend of cabernet sauvignon, merlot and malbec. I'm rarely a fan.

2004 RELEASE
Huge amount of dusty, raisiny character, matched to flavours of tomato bush, raspberry, mint, tobacco and blackcurrant. Lots of dry tannin. Has quite a bit of herbal, dusty character, which some will find off-putting. I did. **DRINK** 2014–2019.

2005 RELEASE
Nice wine, much riper than the 2004, but struggles to impress against the Limestone Ridge and St George of the same year. Raisiny, solid in the amount of fruit weight it delivers, and tightened by a good deal of grapey, sun-ripened tannin. Unexciting. **DRINK** 2013–2020.

Price	$55
Region	Coonawarra
Value	♦♦
Auction	★★★
Score	88 (2004)
	91 (2005)

CABERNET AND BLENDS

Lindemans Reserve Cabernet Sauvignon 2005

2005 RELEASE
Almost too serious for the price. Flavours of eucalypt, earth, dust and tobacco, matched to smoky blackcurrant. It's like a mini Lindemans St George cabernet, complete with a pile of drying tannin. Lip-smacking finish. It will be a better drink in a year's time. **DRINK** 2009–2011.

Price	$13
Region	Padthaway
Value	♦♦♦♦♦
Auction	N/A
Score	87

Lindemans St George Cabernet Sauvignon 2004 & 2005

Of the three Lindemans Coonawarra big gun reds, Limestone Ridge invariably offers the most fun, while St George provides the class. It's true again here.

2004 RELEASE
Take ripe blackcurrant and infuse it with molasses and tar and raisins, and there you have a distinctive flavour profile. Fine, dry tannins cut across the fruity, tarry length of it, creamy, cedary oak fingered throughout. **DRINK** 2013–2023.

2005 RELEASE
Blow me down if it doesn't smell like Coonawarra's red soil – and you know what, it's only 12.9 per cent alcohol. In other words, alcohol warmth does not distract from the land's message. Beautiful sweet fruit. Beautiful earthy accents. Beautiful chalky tannin. This is a cellar star. **DRINK** 2014–2025.

Price	$55
Region	Coonawarra
Value	♦♦♦♦
Auction	★★★★
Score	94 (2004)
	96 (2005)

McKellar Ridge Cabernet Sauvignon Cabernet Franc 2006

The 2005 (93 points) had a lot of folks raving – not something you expect for a Canberra cabernet.

2006 RELEASE
It's much like the beautiful 2005 except denser – its red, inky heart crammed full of blackberries and chocolate, mint and cedarwood. I love cabernet with a hint of lead pencil flavour to it, and this has a dose of it – glory be. Lots of succulent acidity here too. Great cabernet drinking. **DRINK** 2012–2020.

Price	$24
Region	Canberra District
Value	♦♦♦♦
Auction	N/A
Score	92

McWilliam's Hanwood Estate Cabernet Sauvignon 2006

2006 RELEASE
There's the odd small-run wine that beats it, but for the widely available stuff – this is the best ten buck cabernet on the market. You need to specifically look for the 2006 though – the 2005 isn't nearly as good. This tastes of blackcurrant and raisins and toast, and slips down all too easily. Canny red drinkers should snap this one up. **DRINK** 2008–2010.

Price	$10
Region	South Eastern Australia
Value	♦♦♦♦♦
Auction	N/A
Score	87

Majella Cabernet Sauvignon 2005

The Lynn family has been growing grapes in Coonawarra for four decades, and have done so under their own name since 1994. Along with Balnaves, they are the most reliable producer on the Coonawarra strip.

2005 RELEASE
Strong vintage. It's given the wine a forceful sense of purity and generosity, traits to die for in a Coonawarra cabernet. The flavours themselves are of blackcurrant, cedar, toast and chocolate, a touch of Coonawarra mint lifting the aromas from the glass. As always, there's a deal of oak here, but it's folding into the wine even in its youth. Impeccable and impressive. **DRINK** 2012–2019.

Price	$33
Region	Coonawarra
Value	♦♦♦♦♦
Auction	★★★★
Score	94

PREVIOUS
- **1994** Very ripe, very firm. 2003–2008. 89 pts.
- **1995** Lean, perfumed, herbal. 1999–2004. 86 pts.
- **1996** Excellent Coonawarra cabernet, blackcurrant galore. 2004–2012. 92 pts.
- **1997** Warm flavours; developing steadily. 2001–2005. 88 pts.
- **1998** Great structure, lovely depth of fruit. 2006–2012. 94 pts.
- **1999** Elegant, well-powered, lovely drink. 2007–2012. 92 pts.
- **2000** Ripe, generous, sweet. 2002–2012. 93 pts.
- **2001** Concentrated, oak-rich, generous. 2004–2012. 92 pts.
- **2002** Elegant, ripe, sweet. 2005–2012. 91 pts.
- **2003** Generous, curranty, vanillin. 2005–2014. 93 pts.
- **2004** Tangy, curranty, vanillin. 2007–2016. 93 pts.

Majella The Musician Cabernet Shiraz 2006

It's only the third release but it's already established itself as an ever-reliable wine. It's named in memory of the Lynn family's son Matthew, a keen musician.

2006 RELEASE
Another lovely release. Fleshy, fruity, dusty and creamy, the cabernet doing a good deal of the talking, the shiraz simply plumping up the mid-palate. Just take a look at the colour of this! It's dark and blue–black, enough to warm any red drinker's heart. **DRINK** 2008–2011.

Price	$19
Region	Coonawarra
Value	♦♦♦♦
Auction	N/A
Score	89

Maxwell Little Demon Cabernet Merlot 2005

This Maxwell wine is new to the range.

2005 RELEASE
This is nifty red wine drinking. It's a simple hit of blackberried flavour, bitter notes of black olives and tar helping only to set the style – they don't detract from the wine's quality at all. Punchy dark fruit and slightly brandied alcohol. At the price (if you like the bigger end of red wine) this is a good option. **DRINK** 2008–2011.

Price	$16.95
Region	McLaren Vale
Value	♦♦♦♦
Auction	N/A
Score	87

Mike Press Cabernet Sauvignon 2006

If the 2005 Mike Press shiraz was a bargain then the 2005 cabernet was a heart-stopper. It was sold for less than $10 per bottle, and scored a 94 point rating. One for the ages. This 2006 is good too.

2006 RELEASE
It mightn't be quite as good as the 2005 but it's still a gigantic bargain. This is thickly flavoured, syrupy, classily structured and sophisticated – a whole bunch of descriptors you don't expect to use at this price. Lots of lengthy, curranty, pencil-like flavour. Fantastic. **DRINK** 2008–2014.

Price	$10
Region	Adelaide Hills
Value	♦♦♦♦♦
Auction	N/A
Score	92

Mildara Cabernet Sauvignon 2006

This is the White Label Mildara cabernet that seems to move forward and back in priority at Foster's, its parent company. I've long been a fan.

2006 RELEASE
Gosh there is a lot of eucalypt flavour in this wine. If anything can handle it it's cabernet, and with the intensity of the blackcurrant fruit flavour here there's a fair argument that it does. Tannins are long, ropey and impressive, oak is toasty but underplayed, and the persistence through the finish is noteworthy. I'd prefer less of the eucalypt notes, but the quality here is high.
DRINK 2012–2020.

Price	$27.95
Region	Coonawarra
Value	♦♦♦♦♦
Auction	★★★
Score	93

Mildara Cabernet Shiraz 2004

I suspect that this has been caught up in the lack of attention to the Mildara brand, hence 2004 is (I'm told) the current release. Nothing wrong with the wine.

2004 RELEASE
Soft, earthy aromatics, plummy and spicy and minty. Beautiful velvety wine, medium bodied but gorgeous through the mouth. Tannins are unobtrusive but manage to keep the wine honest. Line and length here. It builds beautifully as it sits in the glass. Finishes with a flush of spiced mulberry-like flavours. More or less 60/40 cabernet shiraz. Excellent drinking. **DRINK** 2008–2015.

Price	$27.95
Region	Coonawarra
Value	♦♦♦♦
Auction	★★★
Score	93

Mildara Rothwell Cabernet Sauvignon 2004

This was made for the Jamieson's Run label but it's now coming under Mildara (both owned by Foster's and both Coonawarra-based brands). Confusion aside, it's a cracking cabernet.

2004 RELEASE
Will be beautiful in time. It's a big hit of inky fruit, tempered by graceful tannins. A feast of cassis, mint, sandalwood, cedar and dry chocolate. I love the easygoing strength of this. I love the fruit tannins too. Gorgeous wine. A worthy flagship. **DRINK** 2013–2025.

Price	$75
Region	Coonawarra
Value	♦♦♦♦
Auction	★★★
Score	96

Mitolo Serpico Cabernet Sauvignon 2005

This is made using Italian Amarone techniques. Basically, the grapes are dried on racks prior to them being fermented into wine. This technique can make the wines seem both sweeter (in fragrance and mid-palate) and yet nutty and dry, especially on the finish. Wines made this way, if they're successful, can live for a very long time.

Price	$73
Region	McLaren Vale
Value	♦♦♦♦
Auction	★★★
Score	95

2005 RELEASE
Ravaged with dry, dusty flavours of stewed herbs, coffee beans and earth, the mouth-puckering finish of it offset deliciously by a sweet core of mid-palate fruitiness. Nuts, kirsch, blackberry jam and tar – it tastes exotic, even as a young wine. The true test of this will come in ten years' time, when it is mature. All the signs look excellent.
DRINK 2013–2022.

PREVIOUS
2001 Could develop beautifully. Powerful. 2010–2020. 90 pts.
2002 Layers of smooth, robust flavour. 2012–2022. 94 pts.
2003 Ripe tomatoes, nuts, currants; lots here. 2011–2019. 92 pts.
2004 Intensely herbal but intensely ripe. 2010–2015. 93 pts.

Moondah Brook Cabernet Sauvignon 2005

This is another of the red wines I cut my teeth on in the mid-ish 1990s. I drank a lot of the 1998, and cellared some for a few years – with reasonable results. This release is better balanced than the wines of that era.

Price	$18
Region	Western Australia
Value	♦♦♦♦
Auction	★★★
Score	87

2005 RELEASE
Real cabernet, no getting around that. It's got the sturdy tannin structure, bold length of flavour, notes of leaf matter and gravel and slightly bitter finish that often characterises the variety. There's a high note of eucalypt too. If cabernet is your thing, it's worth hopping into this. If it's not, this won't convert you. **DRINK** 2009–2013.

Moss Wood Amy's Cabernet Sauvignon 2006

The wine formerly known as Glenmore. This is a single vineyard wine and usually a good one; I often think it's the best value wine in the stable. Not this year though.

2006 RELEASE
Lovely flavour but not a great deal of length – making the value here questionable. That flavour profile though, is gorgeous: pencils, dried tobacco, syrupy blackcurrant and toasty oak. It's a fleshy, slightly dilute wine, mouth-watering in its acidity. It's a red that feels refreshing as you swallow each gulp. Drinking it is very enjoyable – as long as you accept the fact that you are paying a little for the name. **DRINK** 2008–2014.

Price	$27
Region	Margaret River
Value	♦ ♦ ♦
Auction	★ ★ ★
Score	87

Moss Wood Cabernet Sauvignon 2004

Moss Wood cabernet has the ability to create the greatest of 'melting moments' in Australian wine. The wines can be so smooth and rich that it feels like they melt in your mouth, the mix of fruit and oak flavour both finely meshed and powerfully built. They're not all like that; but this one is.

2004 RELEASE
Drink it young or drink it old – it'll drink beautifully either way. This is one helluva hedonistic cabernet, packed with mounds of fruit and oak flavour, its silken texture both classy and seductive. Violets, mint, gravel, blackcurrant, dried herbs and a swoosh of vanillin oak. Impeccable. **DRINK** 2009–2022.

Price	$95
Region	Margaret River
Value	♦ ♦ ♦
Auction	★ ★ ★ ★ ★
Score	95

PREVIOUS
1994 Powerful, silken, lengthy. 2008–2018. 94 pts.
1995 Persistent chocolate and blackcurrant. Beautiful. 2008–2017. 94 pts.
1996 Beautifully structured, complex beauty. 2006–2016. 94 pts.
1997 Maturing fast. Savoury, curranty, leathery. 2004–2010. 87 pts.
1998 Spicy, gamey and oak-sweetened. 2006–2012. 89 pts.
1999 Complex, savoury, gamey and curranty. 2008–2016. 94 pts.
2000 Lots of oak but fruit-shy. 2008–2013. 90 pts.
2001 Pure, velvety and generous. 2011–2026. 94 pts.
2002 Savoury but powerful. 2010–2015. 91 pts.
2003 Smooth, medium-bodied, structured. 2012–2017. 90 pts.

Noon Reserve Cabernet Sauvignon 2006

You don't see too many sixteen per cent alcohol cabernets around and if you do, they're rarely as well-balanced as this mild-mannered monster.

2006 RELEASE
Deliciousness plus. This is beautiful. It's sweet, cedary, loamy, currranty and dusty, its cabernet credentials obvious but its fleshy core of ripe, luscious, intense fruit there to be had, and had right now. Mellow, soft tannins play only a minor role – this is all about sweetly ripened cabernet grapes presented in all their dark-hearted glory. **DRINK** 2008–2016.

PREVIOUS
2003 Warm, massive, soft and pure. 2006–2012. 93 pts.
2004 Huge wine, but extremely well handled. 2006–2012. 94 pts.
2005 Gumleaf, currants and lots of heat. 2007–2013. 90 pts.

Price	$25 (Cellar Door)
Region	Langhorne Creek
Value	♦♦♦♦♦
Auction	★★★★★
Score	94

Oliver's Taranga Vineyards Vine Dried Cabernet Sauvignon 2006

This is part of the Oliver's new 'small batch' range, made in only two-tonne lots. It's the kind of thing you can do when you've got 300 acres of vines to play with, as the Olivers have. This wine is a ripper.

2006 RELEASE
If you can find some of this, grab it. It's a luscious, lovely red, full of dust-shot blackcurrant flavour and super-viscous and smooth through the finish. In terms of big reds, it's essentially perfect. It rings very long through the finish, looks and tastes brooding and intense, and has the most supple tannin structure ever invented (OK, maybe I exaggerate – but I like it!). It's not simple either; it's got the lot. **DRINK** 2008–2018.

Price	$28
Region	McLaren Vale
Value	♦♦♦♦♦
Auction	N/A
Score	95

Orlando Jacaranda Ridge Cabernet Sauvignon 2003

Jacaranda Ridge has a loyal following and rightly so; over the years it has produced some lovely wines. This release does not grab me.

2003 RELEASE
It smells lovely but there's something missing in the middle of the palate – and, for that matter, on the finish. Charming, leathery, herbal, mulberried scents run into an angular palate, with flavours of salt, raisins, leather and mulberry pulling inelegantly against one another. The tannins do not glide with the wine; they angle against it. I am being harsher than I would be were it a wine at a quarter of the price, but if you stick your jaw out with a big price on it ... **DRINK** 2008–2014.

Price	$60
Region	Coonawarra
Value	◆
Auction	★★★
Score	87

Over The Shoulder Cabernet Merlot 2005

Oakridge is an excellent winery hamstrung by the fact that a crippled Evans and Tate has owned it for the past half dozen years. Hopefully its future is more prosperous; the wines deserve it.

2005 RELEASE
'Second' labels like this sometimes seem to treat consumers like idiots, but this label is not one of them. This is a really good wine. It's supple, fleshy, curranty and bold, its briary edges simply roping varietal integrity into the show. Structure, flavour and balance. A fine example of winemaking craft. **DRINK** 2008–2012.

Price	$18
Region	Yarra Valley
Value	◆◆◆◆◆
Auction	N/A
Score	90

Parker Coonawarra Estate Cabernet Sauvignon 2004

It might just be me but I never seem to hear all that much about Parker Coonawarra Estate, despite the fact that the wines are generally excellent. My only common criticism of the wines is that they can be over-priced; this wine is not.

2004 RELEASE
I guess there are more obviously impressive versions of Coonawarra cabernet but this is entirely in the classic mould: its curranty, toasty flavour both medium weight and gloriously savoury. There are attractive notes of dried herbs and chocolate and it finishes with a great sense of focus. It's a wine of ripeness and control; as most of the best wines are. **DRINK** 2013–2018.

Price	$29
Region	Coonawarra
Value	◆◆◆◆
Auction	★★★
Score	93

CABERNET AND BLENDS

Penfolds Bin 389 Cabernet Shiraz 2005

Late in 2007 I was lucky enough to attend a tasting of every vintage of Bin 389 ever made. It was an incredibly impressive tasting, and underlined in bold just how good this wine is, and consistently. It was once dubbed 'poor man's Grange'; now it's well and truly a super wine in its own right.

2005 RELEASE
A riot of structured power – fill your cellar up. There's something almost ribald about this. Musk, vanillin, plums, brilliant blackcurrants, integrated mint. Loads of fruity, musky, perfumed tannin, fine, lingering and ripe. This really does have an appetite for seduction: it's the duck's guts. **DRINK** 2014–2021.

PREVIOUS
1995 Entering maturity. Soft and pruney. 2008–2013. 88 pts.
1996 Fresh, expressive, gorgeously structured. 2012–2028. 97 pts.
1997 Game, mint; developing nicely. 2008–2012. 87 pts.
1998 Fine tannin, bold fruit. 2013–2025. 95 pts.
1999 Oak-heavy, but elegantly structured. 2011–2020. 92 pts.
2000 Medium-weight, but genuinely good. 2009–2016. 91 pts.
2001 Oomph, structure, complexity. 2011–2017. 92 pts.
2002 Brooding, tannic, full of promise. 2015–2028. 94 pts.
2003 Raisiny, tannic, slightly disjointed. 2011–2016. 90 pts.
2004 Clean, dark-fruited, balanced. 2016–2025. 93 pts.

Price	$58
Region	South Australia
Value	●●●●●
Auction	★★★★★
Score	96
Past greats	1966, 1976, 1983, 1990

Penfolds Bin 407 Cabernet Sauvignon 2005

The Penfolds reds have had a price hike recently and the one it seems to have affected the most is Bin 407; a strange move considering that it's often the least impressive of the Penfolds Bin range. This release is a beauty, but the price has now moved into Petaluma Coonawarra territory.

2005 RELEASE
Really good. It's a pretty, floral, musky wine, adorned with classy, spicy oak and banged up with fleshy, succulent, grapey tannin. Fruit flavours are in the blackcurrant and dark olive spectrum, but its distinguishing feature is its elegant prettiness. Rare to see a Bin 407 look so classy. **DRINK** 2014–2021.

Price	$44.95
Region	Coonawarra
Value	●●●●
Auction	★★★
Score	93

PREVIOUS
1995 Drying out. Nice leafy, leathery, gamey flavour. 2005–2010. 86 pts.
1996 Effortlessly good. Fruity, smooth and sure. 2012–2020. 92 pts.
1997 Medium-weight, but fading. 2005–2012. 85 pts.
1998 Pure cabernet. Minty, strong, structured. 2011–2018. 92 pts.
1999 Too much tannin for the fruit. 2007–2014. 87 pts.
2000 Minty, pure, attractive. 2010–2018. 92 pts.
2001 Oak-driven, short, awkward. 2008–2013. 86 pts.
2002 Expressive, pure, lengthy. 2013–2023. 93 pts.
2003 Smells great; palate doesn't support it. 2008–2013. 86 pts.
2004 Good structure and varietal character. 2011–2017. 91 pts.

Penfolds Bin 707 Cabernet Sauvignon 2005

I tasted the complete set of Penfolds Bin 707 during 2007, going all the way back to the 1964. I didn't much like the wines of the 1960s or '70s, but slowly came to like the wine through the 1980s and '90s, before really starting to like the wines of the past few years. Perceptions of Bin 707 need to be updated.

Price	$175
Region	Barossa Coonawarra McLaren Vale
Value	♦ ♦ ♦
Auction	★ ★ ★ ★
Score	97

2005 RELEASE
Gorgeous. Just bloody gorgeous. Tannin, fruit, reach, length, seduction, seriousness, the whole shooting match. Galore-ious. Just bloody monumental. Rich blue–black, inky, cassis-like fruit, shot with exquisite oak and tannin.
DRINK 2025–2040.

PREVIOUS
1990 Gigantic seductive flavour, but controlled. 2015–2026. 96 pts.
1991 Super flavour, super length. 2012–2022. 94 pts.
1992 Fresh but weird. 2005–2015. 86 pts.
1993 Tannic, leafy, fading rather than building. 2007–2013. 86 pts.
1994 Big flavoursome bones, big structure. 2011–2020. 94 pts.
1995 Not made.
1996 Almost impossible to fault. 2015–2030. 96 pts.
1997 Smells and tastes good; lacks stuffing. 2009–2015. 87 pts.
1998 Packed with 'wow' factor. Pure, lengthy. 2018–2030. 95 pts.
1999 Strong savoury elements. Nearly outstanding. 2011–2018. 92 pts.
2000 Not made.
2001 Very sweet and ripe, swaggering tannin. 2016–2023. 94 pts.
2002 Stunning flavour and purity. 2023–2035. 96 pts.
2003 Not made.
2004 Very young, very intense, huge future. 2017–2032. 95 pts.

Penley Estate Phoenix Cabernet Sauvignon 2005

The 2005 vintage was a good one in Coonawarra, though Penley seems to have allowed its 'everyday' cabernet to get very ripe. It's a decent wine and I'd happily knock it back, but it probably would have been better if they'd picked it earlier.

2005 RELEASE
Pure Coonawarra. Dusty and herbal and yet abundantly ripe, its currantly, violety, prune-like flavours succulent and fleshy. It surprised me that this was fifteen per cent alcohol; it carries it well. I've deducted points here because it becomes bitter and clumsy on the finish. **DRINK** 2008–2012.

Price	$18
Region	Coonawarra
Value	♦♦♦♦
Auction	★★
Score	86

Pepperjack Cabernet Sauvignon 2006

This wines comes out of the historic Saltram winery in the Barossa. I usually prefer their mid-priced wines to their super-premiums.

2006 RELEASE
Direct hit. Inky, slinky, soft on your tongue and rich to the taste. Hunt around and find it at a good price – and then buy as much of it as you can afford. It's a beautiful, dark-fruited red wine, flooded with blackcurrant and kirsch and chocolate-like flavour, with a mint edge keeping it vibrant. If that's not enough, it smells great too. **DRINK** 2008–2016.

Price	$25
Region	Barossa
Value	♦♦♦♦
Auction	★★
Score	93

Petaluma Cabernet Merlot 2004 & 2005

These two releases are as good as any Petaluma reds released over the past twenty-five years.

2004 RELEASE
Loaded with flavours of cassis, cherries, wood smoke, cedar, malt and loam. It has richness, tannin structure, and savouriness. Great. **DRINK** 2012–2025.

2005 RELEASE
This went within a whisker of taking out the Cabernet of the Year Award. It's an elegant wine but a fantastic one, with dark, olive-like, ripe blackcurrant flavours massaging the palate with both flavour and super-smooth texture. There's malty, spicy oak here too, but the fruit flavours have almost entirely eaten them up – often the best sign of a wine's quality. Captivating. **DRINK** 2013–2023.

PREVIOUS
- **1998** Shy nose, great palate. 2007–2015. 94 pts.
- **1999** Elegant, structured, and beautifully balanced. 2007–2014. 93 pts.
- **2000** Gangly, oaky, tannic and good. 2007–2011. 92 pts.
- **2001** Length, style, sophistication. 2008–2015. 93 pts.
- **2002** Green and herbaceous, but balanced. 2010–2015. 87 pts.
- **2003** Not yet released.

Price	$50
Region	Coonawarra
Value	♦♦♦♦♦
Auction	★★★★
Score	96 (2004)
	96 (2005)

Peter Lehmann Cabernet Sauvignon 2005

2005 RELEASE
I guess it lacks the sweetness some might be seeking but I reckon this is full of bonza cabernet style. It tastes like blackcurrant, toast, vanilla and dust, but it's the personality of it that makes me smile – and want to keep drinking it. This screams 'I am cabernet, and I am proud'. It's really good juice. **DRINK** 2008–2012.

Price	$19
Region	Barossa
Value	♦♦♦♦♦
Auction	N/A
Score	90

Poacher's Ridge Vineyard Louis Block Cabernet Sauvignon 2005

A young vineyard with a big future. Wines are made by renowned winemaker Robert Diletti.

2005 RELEASE
Good easy-drinking wine offering a range of savoury-sweet flavours, its length and depth just shy of deserving higher points. It's rare for me to say this, but the merlot from the same range is significantly better.
DRINK 2008–2012.

Price	$18
Region	Great Southern
Value	♦♦♦
Auction	N/A
Score	86

Polleters Cabernet Sauvignon 2005

A tiny estate with most of the plantings completed in 1996. This is not the last you will hear of Polleters.

2005 RELEASE
Tremendous flavour and tremendous value. Dense blackcurrant and cigar-box aromas/flavours boom through the mouth, classy French oak boosting it further. A mighty wine, but checked and balanced too. This is really something. **DRINK** 2014–2023.

Price	$25
Region	Pyrenees
Value	♦♦♦♦♦
Auction	N/A
Score	94

Red Knot Cabernet Sauvignon 2006

The name only mentions cabernet sauvignon but fourteen per cent of this wine is shiraz. It helps fill out the wine well; the great Aussie blend is more alive and well than is sometimes reported.

2006 RELEASE
Can't help but smile at this one. I just love the punchy sweetness of it; the flavours of toast, coffee, raspberry and blackcurrant; the way it's so easy to knock back and, of course, the honest price of it. I slightly prefer the shiraz of the same label, but this is good too. Succulent and saucy.
DRINK 2008–2010.

Price	$14.95
Region	McLaren Vale
Value	♦♦♦♦♦
Auction	N/A
Score	88

Richard Hamilton Hut Block Cabernet Sauvignon 2006

Years ago the late, great Aussie wine writer Mark Shield wrote a column singing the praises of Hut Block cabernet. I rushed out and bought some, and he was dead right. Forever after both Shield, and Hut Block cabernet, have had a place in my heart.

2006 RELEASE
This tasted a lot better after half an hour in my glass, so open it up and give it a splash in a decanter (the air will do it the world of good). This makes good cabernet look easy. Warm, blueberried, mulberried and (I swear it's true) with a flavoursome sense of inner confidence; it doesn't try too hard, it just tastes damn good. **DRINK** 2008–2014.

Price	$17.95
Region	McLaren Vale
Value	●●●●●
Auction	★★
Score	92

Riddoch Cabernet Shiraz 2004

Been a while since I've liked a Riddoch red but I'm sure on board with this one. Shop around. This would make for a sensational go-to red.

2004 RELEASE
This is what I like to see. A clean-fruited, medium-weight, nicely oaked wine of substance and style, at a reasonable price. Even better, it tastes like you expect Aussie red wine to taste: bright, bold, curranty and just a touch dusty, courtesy of the cabernet. You can swan around with this and feel pretty good about yourself. **DRINK** 2008–2012.

Price	$17
Region	Coonawarra
Value	●●●●
Auction	N/A
Score	89

Ring Bolt Cabernet Sauvignon 2005

It's the Margaret River brand of South Australia's Yalumba winery, and while it's been around for a few years this is the first tempting release.

2005 RELEASE
I love twenty buck wines like this. You can take them anywhere. It's got a lot of soft, smooth, chocolaty charm, and yet it's grainy and earthy too – cabernet's trademark sense of aristocracy very much in evidence. It stands tall in the glass. **DRINK** 2008–2012.

Price	$22
Region	Margaret River
Value	●●●●
Auction	N/A
Score	89

Rosemount Diamond Label Cabernet Sauvignon 2005

A few years ago a friend served this wine at lunch, beside a far more expensive wine. It knocked it over for quality! The quality is slowly getting back to where it was.

2005 RELEASE
We're talking pretty simple stuff here but it packs enough punch to make it well worth considering. It tastes of blackcurrant, toast and eucalypt and is firm and solid enough to stand up to hearty meat dishes (I had it with a chunky beef pie, but I'm a pie fiend). There's the structure and mass of flavour to keep it ticking over for a few years too – I dare say it will taste better in even six to twelve months. Wise buying. **DRINK** 2008–2011.

Price	$15
Region	Multi-Regional Blend
Value	♦♦♦♦
Auction	N/A
Score	88

Rosemount Show Reserve Cabernet Sauvignon 2005

It's been a while since I enjoyed a Rosemount wine, yet I happily tucked into this. This is the best Rosemount red in five years.

2005 RELEASE
Picture-perfect Coonawarra cabernet. Balanced, minty, full of syrupy blackcurrant and then cedary and earthy and undergrowthy through the finish. I first tasted this with its identity masked and it stood out for its smooth, luscious texture and easy, lingering length. It seems totally unforced; drinking it is a pleasure. **DRINK** 2008–2016.

Price	$24
Region	Coonawarra
Value	♦♦♦♦
Auction	★★
Score	93

St Hubert Cabernet Sauvignon 2005

It's been a rocky road for St Hubert over the past fifteen years under various changes of ownership; Foster's is now the boss. Every now and then they produce a stellar wine; this one is middle of the road.

2005 RELEASE
It's got a lot of spreading tannin and it will age well, but there's nothing too much to get excited about here. Indeed, I rate it lower now than when I tasted it six months back. It tastes of mulberry, blackcurrant, chocolate and toast, the finish nicely woven with tannin, but bitter in the aftertaste. The palate too, is starting to hollow out. **DRINK** 2010–2014.

Price	$25
Region	Yarra Valley
Value	♦♦
Auction	★★
Score	86

Saltram Maker's Table Cabernet Sauvignon 2007

This wine is either unoaked or very low in oak, something you almost never saw in Australian red wine until a few years ago. There is now quite a lot of this style of wine around, and it's a very good thing.

Price	$9.95
Region	South Eastern Australia
Value	♦♦♦♦♦
Auction	N/A
Score	86

2007 RELEASE
A big whack of lovely, juicy, lip-smacking fruit flavour. There's even a bit of tannin here too. You can chew on it, gulp at it, sniff it and sip it. It's delicious, in a carefree way – flush with blackcurrant and dark olives. Maybe there's not a lot of length, but boy does it try. Super effort by the Saltram team here. **DRINK** 2008–2009.

Saltram Mamre Brook Cabernet Sauvignon 2005

Mamre Brook shiraz is often good but the cabernet is generally better; a Barossa Valley quirk. Its only issue is that the alcohol is often very high. The 1998, 2002 and 2004 Mamre Brook cabernets were outstanding.

Price	$25
Region	Barossa
Value	♦♦♦♦♦
Auction	★★★
Score	93

2005 RELEASE
It's fifteen per cent alcohol but it carries it well. Actually, it's a smashing drink. There are elements of raisins and tar to the flavours but the main ooze of it is all sweet, ripe blackcurrant, its cedary, seductive oak behaving itself extremely well. Naughty with flavour, but eminently nice to drink – and as you swallow, a great rush of juicy flavour lingers. **DRINK** 2008–2016.

Saltram Winemaker Selection Cabernet Sauvignon 2004

The first release of this was with the 2002 vintage and although it was an advanced, leathery wine, its charm and quality was substantial. The 2004 is fresher and juicier. It's also a single vineyard wine from Dorrien (old school Aussie red lovers prick up your ears now).

Price	$68
Region	Barossa
Value	♦♦♦♦
Auction	★★★
Score	95

2004 RELEASE
Vibrant, lively, vigorous and persistent. This is super quality. It tastes of blackcurrant and background cedarwood and there are flinty, raw, smoky edges, maybe the odd toss of mintiness helping the aroma lift from the glass. It is both substantial and sophisticated.
DRINK 2013–2023.

CABERNET AND BLENDS

Scarpantoni The Brothers Block Cabernet Sauvignon 2004

2004 RELEASE
The flavours are attractive but it lacks the weight to carry the style. It's full of vanillin oak, fresh acidity, dusty blackcurrant and coconut, its easy drinkability 100 per cent spot on. As a humble drink, it's great fun. My only problem is the price. **DRINK** 2008–2013.

Price	$25
Region	McLaren Vale
Value	♦♦
Auction	N/A
Score	87

Seppelt Cabernet Sauvignon 2005

Cabernet from the mountainous Grampians (though these vines grow on the flatlands) region of north-west Victorian doesn't get much press – fortunately. Let's keep it quiet.

2005 RELEASE
It's not a shiraz wannabe – it tastes like real cabernet. It's dusty, currenty, long and minty through the mouth, the rush of chewy tobacco-like flavour and tannin on the finish the kind you usually find in a wine of far higher price. Did someone at Seppelt put the wrong label on this one? Surely it's the wine of a $28 brand. Surely. Must be hard to get good staff these days. **DRINK** 2008–2014.

Price	$18.95
Region	Grampians
Value	♦♦♦♦♦
Auction	★★★
Score	91

Skillogalee Basket Pressed Cabernet Sauvignon Cabernet Franc Malbec 2004

I'm a big fan of Clare reds made with cabernet sauvignon blended with malbec. There's a long tradition of it in the valley, and I dare say it produces the region's best red wines.

2004 RELEASE
If you like a good soft (but full-bodied) red made in a regionally authentic style, try this baby on for size. It's been matured in the Skillogalee cellars for a few years and has started to mellow and soften into an enormously satisfying wine. Flavours of eucalypt, blackberry, earth, vanillin and cloves, the juicy power of it spot on for a dead-of-winter night. **DRINK** 2008–2013.

Price	$28.50
Region	Clare Valley
Value	♦♦♦♦
Auction	★★★
Score	92

Squitchy Lane Vineyard Cabernets 2005

Anyone who's been a fan of AFL football would know the name Mike Fitzpatrick – legendary former ruckman of the Carlton Football Club. This is the red wine he grows.

2005 RELEASE
It's developing steadily but it's a very fine drop. It tastes of eucalypt, earth, sweet raisins and delicious blackcurrant, its dry, elegant tannin profile sure to keep it in reasonable shape over the next half dozen years. I wouldn't quite have it in my 'starting 18', but I'd have it on the interchange bench, ready to make a quick impact on the dinner table. **DRINK** 2008–2013.

Price	$27
Region	Yarra Valley
Value	♦♦♦♦
Auction	N/A
Score	89

Starvedog Lane Cabernet Merlot 2005

There was a time not too long ago when a lot of people thought the Adelaide Hills were too cool for heavier red varieties such as cabernet and shiraz. Whether it's global warming, better grape growing or better site selection – something has changed, and dramatically for the better.

2005 RELEASE
This has the kind of thick wad of flavour that you rarely see in Australian cabernet. It's more of a Bordeaux trait. It gives the wine an expansiveness in your mouth, the flavours of blackcurrant, eucalypt and blackberry coming across as more than the sum of their parts. The reach of fine, filigreed tannin continues the impression. **DRINK** 2012–2019.

Price	$24
Region	Adelaide Hills
Value	♦♦♦♦♦
Auction	★★
Score	92

Stella Bella Cabernet Sauvignon Merlot 2005

Janice McDonald makes the Stella Bella wines and they're always impeccably put together. These are 'gobs of fruit' style wines; they're about structure, pure fruit, brightness and length.

2005 RELEASE
I'd have to be in the right mood but I reckon this is a class act. It's essence of cabernet, in the refined, finely tannined, fragrant style. Lots of gravelly, crunchy, detailed flavour, herbs and blackcurrant. Oak is subservient to the fruit. The finish is juicy and tight, a touch bitter, but in a positive way. It would be an excellent Margaret River cabernet to stick in the cellar and forget about for at least five years. **DRINK** 2012–2020.

Price	$25
Region	Margaret River
Value	♦♦♦♦
Auction	★★
Score	92

Suckfizzle Cabernet Sauvignon 2005

Great cabernet for me is all about fruit weight, yes, but especially about tannin structure. If you don't like tannin, find another grape variety (I'm hard, but fair). This wine is dressed with beautiful tannin.

2005 RELEASE
First rate Margaret River cabernet. Strong, pure, structured, lengthy. Tastes of gravel, blackcurrant, eucalypt, smoke and cedar, the fruit power of it building an irresistible momentum through your mouth. This will age like a champ. One for cabernet's true believers. **DRINK** 2012–2019.

Price	$45
Region	Margaret River
Value	♦♦♦
Auction	★★
Score	93

Tahbilk Cabernet Sauvignon 2004

By all rights the Nagambie Lakes wine region should be prime shiraz country – OK, it is too – but for some reason cabernet sauvignon seems to outperform it. It's the same situation at the Balgownie winery in the nearby region of Bendigo.

2004 RELEASE
An above-average example of this perennial bargain. If you want an inexpensive red to cellar, this is worth checking out. It has an easy, winsome drinkability, the flavours reminiscent of blackcurrant, eucalypt, choc-malt and menthol. The thing I love is that it doesn't seem to be trying all that hard; maybe it's pacing itself for the long haul. **DRINK** 2011–2020.

Price	$18
Region	Nagambie Lakes
Value	♦♦♦♦♦
Auction	★★★
Score	92

Talinga Park Cabernet Merlot 2005

2005 RELEASE
Whomever said that the ten buck red is dead needs their head painted red. This is tasty stuff. I first noticed it in a line-up of a vast number of reds and it stood out for its easy, jubey Ribena-like ripeness, cabernet's trademark dustiness stopping it from tipping into cordial territory. It's not a grand red but it quaffs tidily. **DRINK** 2008.

Price	$9.95
Region	Various
Value	♦♦♦♦
Auction	N/A
Score	84

Taltarni Cabernet Sauvignon 2004

Taltarni had a strong reputation for tannic, gamey, age-worthy wines in the 1970s and '80s – it's arguable that they were part of the modern renaissance of Australian red wine. They seemed to lose their way towards the end of the 1990s, but wine quality is again on the up.

2004 RELEASE
What a classic wine. It's deliciously flavoured but textbook in its balance and structure, the bet that it will age well effectively guaranteed. It tastes ripe and currany and gently minty, the soft, smooth impact of cedary oak as seamless as it is harmonious. Undergrowthy characteristics are layered beneath – all part of the complex, sophisticated appeal of the wine. A beauty. **DRINK** 2010–2020.

Price	$31
Region	Pyrenees
Value	♦♦♦♦♦
Auction	★★★
Score	95

Tapanappa Whalebone Vineyard Cabernet Shiraz 2005

This is (wine industry leader) Brian Croser's new venture – though it's a collaborative effort with some other parties. It's a single vineyard wine of great aspiration. The 2003 was the first release.

2005 RELEASE
The 2003 release of this was good (88 points) without quite being good enough; the 2004 (95 points) was monumentally good. This release is less immediately impressive than the 2004, and certainly not as weighty, but its structure and polish is A-class and its cellaring future seems assured. Fine, elegant, currany fruit, velvety tannins, hay-like, sawdusty French oak and a sweet, jubey finish. They don't come much more classy than this. **DRINK** 2014–2024.

Price	$71.50
Region	Wrattonbully
Value	♦♦♦
Auction	N/A
Score	94

Taylors Cabernet Sauvignon 2005 & 2006

Taylors has won awards for its top-priced wines but I prefer their more affordable offerings.

2005 RELEASE
It's easy to mount the argument that this is Australia's best value cabernet. It can cellar remarkably well too – as does a lot of Clare cabernet. This tastes of blackcurrant, mint, tobacco and choc-vanilla, and lingers in your mouth remarkably well. **DRINK** 2008–2014.

2006 RELEASE
Balance is the thing: the key to all good wine. Vanillin oak, dark fruit, acid, tannin, length of flavour and an all-round feeling of satisfaction. This wine has all the right combinations. Winemaker Adam Eggins – you're a star. Easy five-star value. **DRINK** 2008–2014.

Price	$17.95
Region	Clare Valley
Value	♦♦♦♦♦
Auction	★★
Score	91 (2005)
	92 (2006)

Taylors Jaraman Cabernet Sauvignon 2005

Taylors is a Clare Valley wine company but a few years ago they decided to source grapes from other regions too and to launch the result under the Jaraman name. There have been some good results, but in general the wines have failed to excite.

2005 RELEASE
Sound wine. Nicely structured too. Fresh, minty, currant and persistent, its chalky, powdery tannin an admirable foil to the fresh, dark fruitiness of it. I'd take this one home with me for sure. **DRINK** 2008–2013.

Price	$29.95
Region	Clare Valley Coonawarra
Value	♦♦♦
Auction	★★
Score	91

Tim Adams Cabernet Sauvignon 2004 & 2005

Blends of cabernet and malbec are classic in the Clare Valley; it's the wine style I most look forward to drinking from the region.

Price	$24
Region	Clare Valley
Value	♦♦♦♦♦
Auction	★★★
Score	92 (2004)
	93 (2005)

2004 RELEASE
It's all about balance and – no small thing – natural, effortless complexity. It tastes of bright, pure cassis, dust, earth, mint and coffee grounds, all of it juicy, all of it fresh and more-ish. It has a decent tannin structure, but you hardly notice it. This is a fantastic cabernet blend.
DRINK 2008–2018.

2005 RELEASE
Yep, no-brainer, son of a gun, jump on board. Got it? Right. It's ripe, full, mouth-filling, a lake of blackcurrant and leathery earth. Dead-set perfect Clare Valley cabernet.
DRINK 2008–2014.

Ulithorne Paternus Cabernet Shiraz 2006

A new wine from Ulithorne made in very small quantities – less than 150 dozen.

Price	$35
Region	McLaren Vale
Value	♦♦♦♦
Auction	N/A
Score	93

2006 RELEASE
Strong, grainy, chocolaty, ripped with dust and blackcurrant and firm, bony tannins. One for the long haul. Full of black, teeth-staining, glass-staining, colour and flavour – and yet it's still a wine of line and length. There's no real fun in drinking this as a young wine; it needs to be cellared, preferably for more than eight years. It's a growly engine it's got running though.
DRINK 2012–2020.

Vasse Felix Cabernet Sauvignon 2005

Vasse Felix has a new winemaker in charge – Virginia Wilcox – and judging by these two 2005 reds she's landed herself in a fabulous wine playground. These are excellent reds.

Price	$35
Region	Margaret River
Value	♦♦♦♦♦
Auction	★★★
Score	94

2005 RELEASE
I've had Vasse cabernets that I've loved and others that seemed over-ripe or over-oaked. This one's right in the middle; it's spot on. It's intensely flavoured but to a sensible degree, the oak nestled seamlessly into the wine. There's also a sense of refreshing, lively acidity, the perfect foil to the wealth of clean, bright blackcurrant-like flavour. Flashes of herbs, menthol and cedar also play a role; as does a superb frame of tannin. **DRINK** 2011–2020.

PREVIOUS
1999 Ripe, earthy, smooth and delicious. 2005–2012. 92 pts.
2000 Firm, fruity, tannic and bitter. 2005–2010. 89 pts.
2001 Chocolate, blackcurrant, vanillin; it's yum. 2007–2012. 90 pts.
2002 Lovely, balanced, medium-weight wine. 2007–2012. 89 pts.
2003 Chocolaty, fragrant, fresh. 2009–2014. 91 pts.
2004 Easy-going, smooth and structured. 2010–2015. 91 pts.

Voyager Estate Cabernet Merlot 2004

The quality of Voyager Estate's reds is so good that a lot of its regional neighbours reckon it's not fair – it makes life too hard for them. Sounds like a red drinker's paradise to me.

Price	$58
Region	Margaret River
Value	♦♦♦♦♦
Auction	★★★★
Score	95

2004 RELEASE
Now, I'm a regular lover of Voyager cabernet merlot, but this is an especially good one. The last great one was the 2001, but this 2004 is far tamer in alcohol, and all the better for it. It tastes of chocolate and liquid pencils, cedarwood and oodles of soft, hearty, cassis-like fruit. There's a gravelly underpinning too, which does wonders for the flavour, while keeping the texture smooth. Good but largely unobtrusive structure. Hunt around for a better price than the one listed, and then stock up.
DRINK 2012–2022.

PREVIOUS
1999 Gamey, curranty, bitter tannic finish. 2004–2008. 89 pts.
2000 Good flavour but too much tannin. 2004–2010. 87 pts.
2001 Huge flavour, huge quality. 2010–2020. 95 pts.
2002 Good but struggles for ripeness. 2007–2013. 89 pts.
2003 Terrific cabernet. Balanced, flavoursome, interesting. 2009–2016. 93 pts.

Voyager Estate Girt by Sea Cabernet Merlot 2005

New-ish release in the Voyager portfolio, but a good one. Nice tribute to the ability of Margaret River cabernet to drink well as a young wine.

2005 RELEASE
Grab a steak and a bottle of this, and winter suddenly seems like the best time of the year. Mind, it would go great with a spring lamb too. It's just a lovely drinking wine. Straight, honest, robust flavours, its gravelly, slightly bitter edges swamped by dark currenty fruit. It had me tucking back for more, that's for sure. **DRINK** 2008–2012.

Price	$24
Region	Margaret River
Value	♦♦♦♦
Auction	N/A
Score	90

Warburn Estate Premium Reserve Cabernet Merlot 2006

I'd hardly heard of Warburn Estate before this 2006 release but they are well worth a punt.

2006 RELEASE
I really like drinking this. It has lots of sweet–savoury character – precisely the point of the cabernet merlot blend. It's sweet through the wine's centre, dusty, a touch minty and then plump and juicy through the finish. I'm gobsmacked by the value here; it's quite extraordinary. It drinks well on its own, and would drink well with various meats. This isn't tricked-up sugary drinking; this is stylish drinking. **DRINK** 2008–2011.

Price	$9.50
Region	Barossa
Value	♦♦♦♦♦
Auction	N/A
Score	90

Warrabilla Reserve Cabernet Sauvignon 2006

Andrew Sutherland Smith makes the biggest of red wines, some of them over seventeen per cent in alcohol. Often, remarkably, they taste balanced and good.

2006 RELEASE
Lots of good, dark, intense, value-for-money drinking here. It tastes of dust, cedarwood, tar and blackcurrant, the lot mixed into a mass of sweet (almost) overwhelming flavour. It finishes dry and grapey, and sits both firmly and proudly in the monster red category. **DRINK** 2008–2013.

Price	$22
Region	Rutherglen
Value	♦♦♦♦
Auction	★★★
Score	89

Wine by Brad Cabernet Merlot 2005

The label for this wine is in a retro cartoon style – I like it rather a lot. It's not intimidating. The only problem with it is that it's often assumed that the wine's quality will be gimmicky; it is not.

2005 RELEASE
A very good Margaret River red at an excellent price. It tastes regional: curranty, gravelly, tipped with mint and then chocolaty through the finish. It's satisfying and good. Why aren't there more sub-$20 Margaret River reds as good as this? **DRINK** 2008–2012.

Price	$18
Region	Margaret River
Value	♦♦♦♦♦
Auction	N/A
Score	89

Wirra Wirra The Angelus Cabernet Sauvignon 2005

Angelus is the name of the bell that sits on top of the Wirra Wirra winery. They ring it at the start and end of each vintage – and when things get a bit too rowdy. Sound like my kind of people.

2005 RELEASE
Massed with dark, chocolaty, dusty fruit flavour, the impact and style of it as impressive as one another. This is the kind of red to drink in the middle of winter after you've just achieved something important; it's a statuesque, saturated wine worthy of a grand occasion. Bigger is not always better when it comes to red wine, but this is an example of bigger being a belter. Deep, sustained, beautiful. **DRINK** 2012–2022.

Price	$60
Region	McLaren Vale
Value	♦♦♦♦
Auction	★★★★
Score	95

Wolf Blass Grey Label Cabernet Sauvignon 2006

A few years ago Wolf Blass chief winemaker Chris Hatcher mentioned that they were trying to tone down the heavy use of oak on the Wolf Blass Langhorne Creek reds. This though is a substantially oak-driven wine – not that there's anything wrong with that.

2006 RELEASE
Full of creamy, coffeed, toasty oak, like an oil slick of smooth sweetness sliding over the blueberried, blackberried, minty fruit flavour. I've served this to folks and they have loved it, but to me it lacks power through its centre (especially for forty bucks). **DRINK** 2008–2014.

Price	$40
Region	Langhorne Creek
Value	♦♦
Auction	★★
Score	89

Woodlands Cabernet Merlot 2005 & 2006

Woodlands is in the same part of Margaret River as Cullen, Moss Wood and Vasse Felix. It's been kicking hefty goals in recent years.

2005 RELEASE
A beautiful drink. Soft, mulberried, curranty flavour is matched to cedarwood and regional gravel/eucalypt flavour. It's structured and flavoursome. Exceptional value for a Margaret River cabernet. **DRINK** 2009–2016.

2006 RELEASE
The 2006 vintage was pretty much a dog of a year for reds out west but this has come up trumps. It tastes of autumn leaves, raspberries, blackcurrant and toast and, while the cool year is evident, the yum factor is still high. **DRINK** 2008–2014.

Price	$20
Region	Margaret River
Value	♦♦♦♦♦
Auction	N/A
Score	91 (2005)
	88 (2006)

Woodstock Cabernet Sauvignon 2005

2005 RELEASE
A good red wine. It doesn't taste much like cabernet but it does taste bloody good: succulent, plummy, cherried fruit washing through the wine, every drop of it delicious. Toasty, grainy oak adds interest and a slight mintiness adds lift and life to the wine's fragrance. **DRINK** 2008–2013.

Price	$20
Region	McLaren Vale
Value	♦♦♦♦
Auction	N/A
Score	90

Wynns Coonawarra Estate Black Label Cabernet Sauvignon 2005

They've been putting a lot of work into the Wynns Coonawarra vineyards over the past few years, and the work is now starting to pay off. Look forward to a resurgent Wynns.

2005 RELEASE
The best Black Label cabernet since the 1998. It's an old style, classic wine of briary leaf highlights in what is, essentially, a blackcurrant-filled wine. Pretty, floral aromatics make it a delight to smell, and it has the tannin structure to age beautifully. **DRINK** 2011–2016.

PREVIOUS
- **1990** Still tastes brooding and pure. 2003–2014. 93 pts.
- **1991** Marriage material. Tremendously well structured. 2004–2014. 94 pts.
- **1992** Unattractive. Sour and lacklustre. 1997–2002. 81 pts.
- **1993** Lovely mix of ripeness and leafiness. 2003–2011. 89 pts.
- **1994** Pruney, tannic, unbalanced. 2003–2009. 87 pts.
- **1995** Nice and leathery; fading. 2002–2007. 86 pts.
- **1996** Medium-weight, perfectly balanced. 2008–2014. 93 pts.
- **1997** Drinker's wine. Casually sophisticated. 2006–2013. 87 pts.
- **1998** Beautiful components. Needs more time. 2010–2018. 92 pts.
- **1999** Will age stylishly. Balance and purity. 2008–2016. 93 pts.
- **2000** Smooth, firm, competent. 2004–2010. 89 pts.
- **2001** Dark fruit, great palate; falls away. 2010–2020. 88 pts.
- **2002** Explosive floral fragrance. Smooth palate. 2012–2019. 92 pts.
- **2003** Classically styled. Needs a little more. 2012–2017. 89 pts.
- **2004** Great potential. Pure blackcurrant and violet. 2014–2022. 91 pts.

Price	$25
Region	**Coonawarra**
Value	♦♦♦♦♦
Auction	★★★★★
Score	**93**

Wynns Coonawarra Estate John Riddoch Cabernet Sauvignon 2005

John Riddoch cabernet has had its grand moments in the past, but also the odd over-oaked disappointment. It's back here as a balanced, substantial wine of genuine, beguiling quality.

2005 RELEASE
A big, dark, strapping wine of profound varietal character. Flavours of olive and blackcurrant, mint and cedar. Swaggering tannin. Long grainy finish. Beefy and intense, but not in any way over the top. This is the prototype of what a John Riddoch cabernet should be. Simply outstanding. **DRINK** 2015–2025.

PREVIOUS
1998 Bulky, oak-driven; great substance. 2008–2016. 94 pts.
1999 Beautiful marriage of oak and fruit. 2009–2020. 93 pts.
2003 A treat. Dusty, composed, ethereal. 2012–2020. 94 pts.
2004 Super-tight, super-dusty, super-elegant. 2020–2030. 94 pts.

Price	$75
Region	Coonawarra
Value	♦♦♦♦
Auction	★★★★
Score	97

Wynns Coonawarra Estate Messenger Cabernet Sauvignon 2005

Wynns winemaker Sue Hodder points out that some of the estate's vineyards are 'among the most important cabernet vineyards in the country, and deserve to be given recognition.' Messenger is a dry-grown vineyard at the southern end of the region.

2005 RELEASE
Pure, floral, silken cabernet. Just a beautifully balanced wine. Lengthy, flavoursome, fine-grained tannins ripple through the finish. This is not a big, plush, heavy flavoured wine, but it feels lovely in your mouth, and lingers on for a good long while after you've swallowed – the sign of red wine excellence. **DRINK** 2012–2023.

Price	$35
Region	Coonawarra
Value	♦♦♦♦♦
Auction	★★★★★
Score	94

Xanadu Dragon Cabernet Merlot 2006

Xanadu has had its ups and downs, but since the Rathbone family took over a couple of years back, quality has rapidly headed north.

2006 RELEASE
Really good. Flavoursome, chocolaty, brimming with succulent cherried flavour and punchy and impressive through the finish. Super mid-week wine. **DRINK** 2008–2010.

Price	$16
Region	Margaret River
Value	♦♦♦♦♦
Auction	N/A
Score	89

Yalumba Menzies Cabernet Sauvignon 2004 & 2005

The Menzies Coonawarra vineyard has been in Yalumba hands since 1993, and it's always produced wines full of herbal, dusty flavours. It's never been one of my favourites. The 2005 marks a new era for this vineyard and label.

2004 RELEASE
This has picked up the odd gold medal at wine shows, but it's not for me. It's fragrant, ashen, spicy, but unfortunately full of gravelly, dried herb and tomato-leaf characters. Its tannins are minty, mulberried, dry and somewhat hard. **DRINK** 2012–2016.

2005 RELEASE
Yalumba see this wine as the future of Menzies, and boy I hope they're right. It's curranty, mulberried, straight and long – archetypal line-and-length red wine – with minty tannins and real length. Huge cellaring potential. Great varietal purity, and yet greatly elegant. **DRINK** 2014–2022.

Price	$46.95
Region	Coonawarra
Value	♦♦♦
Auction	★★
Score	87 (2004)
	95 (2005)

Yalumba Signature Cabernet Sauvignon Shiraz 2004

There was a long period when the Signature was Yalumba's top red, and while there are a couple of wines that now outrank it in price, it's still arguably the best all-purpose wine in the portfolio. It's certainly reliable.

2004 RELEASE
This spends two years in oak, and a further two years in bottle, prior to its release. It's fifty-five per cent cabernet sauvignon. It's strong with minty, mulberried fruit flavour, the mintiness making the wine's ultimate blackberried depth remain fresh and fragrant. Toasty oak sits in the background. Lively acidity. It should age like a charm.
DRINK 2014–2023.

PREVIOUS
1999 Structured, flavoursome, balanced. 2006–2012. 92 pts.
2000 Smooth, coffeed, early-drinking. 2005–2010. 90 pts.
2001 Toasty, leathery, generous. 2008–2015. 94 pts.
2002 Ripe, luscious, lingering. 2006–2018. 93 pts.
2003 Smooth, minty, blackberried. 2010–2016. 91 pts.

Price	$46.95
Region	Barossa
Value	♦♦♦
Auction	★★★★
Score	94

Zema Estate Cabernet Sauvignon 2004

Zema is a family-run estate in the heart of Coonawarra. It hand-picks its vines, and often grows them without irrigation too. It's called sustainable farming.

2004 RELEASE
Classically styled if not quite classic quality. It's a nice wine though. It carries a nice hit of blackcurrant-like flavour, notes of mulchy, dried leaf matter hanging about the edges. The oak's been handled well too, contributing creamy, cedary tones and it then finishes fleshy and ripe. The thing is, it's a very nice drink, and should drink well for as long as a decade. **DRINK** 2009–2016.

Price	$26
Region	Coonawarra
Value	♦♦♦
Auction	★★★
Score	91

CABERNET AND BLENDS

MERLOT, GRENACHE, ITALIANS, SPANIARDS

+ blends

The best of wines, the worst of wines – there's probably more fun to be found in this chapter, but more pitfalls too. Nothing quite excites like a great nebbiolo, or indeed goes better with a meaty pizza than really good sangiovese ... though those who love a great grenache blend or tempranillo would likely argue the point.

Of course, that's if you're in at least semi-serious mode ... there are also sweet reds here, gamays, funky new blends and some really good value quaffers. The more red wine I drink the more days of the week I find myself wanting something unusual. This chapter highlights the best of what I've found.

TOP TEN OF THE YEAR
1   Pizzini Il Barone 2004
2   Vinea Marson Nebbiolo 2006
3   D'Arenberg Twentyeight Road Mourvedre 2005
4   Hewitson Old Garden Mourvedre 2006
5   Vinea Marson Sangiovese 2006
6   Luke Lambert Nebbiolo 2006
7   D'Arenberg Derelict Vineyard Grenache 2006
8   Castagna Un Segreto Sangiovese Syrah 2005
9   Burge Family Winemakers Olive Hill Shiraz Mourvedre Grenache 2005
10 Arrivo Rosato di Nebbiolo 2007

Adam's Rib The Red 2005

This is made by Adam Castagna, son of winemaker Julian Castagna. Clever winemaking clearly runs in the family.

2005 RELEASE
It's a mighty lovely blend of merlot and shiraz. Go flavour hunting and you see notes of roasted coffee, blueberry, five-spice and mulberry – though really, take a sip and all you can think is how interesting, and delicious, it tastes. It's well balanced and blessed with ripples of very fine, very ripe tannin. It is one of the discoveries of the year.
DRINK 2008–2014.

Price	$35
Region	Alpine Valleys Beechworth
Value	♦♦♦♦♦
Auction	N/A
Score	93

Anvers Razorback Road Shiraz Cabernet Sauvignon 2005

This wine technically comes from the Adelaide Hills but the vineyard, at Kangarilla, is so close to the McLaren Vale region that its flavours are more likely to be robust and chocolaty than elegant and ashen.

2005 RELEASE
Solid red wine of length, structure and class. Tastes of malt, blackcurrant, pencils and cedar, the juicy mid-palate swishing heartily onto a chalky, tannin, fruity finish. This has all the right boxes ticked, at a good price.
DRINK 2009–2014.

Price	$20
Region	Adelaide Hills
Value	♦♦♦♦
Auction	N/A
Score	89

Arrivo Nebbiolo 2005

The first release was the 2004 and it was a cracker (93 points). Look out for the upcoming 2006 Arrivo Lunga Macerazione – it was left fermenting on its own grape skins for a whopping seventy-two days, and sounds fascinating in all respects.

2005 RELEASE
It's very nearly in the class of the 2004 but it's slightly marred by exuberant notes of eucalyptus, which stick daggers into this wine's Italianate heart. It's otherwise a leathery, tarry, juicy wine, fronted with tannin and then long and (appropriately) bitter through the finish. It drinks a lot better after a few hours in a decanter; this bottle tasted significantly better on the second night.
DRINK 2010–2016.

Price	$60
Region	Adelaide Hills
Value	♦♦♦
Auction	N/A
Score	92

Arrivo Rosato di Nebbiolo 2007

This book was meant to be a Rosé Free Zone, but a few were so good that I couldn't hold them back. This is a first release, and it is absolutely fabulously gorgeous.

2007 RELEASE
Think of sweet, ripe red table grapes pureed and then cleaned up into a bright, translucent liquid – the slightly herbal grip of their skins still detectable in the juice. Then add alcohol, and imagine flavours of grapey, Turkish delight-like flavour. If that sounds delicious to you, then whammo, we're onto something seriously special here. If it sounds a bit light and sweetish for your tastes – then this won't be for you. Admittedly, it will drink far better in autumn, spring and summer than it will in the upcoming winter. **DRINK** 2008–2010.

Price	$26
Region	**Adelaide Hills**
Value	♦♦♦♦♦
Auction	N/A
Score	94

Blue Poles Merlot Cabernet Franc 2005

One of the great 'insider' gags of the movie *Sideways* is that the 'merlot hating' lead character, Miles, openly lusts after the Bordeaux wine Cheval Blanc. The gag is that Cheval Blanc is a blend of cabernet franc and, you guessed it, merlot.

2005 RELEASE
It walks to its own beat, that's for sure. It tastes like unsweetened chocolate and dried flowers, a combination which might sound a bit austere – but doesn't come across that way. It tastes yummy actually, and stylish, and with its low (12.7 per cent) alcohol it moves freely and smoothly through the finish, minus any alcohol heat. You have to be in the mood for it, but it is good. **DRINK** 2008–2012.

Price	$24
Region	**Margaret River**
Value	♦♦♦♦
Auction	N/A
Score	90

Brown Brothers Barbera 2005

Brown Brothers is a traditional, family-owned company of long standing. And yet, of late, it has started to slay them in the marketplace with either fun and funky styles (see below) or unpretentious quaffers. If you can't beat 'em ...

Price	$15.90
Region	Milawa
Value	♦♦♦♦♦
Auction	N/A
Score	87

2005 RELEASE
I might be being a bit harsh with the drinking window here because there's more fruit weight than you might expect – which should hold it in reasonable shape. It delivers a nice dose of dark cherried, spicy, slightly herbal flavour and rings sound and succulent through the finish. Damn it, it's a mighty tasty quaffer. **DRINK** 2008–2010.

Brown Brothers Dolcetto Syrah 2007

There's even more interest in sweet-styled table wines than usual right now and that interest has spread to sweet reds. Yes, sweet reds. Brown Brothers has long been the market champion of this kind of thing, and they're still showing others how to do it.

Price	$15.90
Region	Milawa
Value	♦♦♦♦♦
Auction	N/A
Score	85

2007 RELEASE
Hang on a minute, I have to remove my snob's hat. Right, that's better. Now what do I think of this? Hey, I like it! Wash your mouth out Mattinson! Look, it's by no means a sophisticated wine, and the sugary sweetness of it is obvious. There's a dryness through the finish though, and a clean, fresh, fruit-driven energy to the way it rollicks across your tongue ... I'll say one thing, it's hard not to smile after each mouthful. Chill it slightly (in cool weather and hot) and it drinks like a bloody ripper. **DRINK** 2008.

Brown Brothers Everton Red 2006

Brown Brothers makes wine for the people. It's not about ego, it's about making wines that people love to drink. This wine (a blend of cabernet sauvignon and shiraz) and the 2006 graciano are the perfect examples.

Price	$15.90
Region	Milawa
Value	♦♦♦♦♦
Auction	N/A
Score	85

2006 RELEASE
Juicy, lively, refreshing, packed with medium-weight, sweet-styled fruit flavour – no wonder it's so popular. This is a really good quaffing wine. It tastes of redcurrants and dried leaves and it leaves your mouth feeling fresh – and ready for more. **DRINK** 2008.

Brown Brothers Zibibbo Rosa NV

This isn't really a red but it does have a pink/red hue and it's such a phenomenon that it 100 per cent deserves a place in this book. It's made with muscat of Alexandria grapes and, let's face it, Zibibbo is a very cool name.

NV RELEASE
As a fine wine it's crummy but as a fun wine it's got it going on. Serve this when you want people to like you. Sweet, grapey, strawberried and, how can I say it and keep my testosterone intact … fluffy in the mouth. It was never meant to be contemplated (or written about) but it is meant to be drunk, and in a light, sweet way it's very good for that. The alcohol is a modest eight per cent. **DRINK** 2008.

Price	$15.90
Region	Victoria
Value	♦♦♦♦♦
Auction	N/A
Score	85

Burge Family Winemakers Garnacha Dry Grown Grenache 2005

Garnacha is a Spanish word for grenache. Whether or not Rick Burge's grenache is made in a Spanish style comes second in importance to the whip-cracking enjoyment of saying the word out loud. Garnacha!

2005 RELEASE
There might be a bit too much warming alcohol here but the flavours are so complex that it's easy to forgive. It tastes of red pebbles (I swear it does) along with raspberry, aniseed, dry chocolate, smoke and old wood, and while there is a swing of succulent acidity it's a wine ultimately defined by its warm, chalky tannin structure. I love drinking this – I reckon it's the goods. **DRINK** 2008–2014.

Price	$25
Region	Barossa
Value	♦♦♦♦
Auction	★★★
Score	91

Burge Family Winemakers Olive Hill Shiraz Mourvedre Grenache 2005

A single vineyard wine (sitting on a ridge of limestone) from one of Australia's most interesting winemakers. Interestingly, Rick Burge has begun using biodynamic preparations in his vineyards.

2005 RELEASE
Olive Hill is in the southern, or Lyndoch, sub-region of the Barossa and from 2005 it has produced a stellar wine. I hate to say it but Burge could easily charge fifty bucks for this. It tastes of plums, smoke, graphite and chocolate but the thing that really makes it stand out is its length: it rings on for a good long time once you've swallowed. It's the mark of excellence. **DRINK** 2008–2014.

Price	$32
Region	Barossa
Value	♦♦♦♦♦
Auction	★★★
Score	94

Cape Mentelle Zinfandel 2005

They've had their ups and downs with it but Cape Mentelle was one of the first to plant zinfandel in Australia – and they're easily one of the two or three best producers of it. It's notoriously high in alcohol.

2005 RELEASE
No shrinking violet at 15.5 per cent alcohol, but for all its warm, mighty flavour there's a noteworthy attempt at restraint, with cool, long tannins twisting through flavours of tar, blackberry, coffee and wood sap. Don't be concerned: the flavour is still mega-applied. **DRINK** 2008–2014.

Price	$53
Region	Margaret River
Value	♦♦♦
Auction	★★★
Score	92

Cascabel Tempranillo 2007

If you'd said five or six years ago that the Spanish grape tempranillo would spread like wildfire through Australia, wine people would have thought you were mad. But it's happened. Cascabel was one of the leaders of the charge.

2007 RELEASE
This is the best Cascabel tempranillo I've tasted. Unlike a lot of 'alternative' varieties it's user-friendly too, with succulent aniseed and strawberry flavours mixing easily with the variety's trademark sour dark cherries and sundry splashes of dried herbs. It's all about fresh, naturally structured fruit flavour, and I don't mind if I do have another glass. **DRINK** 2008–2011.

Price	$20
Region	McLaren Vale
Value	♦♦♦♦♦
Auction	★★★
Score	90

Castagna Un Segreto Sangiovese Syrah 2005

Julian Castagna usually makes a super premium sangiovese (called La Chiave) but the 2005 vintage proved too much of a temptation. He believes that sangiovese/shiraz blends could be the future of Australian wine, and for a few years he's wanted to make a top-tier version to help establish his point. This 2005 does so emphatically.

2005 RELEASE
The sweet, supple generosity of shiraz and the tangy, savoury excitement of sangiovese. It sounds good and tastes even better. Kirsch, smoke, hazelnuts, menthol, ground spice, both sour and sweet blackberries – it's a fascinating parade of flavours. Outstanding wine.
DRINK 2010–2017.

Price	$75
Region	Beechworth
Value	♦♦♦
Auction	N/A
Score	94

Chapel Hill Il Vescovo Tempranillo 2006

Chapel was a regular drink at my place through parts of the 1990s, but wine quality seemed to fall away through the first half of this decade. Great to see some good wines coming through again.

2006 RELEASE
Bangs of smoky, meaty fragrance here, the perfect match for barbecued meats. The palate continues the theme, adding sour cherries and Asian spices. It all stops a little short – but it's a lot of fun while it lasts. **DRINK** 2008–2011.

Price	$20
Region	Adelaide Hills
Value	♦♦♦
Auction	N/A
Score	87

Chapel Hill Sangiovese 2005

Sangiovese and McLaren Vale seem like a pretty good fit. Indeed, there's an argument that a number of Italian and Spanish grape varieties will grow well – and make good wine – in the hills of the Vale.

2005 RELEASE
Fan of this. It's seductively savoury. It tastes of nuts and cherries and wood smoke, low-input chocolaty oak intelligently applied. Juicy, savoury and satisfying.
DRINK 2008–2012.

Price	$20
Region	McLaren Vale
Value	♦♦♦
Auction	N/A
Score	89

Charles Melton Nine Popes 2005

The quality and style of this wine has been important in the evolution of Australian wine; it has spawned countless imitators. Most years I'm a big fan.

2005 RELEASE
I was tempted to be cruel at first. It opened poorly, the flavours lacklustre. It seemed to be all arms and legs, with not a lot of weight on them either. Given time to breathe it got better, with minerally, raspberried, licoricey, earthy flavours giving it a sweet, savoury appeal. The finish seemed to get sweet and longer too, making it a satisfying drink. I reckon it needs five years in the cellar.
DRINK 2012–2019.

Price	$49
Region	Barossa
Value	♦♦♦♦
Auction	★★★
Score	89

Coriole Nebbiolo Rose 2007

Coriole reckon this is a rosé for grown-ups. Not often I'm called that.

2007 RELEASE
Another rosé that is just too good to leave out – and while it was released for the 2007/2008 summer, it'll still be beaut drinking this spring and summer (and maybe even the summer after). It's chewy and tannic for a rosé, its flavour in the dried herb and chalk-splashed cherry spectrum. For a rosé, it's also very, very good. **DRINK** 2008–2010.

Price	$18
Region	Langhorne Creek
Value	♦♦♦♦♦
Auction	N/A
Score	91

Coriole Sangiovese 2006

Time flies. This, believe it or not, is the twentieth release of Coriole sangiovese. Hard to call it an 'alternative variety' when it's been around for two decades!

2006 RELEASE
Tough guy sangiovese. Take a sip and it coats your mouth in dry, punchy tannin, the force of it greater than the sum of your expectations. Along with all that chewy dryness comes a swagger of sour, nutty, cherry-like flavour, the odd hint of game both evident and enjoyable. Sangiovese always likes to be drunk with food; this release demands it.
DRINK 2009–2014.

Price	$20
Region	McLaren Vale
Value	♦♦♦♦
Auction	★★★
Score	89

Craggy Range Sophia Merlot Cabernet Franc 2005

There was a brief moment in time when it looked like cabernet would be the variety for New Zealand to hang its hat on – before sauvignon blanc and pinot noir took over. This wine though, confirms the original excitement.

2005 RELEASE
What a classy wine. It's just so flavoursome, so soft, so rich in its chocolaty, currenty, pencily flavour, and yet so even-tempered in the way it presents its power. It croons its flavours with a gravelly voice. Simply, there is a lot to adore here. **DRINK** 2012–2019.

Price	$85
Region	Hawke's Bay, NZ
Value	♦♦♦
Auction	★★★★
Score	94

Cullen Mangan 2006

This unusual blend of merlot (fifty per cent), petit verdot (thirty-six per cent) and malbec (fourteen per cent) has been part of the Cullen range for a half-dozen years, but it's just now settling into its stride. The early vintages were explosions of raw fruit flavour; now it's a more structured, 'serious' wine.

2006 RELEASE
Hard work to drink now – if you must, pour it into a decanter and leave it there for an hour or two prior to starting in on it. It's tight and minerally, earthy and blueberried, the mid-palate a touch lacking but the style of it rigid and assured. Good result from a tough vintage. **DRINK** 2010–2018.

Price	$45
Region	Margaret River
Value	♦♦♦♦
Auction	★★★★
Score	91

D'Arenberg Derelict Vineyard Grenache 2005 & 2006

D'Arenberg has been a modern champion of McLaren Vale grenache; indeed it's made sure that a lot of the best vineyard sites have stayed planted with grenache.

2005 RELEASE
You little beauty. Minerals, violets, blackberries, asphalt, cedarwood – this is a pristine little number, chocked full of personality. I'd be absolutely raving about this – except that the 2006 is even better. **DRINK** 2010–2020.

2006 RELEASE
A profound grenache. Incredibly well structured and fruited, the silken, blueberried, cherried fruit shot with minerals and gun smoke and then pulled tight and long by superfine tannins. Grenache is only ever medium weight but this is at the upper end of it, its texture and weight both thick and ravishingly smooth. Grenache of the Year. **DRINK** 2011–2020.

Price	$30
Region	McLaren Vale
Value	♦♦♦♦
Auction	N/A
Score	94 (2005)
	95 (2006)

D'Arenberg The Peppermint Paddock Sparkling Red Chambourcin NV

D'Arenberg has persisted with this unusual wine for a number of years; I reckon it's just about to hit pay-dirt. This is excellent stuff.

NV RELEASE
Fascinating wine – and quite delightful. It's full of glossy, charming, dark cherry-like flavour, but bolted to these are notes of sap, ink, chocolate and fresh, slightly unripe plums. I mean all those descriptors in a positive sense. It's a refreshing wine, yet complex and immediately appealing. It's a beautiful colour and a beautiful drink. **DRINK** 2008–2013.

Price	$28
Region	McLaren Vale
Value	♦♦♦♦
Auction	N/A
Score	92

D'Arenberg The Ironstone Pressings Grenache Shiraz Mourvedre 2005

Top-notch examples of this blend can age for twenty years plus. I suspect this might be one of them.

2005 RELEASE
It smells great. You stick your nose into it and a blast of sweet, raisiny, tobacco-like aromas gush at you. It smells so good that you could go on smelling it all night – if you were a looney, and if your mouth wasn't watering so much. There's a lot of earthy, raspberried tannin here too, plus a pool of licorice and blueberry-like fruit flavour. It's worthy of equal-top billing in the D'Arenberg stable.
DRINK 2008–2020.

Price	$65
Region	McLaren Vale
Value	♦♦♦
Auction	N/A
Score	93

D'Arenberg Twentyeight Road Mourvedre 2006

2006 RELEASE
A great mourvedre. This is the wine of a winery on song. It's pure, warm, interesting, full of flavour – and yet structured and savoury too. A mourvedre with the lot, please. It tastes of tar, violets, orange blossom, kirsch and boysenberries. It's a boomer. A tannin structure to die for. Yummo. **DRINK** 2012–2022.

Price	$35
Region	McLaren Vale
Value	♦♦♦♦
Auction	★★★
Score	95

De Bortoli Merlot Sangiovese 2006

De Bortoli has been making some interesting wines out of its extensive King Valley vineyard over the past few years. This is an excellent example.

2006 RELEASE
Charming mix of bright, syrupy blueberried fruit flavour and more savoury, smoky, tarry influences – exactly why I reckon this is a super quaffer. It gets the mix of savouriness and sweetness pretty much exactly right, the kick of grippy tannin on the finish bound to melt away beside food – charry Greek lamb would be great with this.
DRINK 2008–2010.

Price	$14
Region	King Valley
Value	♦♦♦♦♦
Auction	N/A
Score	89

Eldridge Estate Gamay 2006

Gamay isn't exactly your flavour-of-the-month variety, but its juicy acidity and refreshing appeal makes it a winner in my books. Think of it as a half-way house between pinot noir and sangiovese. It's a passion of Eldridge Estate's David Lloyd.

2006 RELEASE
There's an effortless, succulent firmness to this that would make it a monty for the table; this is a food wine par excellence. Juicy, smoky acidity, notes of strawberry and sour cherry, the odd flash of dried herbs and a lingering, mouth-watering finish. It has both gorgeous line and length and a sense of light-weighted 'presence' in the mouth. Boy I could go this with duck, or even osso buco. **DRINK** 2008–2013.

Price	$30
Region	Mornington Peninsula
Value	♦♦♦
Auction	★★★
Score	91

Fifth Leg 2006

Made by the wonderful Devil's Lair winery in Margaret River. It's a blend of cabernet sauvignon, merlot and shiraz.

2006 RELEASE
Confession: it was a cabernet that made me go mad over wine, and I've had a bias towards it ever since. This partly explains why I like this wine so much. It has a dry, dusty succulence to it, the tannins and finish dry but the core of it curranty and flavoursome. It doesn't have the length to warrant higher marks and I'd want to pick it up on discount, but knocking a glass or four of this back is no chore at all. **DRINK** 2008–2011.

Price	$19
Region	Western Australia
Value	♦♦♦♦
Auction	N/A
Score	87

Fox Gordon By George Cabernet Tempranillo 2005

Blends like this are part of the future of Australian wine – unusual blends that almost no-one else in the world does, but which work terrifically. Hats off to Fox Gordon here.

2005 RELEASE
The 2004 of this was really good, though I thought the alcohol level was a little too high. No such problem here. This is a firm, tasty, chewy red, full of flavour and personality. Flavours of fennel, blackcurrant, dried herbs and malt. It's fresh, dark, weighty and deeply, deeply satisfying. **DRINK** 2008–2013.

Price	$20
Region	McLaren Vale
Value	♦♦♦♦♦
Auction	N/A
Score	91

Galli Estate Tempranillo Grenache Mourvedre 2006

The bottle label says that this blend was chosen for 'leisurely relaxed enjoyment'. At a stated strength of fifteen per cent alcohol, you're likely to become very relaxed, very fast.

2006 RELEASE
Chunky, chocolate flavour with lots of (too) warm aniseed-like flavour. Indeed why this wine was left to ripen so long I'm not quite sure – not only has it made the wine leap with alcohol, but it's also made it raisiny and flaccid. That said, the bang for buck here is pretty good. It just could have been better. **DRINK** 2008–2010.

Price	$19
Region	Heathcote
Value	♦♦♦♦♦
Auction	N/A
Score	91

Gemtree Tadpole Shiraz Cabernet Sauvignon 2006

For every dozen of this bought $2 is donated to Greening Australia. It is part of a growing trend in Australian wine to look after the land in which it is grown.

2006 RELEASE
Strong, firm, warm wine of decent concentration. Very good at the price. Toasty oak, mulberried flavour, a bright red berried finish and both sound and clean throughout. The alcohol is a little too obvious – but at the price, who's complaining. **DRINK** 2008–2010.

Price	$14
Region	McLaren Vale
Value	♦♦♦♦
Auction	N/A
Score	86

Glaetzer Wallace Shiraz Grenache 2006

A bit of grenache blended in with shiraz often gives the wine a fresh, redcurrant character. I particularly enjoy it in those red wines I want to hook into while they're young.

2006 RELEASE
Meaty, grunty, dark fruit flavour, made more complex by tastes of pan juices, raspberries and toast. Lovely smoothness through the mid-palate, before tough, chewy tannins take over. I've seen this wine sold at a tick under $20 – and at that, it's lip-smacking value. **DRINK** 2008–2014.

Price	$20
Region	Barossa
Value	♦♦♦♦♦
Auction	★★
Score	89

Gramp's Grenache 2006

Grenache is a love it or hate it variety. Its detractors point to either its lightness of flavour or its predilection to being sweet and candied; its supporters to its great gritty tannin, suitability (and hence sustainability) to our climate, and ability to produce intoxicating perfumes. If you want to know which camp you sit in, this wine is the perfect start.

2006 RELEASE
This has everything grenache lovers adore. It smells terrific, like breathing in a bag of jubes and musk-sticks and raisins, the palate then flowing directly on from the aroma of it. There's the taste of licorice in there too – but separating the flavours from its overall effect is absurd. For a wine made with grenache, it tastes perfect. DRINK 2008–2013.

Price	$15
Region	Barossa
Value	♦♦♦♦♦
Auction	★★
Score	92

Hardy's Oomoo Grenache Shiraz Mourvedre 2006

I had my doubts about the 2005 version of this but the 2006 is good, medium-weight, red-fruited drinking.

2006 RELEASE
It tastes sweet and spicy but its most obvious distinction is how easily it slips down. This is one tempting little sucker. It tastes of raspberry, cherries, sand, cedarwood and woodspice, and the more you drink of it the more complexity you notice – or that's my argument anyway. Nice wine. DRINK 2008–2011.

Price	$18
Region	McLaren Vale
Value	♦♦♦♦
Auction	N/A
Score	88

Hardy's Tintara Grenache 2004

This is the premium Tintara wine in the heavy etched bottle. When it was first launched in the mid to late 1990s it caused quite a stir, but the label has been deadly quiet in recent years. This 2004 is very solid.

2004 RELEASE
Nicely structured, nicely focused, ripped with spice and sour cherry-like flavour and then long and juicy through the finish. Its savouriness is very attractive, as are its high notes of raspberry and roses. This could be gorgeous in five to seven years. DRINK 2009–2016.

Price	$35
Region	McLaren Vale
Value	♦♦♦♦
Auction	★★★
Score	93

Hardy's Tintara Tempranillo 2004

Strange that Hardy's has held back this release for a year or two but I suspect that the wine needed extra time in bottle to soften. It's not an unusual requirement of tempranillo.

2004 RELEASE
A good example of why a lot of people reckon tempranillo has a future in McLaren Vale. It's dry, sour–sweet, has good juicy length and an attractive overtone of roasted nuts. It needs to be consumed with food, but it's arguably the best of this range. **DRINK** 2008–2014.

Price	$18
Region	McLaren Vale
Value	♦♦♦♦
Auction	★★★
Score	88

Hewitson Baby Bush Mourvedre 2006

This is the first release of a ten-year-long pet project of Dean Hewitson's. He took vine cuttings from the oldest living mourvedre vineyard on the planet, and grew these cuttings as 'bush vines', which means they are not trellised in any way.

2006 RELEASE
I reckon this is bonza. It's tarry and blueberried and interesting, the depth of it made to look easy by its satiny, grapey texture. I pretty much guarantee that you will love this. It's lusciously fragrant too, long and succulent, and (just quietly) does a decent job at getting my blood racing. **DRINK** 2008–2015.

Price	$28
Region	Barossa
Value	♦♦♦♦♦
Auction	N/A
Score	94

Hewitson Miss Harry 2006

A mighty good value blend of grenache, shiraz and mourvedre.

2006 RELEASE
Clean, ripe, controlled. Excellent mid-weight drinking. Gets the mix of spicy grenache-like flavour and sweet dark shiraz flavour exactly right, the exotic leathery appeal of mourvedre needing only time to show its worth. This was one of the first wines to waltz easily into the pages of this book. Look for the supple tannins – they're a piece of textbook craftsmanship. **DRINK** 2009–2014.

Price	$22
Region	Barossa
Value	♦♦♦♦♦
Auction	N/A
Score	93

Hewitson Old Garden Mourvedre 2006

Some mad folks reckon that mourvedre is the Barossa Valley's best performing red grape. A couple of recent tastings have made me think the mad folks aren't far wrong.

2006 RELEASE
Part of the price is rarity – this is picked off a very small patch of the world's oldest living mourvedre vines (planted in 1853) – but the quality too is extremely high. It's like a good, rich South Australian shiraz complete with all the dark fruited treats you'd expect, with an X-factor attached. Describing that X-factor isn't easy, but it has something to do with the orange rind, spice-box and old dry tobacco flavours that cavort through the wine. It's marvellous to admire, but even better to drink. **DRINK** 2011–2019.

Price	$50
Region	Barossa
Value	♦♦♦♦♦
Auction	N/A
Score	96

Hugh Hamilton The Mongrel Sangiovese 2006

This wine is mostly sangiovese, though small amounts of merlot and tempranillo have also been blended into it. I'm a fan.

2006 RELEASE
OK, so this recommendation is a little out of left field. Purists would argue, rightly, that this wine tastes little like a true expression of sangiovese, in that it's not all that savoury. Indeed there is a distinct sweetness to both the smell and taste, and I'd even admit to there being suggestions of orange juice on the nose. That said, it tastes bloody excellent. It boasts flavour of sweet and sour cherries, dried tobacco and blood plums. Its tannins are ripe and chewy. In short, if you forget the word sangiovese and just drink it – it's a ripper. **DRINK** 2008–2010.

Price	$19
Region	McLaren Vale
Value	♦♦♦
Auction	★★★
Score	88

Innocent Bystander Sangiovese Merlot 2006

You know those folks who make running or swimming or tennis look easy – when it can so often look hard? That's what this wine is like; it makes red winemaking look easy.

2006 RELEASE
The mix of mulberry fruit flavour and almond-like nuttiness here is enormously enjoyable. I've found my 'sangio' of choice for this season. It's superbly structured, the tannins light and feathery and yet pervasive, reaching out to all corners of the mouth. There's the lightest touch of creamy oak. This wine is not a show pony; it's not supposed to knock you out with its sexiness. It's simply yum. **DRINK** 2008–2013.

Price	$19.95
Region	Yarra Valley
Value	♦♦♦♦♦
Auction	★★★
Score	92

Izway Mates GMS 2006

New-ish brand put together by Craig Isbel and Brian Conway. All the releases have been good so far. This wine is a blend of grenache, shiraz and mataro.

2006 RELEASE
Totally delicious. Don't really know how they can afford to offer this quality at this price. It tastes of luscious, bright, smoked blackberries and raspberries, edges of ground spice giving it an exotic glow. Beautifully bright, bold wine. **DRINK** 2008–2012.

Price	$19.95
Region	Barossa
Value	♦♦♦♦♦
Auction	★★★
Score	92

Jim Barry Three Little Pigs Shiraz Cabernet Malbec 2004

Always love seeing cabernet and malbec blended together, particularly out of the Clare Valley. The shiraz portion can't hurt either.

2004 RELEASE
Intensely regional red wine. Minty, mulberried, leathery – though the flavours are rather irrelevant. It's all about a solid, smooth, ripe hit of flavour at an affordable price – and at both it succeeds admirably. I served this to some friends one night and everyone wanted me to write down the name of it. **DRINK** 2008–2013.

Price	$19
Region	Clare Valley
Value	♦♦♦♦
Auction	N/A
Score	88

John Duval Wines Plexus Shiraz Grenache Mourvedre 2005

Shiraz–grenache blends are often considered of lower caste to pure shiraz in Australia, but it ain't necessarily so. These wines may be lighter, but they're often more complex, savoury and food-friendly. They can also cellar surprisingly well.

2005 RELEASE
Shortly after opening this I turned the computer off and headed to an early dinner – bottle locked in my claws. It demanded to be drunk. It's layered with flavour – spice, plums, kirsch, olives, licorice – and bursts through your mouth with precision control. The flavours are delivered in ultra smooth fashion – well, how much of the bottle do you think I actually shared? **DRINK** 2008–2015.

Price	$38
Region	McLaren Vale
Value	♦ ♦ ♦
Auction	★ ★ ★
Score	92

Kalleske Basket Press Clarry's Red 2006

Kalleske's full-blown Greenock Shiraz (Greenock is a sub-region of the Barossa Valley) is magnificent and worth hunting down. This Clarry's is a blend of grenache and shiraz, though it's the one I'm punting on. It's outstanding value.

2006 RELEASE
Everything you could ask of a well-priced, well-played, well-I've-already-finished-a-glass-of-it red wine. It tastes of raspberry, blackberry and coal, is flecked with spice, has a decent set of tannins on it and pushes nicely through the finish. Dark, juicy, fun. **DRINK** 2008–2012.

Price	$19
Region	Barossa
Value	♦ ♦ ♦ ♦ ♦
Auction	★ ★ ★
Score	90

Kurtz Boundary Row Grenache Shiraz Mataro 2005

This was aged in all-French oak barrels for eighteen months – and it's still being put out at only $15. Schtonking value really.

2005 RELEASE
There's a lot of sweet, spicy fruit here and I can tell you something for free, this is incredibly easy to drink (a fact learned the easy way). Jubey, raspberried, leathery fruit, wrapped in an exceptionally juicy package. It would be easy as pie to drink this regularly – with pie. Or pizza. Or spag bog. **DRINK** 2008–2011.

Price	$15
Region	Barossa
Value	♦ ♦ ♦ ♦ ♦
Auction	N/A
Score	87

Kurtz Siebenschlafer Seven Sleepers 2005

Gotta say I love the name 'siebenschlafer'. Made me want to head to a bistro and call out 'More siebenschlafer please!' in my best Schwarzenegger voice. The word, apparently, refers to weather conditions on 27 June each year, and how rain (or no rain) on that day will effect the seven weeks thereafter. The wine is a blend of six red varieties.

Price	$12.50
Region	Barossa
Value	♦♦♦♦♦
Auction	N/A
Score	86

2005 RELEASE
Very tasty. Very good value. A lovely mouthful of wine, soft and spicy and yet shot with sweet aniseed-like flavour. Looking for a wine you can pull out anytime, free of guilt? Grab a dozen of these. **DRINK** 2008–2010.

Langmeil Fifth Wave Grenache 2005

This is produced from fifty-four-year-old grenache vines grown on the Barossa hillside, in sandy soils. It's cropped very low – often at only one tonne to the acre.

Price	$30
Region	Barossa
Value	♦♦♦
Auction	★★
Score	91

2005 RELEASE
It's quite a gorgeous drink. It's fragrant, riddled with fresh leather-like flavour, raspberried and musky and doused with spice. There's quite a bit of alcohol warmth, but the softness and texture is exquisite. There are even some flavours of ripe tomatoes here – to add interest. My only query is that it seems to stumble over itself through the finish; time could easily correct this. **DRINK** 2009–2014.

Longhop Old Vine Grenache 2006

Domenic Torzi is the man behind this wine. He's a fierce believer in the Adelaide Plains as a place to grow grapes – despite the fact that most of them have been overtaken by residential housing. The odd vine survives ... hence, Longhop.

Price	$19
Region	Adelaide Plains
Value	♦♦♦♦
Auction	★★★
Score	87

2006 RELEASE
Big hit of alcohol, but wow, what a mound of flavour. You don't often see monsters like this at this kind of price. Flavours of aniseed, raspberry, sand, loam, cedar and brandy. Good structure too. Sorry, in a hurry. Gotta drink me some more of this. **DRINK** 2008–2011.

Luke Lambert Nebbiolo 2006

Nebbiolo is a holy grail of a lot of Australian winemakers. It's a tough, tannic, difficult variety, akin to a stronger, more challenging, more Italian version of pinot noir. Luke Lambert is one of a very small band to be making real progress with it.

2006 RELEASE
Juicy, tannic, muscular, floral – music to the ears of all nebbiolo lovers. This looks very, very promising. Nebbiolo is notorious for needing both years of cellaring and hours of decanting once it is opened, to taste its best. Only time will tell whether the promise of this wine results in anything substantial. Patience, patience. But I've placed a bet with my own money on this one. **DRINK** 2013–2020.

Price	$33
Region	Heathcote
Value	♦♦♦♦♦
Auction	★★★★
Score	94

McWilliam's Hanwood Estate Merlot 2006

I basically have a rule that I don't drink ******* merlot (to steal a quote from the movie *Sideways*), but I'd make an exception for this.

2006 RELEASE
High gluggability factor. There's a term for you. Sweet mulberried flavour with raspberries and plums. No great length of flavour, granted, but it chugs with pasta very smartly. **DRINK** 2008–2009.

Price	$10
Region	South Eastern Australia
Value	♦♦♦♦
Auction	N/A
Score	84

Maxwell Four Roads Shiraz Grenache Viognier 2005

This is mostly shiraz (eighty-eight per cent) with bits of grenache and (the white grape) viognier to help get the aromas jumping. It's worked pretty well.

2005 RELEASE
I dare say this would have been tough work without the softening influences of grenache and viognier. It smells good but the tannins are firm (too much so) and the warmth of the alcohol noticeable. What I do like though, is the intensity of the cherry-plummed fruit, here shot through with notes of spice and sand. The wine probably needs another eighteen months to provide more mellow drinking. **DRINK** 2009–2011.

Price	$19.95
Region	McLaren Vale
Value	♦♦♦
Auction	N/A
Score	86

Mayford Tempranillo 2006

Mayford is a new (and handsomely designed) label from Victoria's Alpine Valleys. It's a beautiful vineyard in a hidden valley, and judging by this release – it has quite some potential.

2006 RELEASE
It's got nice flavour but what got me really excited was the tannin structure. It's far above average. It tastes of nuts and cranberries, plums and chocolate, though in many ways it is not a fruit-driven wine; it has flavour, but structure is more its bag. I'd love to drink this in three or four years' time. **DRINK** 2009–2013.

Price	$27.50
Region	Alpine Valleys
Value	◆◆◆◆
Auction	N/A
Score	92

Noon Eclipse 2006

This is the wine the Noon family produces from their home vineyard in McLaren Vale. Grapes from these old vines are hand-picked and fermented in old open tubs, before being basket-pressed into oak barrels. It's careful, considered winemaking, threaded with character. Noon's cellar door is the best place to find this.

2006 RELEASE
The alcohol is high (15.5 per cent) but this doesn't have the distracting warmth that it has had in some years; the deliciousness of this is left to flow freely here. It tastes of dried plums, asphalt, blueberries and spice, the blend of grenache and shiraz working harmoniously, and well. The finish is glycerol and sweet, the tannin structure almost assertive – though not quite. **DRINK** 2011–2020.

Price	$25 (Cellar Door)
Region	McLaren Vale
Value	◆◆◆◆◆
Auction	★★★★
Score	93

Nugan Estate Frasca's Lane Vineyard Sangiovese Merlot 2005

Nugan Estate buys grapes from a range of different regions, in search of suitable region/variety matches. Both merlot and sangiovese work very well in the King Valley.

2005 RELEASE
This needs a couple of years to relax in the bottle but it will make for yummy drinking. It's fleshy, savoury, meaty and peppery, its heart of mulberried fruit flavour both sour and sweet at once. It's full of juicy acidity and carries quite a deal of tannin, but store it for eighteen months in a cool, dark place and it will really shine. **DRINK** 2009–2014.

Price	$22
Region	King Valley
Value	◆◆◆◆
Auction	N/A
Score	89

Penfolds Bin 138 Shiraz Grenache Mourvedre 2005

The artist formerly known as Penfolds Old Vine has, since the 1998 vintage, joined the Bin Range as secret agent 138. It's uniformly under-rated in the market place. It's aged in all old oak and generally has its alcohol level well under control. Shop around.

2005 RELEASE
Tar, roses, guns. Lots of cuddly blueberry and raspberry fruit flavours, flooding over burnt sugars, violets and aniseed. This will drink better the longer it's been in bottle – it's a sleeper. **DRINK** 2008–2015.

PREVIOUS
1994 Pretty, chewy, powerful. 2003–2010. 89 pts.
1995 Tar and caramel; fading. 2008–2013. 85 pts.
1996 Exotic, complex, tar and roses. 2008–2015. 93 pts.
1997 Tough tannins but a pretty wine. 2006–2014. 88 pts.
1998 Porty, tarry, charmless. 2007–2016. 87 pts.
1999 Rustic, developed, ready. 2008–2011. 89 pts.
2001 Sweet, toffeed, gamey. 2008–2013. 87 pts.
2002 Polished, fruity, smooth. 2008–2018. 91 pts.
2003 Tannic, perfumed, fruity. 2006–2012. 87 pts.
2004 Succulent, fleshy, delicious. 2012–2023. 93 pts.

Price	$33
Region	Barossa
Value	♦♦♦♦
Auction	★★★
Score	91

Penny's Hill Specialized Shiraz Cabernet Merlot 2005

Penny's Hill is a super producer, worth seeking out. It's a great spot for lunch too if you're ever in the area.

2005 RELEASE
Yes, it's a big, rich red wine (fifteen per cent alcohol) but there's a freshness to this wine that makes its big, warm flavour super-quaffable. Mind, the wine will cellar well too – what I'm saying is that the flavours of blackberry jam, dust and pipe-smoke come air-brushed and buffed clean. Great red-wine drinking. **DRINK** 2008–2016.

Price	$22
Region	McLaren Vale
Value	♦♦♦♦♦
Auction	★★★
Score	91

Pepperjack Shiraz Grenache Mourvedre 2006

Price	$25
Region	Barossa
Value	♦♦♦
Auction	N/A
Score	88

If there's one thing Barossa winemakers hate you harping on about it's alcohol levels; most fail to see a problem. Alcohol levels in Australian red wines though, have gone up significantly over the past twenty years in the chase for riper, sweeter flavours. These flavours are often glorious in themselves; the problem comes when the first thing you smell in a wine is alcohol, and the last thing you taste is alcohol.

2006 RELEASE
Soft, spicy, flavoursome and delicious. Lovely red wine, full of glycerol, dark cherry-like flavours mixed admirably with raisiny, chocolate sweetness. Its fifteen per cent alcohol shows very keenly on the finish though. Pity. Everything else about it is good. **DRINK** 2008–2012.

Peter Lehmann Clancy's 2005

Price	$17
Region	Barossa
Value	♦♦♦♦♦
Auction	N/A
Score	90

Lovely blend of shiraz, cabernet and merlot, each of the three varieties making a noticeable, and positive, contribution. You should be able to find a much better price than the full-tote price listed here.

2005 RELEASE
It tastes of mulberries, plums and chocolate but that's essentially irrelevant; the main thing is that it tastes good. It's got soft, velvety tannin and a chewy hit of medium-weight flavour. As a drink-now red I reckon it's spot-on. **DRINK** 2008–2012.

Picardy Merlot Cabernet Sauvignon Cabernet Franc 2005

Price	$20
Region	Pemberton
Value	♦♦♦♦♦
Auction	★★
Score	91

Picardy has been in operation since 1993 but in my books the reds are just now hitting their straps. The 2005 vintage releases are fantastic.

2005 RELEASE
A pure slice of stylish red wine for twenty bucks. I don't earn a great deal, but I figure that to be a pretty handsome deal. It tastes of graphite, dark chocolate, new French oak and mulberry. It even tastes of something intangible – something exotic – something like class. This is fifty-three per cent merlot, twenty-four per cent cabernet sauvignon and twenty-three per cent cabernet franc.
DRINK 2011–2016.

Pillar Box Red 2006

This wine is made by the prestigious Henry's Drive outfit in Padthaway. It's a blend of cabernet sauvignon, merlot and shiraz.

2006 RELEASE
I keep wanting to like this wine because the price is so good and the packaging looks cool, an all-red label with small white writing. But the wine itself just keeps falling short of expectations. There's enough flavour – it tastes like blackcurrant and menthol – but the aftertaste is bitter and the tannins are bunchy and clubby. The best thing about this wine is its price. **DRINK** 2008–2010.

Price	$13
Region	Padthaway
Value	♦♦♦
Auction	N/A
Score	83

Pizzini Il Barone 2004

It's the age of interesting red blends and this is one of the most interesting of all: it's made using shiraz, cabernet sauvignon, sangiovese and nebbiolo.

2004 RELEASE
The kind of wine that gets me excited – it's so full of complexity and intensity. Raisins, blackcurrants, lots of savoury earthiness and a lovely splash of licoricey tannins. A truly beautiful, lengthy, textural wine. **DRINK** 2010–2017.

Price	$43
Region	King Valley
Value	♦♦♦♦
Auction	N/A
Score	95

Pizzini Nebbiolo 2003

Pizzini's 1998 and 2002 nebbiolos were fantastic, and are worth hunting down. This 2003 is very close to their league.

2003 RELEASE
Give it a lot of air (I drank this over two nights, and it was much better on night two) and the daring complexity of this shines through. It smells floral and earthy and tastes it too, notes of tar and Fanta giving it an exotic edge. Muscular tannin, svelte texture, succulent acidity and excellent length. This baby's the goods. **DRINK** 2010–2017.

Price	$45
Region	King Valley
Value	♦♦♦♦
Auction	N/A
Score	93

Pizzini Sangiovese 2005 & 2006

The Pizzini family has won the battle as Australia's leading exponent of 'Italian varieties'. Truth is that all their wines (generally) are very good or better.

2005 RELEASE
This wine took a while to get going, but has really started to settle down and provide excellent drinking pleasure. It leans towards the savoury side of things, as a sangiovese should, but there's also a core of ripe, nutty, cherried fruit flavour and chewy tannins to match. I'll say one thing for certain: it drinks terrifically with pizza. It will taste even better – more mellow, and more complex – in a year or two. **DRINK** 2008–2012.

2006 RELEASE
The best Pizzini sangio yet. You could stack this up against a real-deal Italian Chianti Classico (the home of sangiovese) and it would fare really well, such is its structured, savoury, lip-smacking class. It tastes of dried cherries and almonds, and feels both juicy and attractively chewy. It's worth pulling out your best glassware for this. **DRINK** 2008–2013.

Price	$24
Region	King Valley
Value	♦♦♦♦♦
Auction	N/A
Score	93 (2006)
	91 (2005)

Poacher's Ridge Vineyard Louis Block Merlot 2005

The Great Southern region may not be synonymous with merlot, but it has produced the odd classic.

2005 RELEASE
What a beautiful wine. Classically structured and fruited, its classy mix of plummy, cedary, currany flavour a joy to both sit on and admire – and drink of heartily. A beautiful mix of medium-bodied elegance, and ripe satisfying flavour. Value through the roof. **DRINK** 2008–2013.

Price	$18
Region	Great Southern
Value	♦♦♦♦♦
Auction	N/A
Score	92

Port Phillip Estate Quartier Barbera 2006

There's not a lot of barbera grown on the Mornington Peninsula but this is great juice. The 2005 was better, but the 2006 is good.

2006 RELEASE
Lots of juicy, cherried, berried, cedary flavour, the ripe succulence of it really getting your saliva working. I kept wanting to dive back into it. It all gets a bit much, a bit loose – which is where the 2005 is better, and more controlled – but there's lots of fun with this wine, don't worry. **DRINK** 2008–2011.

Price	$25
Region	Mornington Peninsula
Value	♦♦♦
Auction	★★
Score	89

Primo Estate Il Briccone Sangiovese Shiraz 2005

There's a feeling in some Australian wine circles that blends of sweet-centred shiraz and savoury, naturally acidic sangiovese are the way of the future. Tastes good here.

2005 RELEASE
Beefy shiraz and savoury, nutty sangiovese – the marriage working pretty well. It's a good drink. The shiraz here comes complete with love-handles of porty, high alcohol flavour though, which works against the grain of the blend's intention. That said, there's a deal of full-bodied interest/flavour here. **DRINK** 2008–2012.

Price	$22
Region	McLaren Vale
Value	♦♦♦♦
Auction	★★
Score	89

Primo Estate Merlesco Merlot 2006

A few years ago some wondered why Australian wine producers didn't make 'unoaked' red wines, made to be served young and fresh. Suddenly a number of Australian producers make such a wine.

2006 RELEASE
It's fruity and tasty and slips down easy, and it's very hard to slug on it without wanting to jump on the phone and order a pizza. Indeed, I'm writing this review with the point of my nose because both of my hands are tied behind my back – hence no pizza for me. A good weeknight drink. **DRINK** 2008–2009.

Price	$18
Region	McLaren Vale
Value	♦♦♦♦
Auction	N/A
Score	86

Ravensworth Sangiovese 2006

If you're not familiar with the name Ravensworth it's worth sticking it in your memory bank. It's one of a growing number of exciting Canberra district wine producers, and this sangiovese and the winery's shiraz and viognier are all very good.

2006 RELEASE
I'm not sure that it tastes much like traditional sangiovese – it tastes like there's a dab of viognier been blended in – but I am sure that it's a lovely wine to drink. This is worth taking a punt on. It tastes of dried tobacco, licorice, blackberry and sweet stone fruits, and it ain't half hard to knock back a few glasses of it. **DRINK** 2008–2011.

Price	$18.50
Region	Canberra District
Value	♦♦♦♦♦
Auction	N/A
Score	88

Rolf Binder Christa Rolf Shiraz Grenache 2005

When it comes to Barossa Valley reds I often prefer the mid-priced wines to the super-duper premiums; the balance between flavour and drinkability is often better. Here's an excellent example.

2005 RELEASE
There's a deal of toasty, sawdusty oak here but it tastes damn gorgeous, particularly as it's matched to generous flavours of blueberry and raspberry. Just feel how velvety this wine is! Because of those red fruit flavours it's not the heaviest of wines, but the easy-going complexity, grapey tannins and smooth application of oak make for an extremely enjoyable wine. **DRINK** 2008–2013.

Price	$22
Region	Barossa
Value	♦♦♦♦
Auction	★★★
Score	91

Rosemount Show Reserve GSM 2004

Rosemount is now packaging its show reserve wines in the same bottle as its lower priced offerings, a move that harmonises the brand, but is bound to confuse customers. The quality of the wine here does not transcend the confusion. Grenache, shiraz, mourvedre blend.

2004 RELEASE
There are attractive raspberried, spicy, minerally smells and flavours, the palate soft-centred and the finish almost satisfying. Problem is that the wine lacks personality, depth and real value for money. **DRINK** 2008–2013.

Price	$24
Region	McLaren Vale
Value	♦♦
Auction	★★
Score	86

Rutherglen Estates Durif 2006

Durif has a blood-and-thunder reputation – the wines can be big and tough, and take a few years to soften. This wine is a more modern version, in the sense that it can easily be drunk young.

2006 RELEASE
I'd probably shop around to get this at the keenest price possible, but anything around or below the listed price is good buying in my books. It's a sizeable wine, leathery and pruney, blackberried and raspberried, the mix of rustic and bright-fruited flavours decidedly attractive. A very good red option. **DRINK** 2008–2011.

Price	$19.95
Region	Rutherglen
Value	♦♦♦♦♦
Auction	N/A
Score	89

Rymill MC² 2004

This is a blend of cabernet sauvignon, merlot and cabernet franc. It seems to have become leaner in style over the past few years.

2006 RELEASE
Needs a stint in the decanter to open up and build flesh. It's a leaner style of Coonawarra red, with dust and herbs and juicy raspberry flavours carrying the day. It's also quite tannic, making accompanying food an essential to the enjoyment of this wine; by itself it tastes too lean, but with roast meats it flourishes. **DRINK** 2008–2012.

Price	$17
Region	Coonawarra
Value	♦♦♦
Auction	★★
Score	86

S.C. Pannell Nebbiolo 2005

2005 RELEASE
Here's where things get interesting. Every time anyone releases a 'serious' nebbiolo in Australia a whole gang of folks prick up their ears, in the hope that they can get a decent nebbiolo fix. This one has excellent components: flavours of tar, jubes, aniseed and roses, though these flavours are muddied somewhat by an intrusive level of alcohol. Its tannins are tough to the point of pulling the wine up short, but I suspect that time will ease this problem – or I hope so. Well worth keeping an eye on. **DRINK** 2010–2015.

Price	$55
Region	Adelaide Hills
Value	♦♦♦
Auction	N/A
Score	89

S.C. Pannell Pronto Red 2006

2006 RELEASE
Easily my favourite drink in the S.C. Pannell range. It tastes of iodine, blackberry, minerals, earth and plums, a dry aniseed-like flavour lingering through the aftertaste. There's a lot of dry, gritty tannin too, which works with the style of it beautifully. This would be great with barbecued meats. It's a blend of grenache, shiraz and touriga. **DRINK** 2009–2013.

Price	$28
Region	McLaren Vale
Value	♦♦♦♦
Auction	N/A
Score	91

S.C. Pannell Shiraz Grenache 2005

Steve Pannell's not only a member of a famous winemaking family (his parents Bill and Sandra founded both Moss Wood and Picardy), but he's the former head winemaker at South Aussie wine giant Hardy's. He knows his stuff!

2005 RELEASE
Classy, textured, bold and brilliant. Blackberries, sweet sawdusty oak, minerally tannins and a tarry aftertaste. It all gets a bit warm and brandied on the finish, but it's a schmick wine. Drink it young, or as a ten-year-old. **DRINK** 2008–2015.

Price	$55
Region	McLaren Vale
Value	♦♦
Auction	N/A
Score	92

St Hallett GST 2007

Great name for a wine I reckon, especially for consumption around the end of the financial year. It's a juicy, bright, slightly lighter red wine – but the enjoyment factor is very high. Blend of the grenache, shiraz and touriga grape varieties.

2007 RELEASE
There's a lot of aniseed-like flavour here and quite a bit of chunky tannin too, the sweet grip of it made to work beautifully with Asian-styled meat dishes. Personally though, I can drink this kind of wine anytime, anywhere – I love the mix of rustic, earthy flavour and succulent fruit sweetness. **DRINK** 2008–2013.

Price	$21
Region	Barossa
Value	♦♦♦♦
Auction	★★
Score	90

Smithbrook Merlot 2005

Smithbrook has had a long investment in merlot and has produced some of Australia's best. This release doesn't quite make it for me.

2005 RELEASE
It smells and looks great – pencils, blackcurrant, smoke and eucalypt – and for the most part it tastes it too, though the flavours then finish bunchy and short. I'd be all over it if it was ten bucks cheaper – but not at this price. **DRINK** 2008–2013.

Price	$25
Region	Pemberton
Value	♦♦♦
Auction	★★
Score	86

Taylors Eighty Acres Cabernet Shiraz Merlot 2005

Taylors has been galloping along in recent years, which just goes to show that there's still a significant place for medium-sized family-owned wine companies in Australia. The original Clare Valley block the Taylors' bought, back in 1969, was eighty acres in size – hence the name of this new range.

2005 RELEASE
It might be a touch too tannic for the price (there's a good chance you'll find this wine on discount) but I'm a tannin freak, so that's fine by me. This tastes dusty, chocolaty, raisiny and dry through the finish, though it does not lack sweet ripe fruit through the mid-palate. Bonza at the price. I'm impressed. **DRINK** 2008–2010.

Price	$16.95
Region	Clare Valley
Value	♦♦♦♦♦
Auction	N/A
Score	90

The Pawn En Passant Tempranillo 2006

Tempranillo sounds like a good idea in Australia – it's quite happy in the heat – but I've taken some convincing on the quality of the wines produced. Wines like this are turning me around.

2006 RELEASE
Blatantly scrummy yummy but with a Euro edge. Its dry, chalky, juicy finish is a lovely foil to the ripe, cherried, plummy core promises of the wine's central flavours. Stylishly packaged too. **DRINK** 2008–2013.

Price	$25
Region	Adelaide Hills
Value	♦♦♦♦
Auction	N/A
Score	91

The Pawn The Gambit Sangiovese 2006

Tom Keelan works in Langhorne Creek by night, but has a secret love of some of the more unusual varieties being grown in the Adelaide Hills regions. He's a vineyard manager and knows good grapes when he sees them – as these wines amply show. An exciting new brand.

2006 RELEASE
Jolly good wine. Mega savoury. Full of flavours of bacon fat and sun-dried cherries, cedar and dried herbs. There's a hunk of chewy tannin here too, which works well with the style and shape of the wine. Lots of juicy acidity. **DRINK** 2008–2013.

Price	$25
Region	Adelaide Hills
Value	♦ ♦ ♦ ♦
Auction	N/A
Score	92

Tim Adams The Fergus 2005 & 2006

This is a blend of mostly grenache (sixty-three per cent) with cabernet sauvignon, cabernet franc, merlot and malbec also contributing.

2005 RELEASE
This shows its alcohol too keenly. It seems gluggy and loose in the mouth, its tarry, pruney fruit flavours inky and impressive, but lacking in charm. **DRINK** 2008–2009.

2006 RELEASE
Again there is alcohol warmth here but I like the flavours quite a lot. It's full of tar and raspberry, but the best thing is that there are highlights of lavender and violet. It tastes quite a bit like a decent Spanish red, which is a serious compliment. Excellent value here. **DRINK** 2008–2012.

Price	$19
Region	Clare Valley
Value	♦ ♦ (2005) ♦ ♦ ♦ ♦ (2006)
Auction	★ ★
Score	85 (2005) 91 (2006)

Torbreck Juveniles 2007

This is Torbreck's everyday quaffer – a blend of grenache, mataro and shiraz. It's the one with the reversed, blue and red label.

2007 RELEASE
It's always a perfumed, spicy wine, the fruit flavour of it awash with burnt sugar, aniseed and raspberries. This is a very good release, full of warm, medium-weight flavour, the alcohol sticking out a touch but the tannins gritty, chewy and well formed. Nice drink. **DRINK** 2008–2010.

Price	$24
Region	Barossa
Value	♦ ♦ ♦
Auction	★ ★
Score	87

Turkey Flat Grenache 2006

Over the past couple of years they've reduced the amount of new-oak flavour in their wines, a fact that has some rejoicing, and others scratching their heads.

2006 RELEASE
Can a wine be sexy? Probably not, but this comes close. It gives a big hit of sweet licorice-like flavour, and for the most part that's all you can taste – deliciously, and thankfully. Look harder though, and you find flavours of cedarwood, raisins and hay, with quite a bit of tannin chomping through the finish. It tastes a bit like an Italian Amarone, not that you need to be familiar with one of those to thoroughly enjoy drinking this wine.
DRINK 2008–2015.

Price	$22
Region	Barossa
Value	♦♦♦♦
Auction	N/A
Score	91

Vinea Marson Nebbiolo 2006

Winemaker Mario Marson has worked at cult wineries Mount Mary in the Yarra Valley and Jasper Hill at Heathcote – as well as at a number of Italian wineries. He knows his stuff, and the wines show it.

2006 RELEASE
It's a classically styled nebbiolo – so you have to like mouth-puckering tannin to enjoy this wine. It's orange-crimson in colour and to look at it there's nothing dense about it, but it sure does not lack power. Lots of acidity, lots of cherry and tobacco flavour, low oak input and the most gorgeous display of liquid roses – it's the only way I can put it. This is a super nebbiolo. Given time in the cellar it will shine. I'm getting on the phone now ... **DRINK** 2011–2018.

Price	$39
Region	Heathcote
Value	♦♦♦♦♦
Auction	N/A
Score	95

Vinea Marson Sangiovese 2006

Vinea Marson has impressed over the past couple of years, but these 2006 releases are a loud bugle call: a star has been born.

2006 RELEASE
This is on the money. Indeed, this is fabulous. It tastes like almonds, dark cherries, powdery chocolate, kirsch and tar, and its wealth of tight, focused, superfine tannin has all those interesting flavours tied to the spot. It's juicy, it's long, and its flavours are thick enough to satisfy, but savoury enough to stay true to the grape variety. This is a super sangiovese. **DRINK** 2011–2018.

Price	$33
Region	Heathcote
Value	♦♦♦♦♦
Auction	N/A
Score	95

Wirra Wirra Church Block 2006

This is a blend of cabernet sauvignon, shiraz and merlot. It routinely outperforms its price.

2006 RELEASE
Tip-top red wine drinking. The more I drank of it the more perfect it seemed – I think I'm going to have to nab me a case. It's perfectly balanced and perfectly powered, bangs of blackcurrant and blackberry-like flavour easing into fine, perfectly ripened tannins. Oh how I wish that all reds at this price were as good as this. **DRINK** 2008–2012.

Price	$23
Region	McLaren Vale
Value	●●●●●
Auction	★★★
Score	92

Wirra Wirra Scrubby Rise Red 2006

It's the lowest priced red in the Wirra Wirra range but the value is better than good. It's a blend of shiraz, cabernet sauvignon and petit verdot.

2006 RELEASE
The good thing about this is that it's full-bodied – I like medium-bodied wine but it's great to have a full monty option at an affordable price. It tastes of ground coffee, deli meats, blackberry jam and plums, and it keeps itself fresh and nice right to the bottom of the bottle. **DRINK** 2008–2011.

Price	$16.50
Region	McLaren Vale
Value	●●●●●
Auction	N/A
Score	88

Wrattonbully Vineyards Tempranillo 2006

Expect to see a lot more tempranillo on the market over the next ten years; there are too many influential folks too interested in it for it to fade away. This one is produced by the Hill Smith family – the family behind Yalumba. They reckon Wrattonbully is a great place to grow this variety.

2006 RELEASE
It's a sweet–sour wine with flavours of hazelnut and dark cherries, minerally tannins edging through the finish. The wine is fourteen per cent alcohol but it seems warmer than that, perhaps because the mid-palate lacks oomph, and there's a vague sense of 'saltiness' to the wine. The wine is reasonable quality, but I'm finding it difficult to get excited. **DRINK** 2008–2010.

Price	$18.50
Region	Wrattonbully
Value	●●●
Auction	N/A
Score	84

Yalumba Bush Vine Grenache 2005

Yalumba's reds in the $12 to $20 bracket have done terrifically in recent years – they're big on 'drinkability'.

2005 RELEASE
Immensely drinkable wine – you just want to keep hooking into it. Sweet raspberries, minerally tannins, a ring of bitterness and a good punch of flavour through the finish. It's not big and heavy, but it is lovely to drink.
DRINK 2008–2009.

Price	$17.95
Region	Barossa
Value	♦♦♦
Auction	N/A
Score	86

Yalumba Mourvedre Grenache Shiraz 2006

Some say mataro, some say mourvedre, they're both the same grape. It's a beautiful blender with shiraz.

2006 RELEASE
Fresh, vibrant quality. Super-juicy, super-fruity, blueberries and raspberries, fennel and fresh leather. Notes of smoky oak run through the wine's dry, lengthy tannin. The 2005 (90 points) was good but I like this release a lot more.
DRINK 2009–2015.

Price	$29.95
Region	Barossa
Value	♦♦♦♦
Auction	★★★
Score	93

Yalumba Tempranillo Grenache Viognier 2006

Yalumba have a lot of faith in the tempranillo grape. Stay tuned for a lot more evidence of it.

2006 RELEASE
Tempranillo will be a big thing in Aussie wine – because it's good, and also because it's good in a lot of different kinds of regions (everywhere from the Barossa to Canberra, McLaren Vale to Bendigo). It could be the new shiraz! It goes great with tomato-based dishes too. This wine has lots of rich, perfumed flavour, yet lots of juicy, refreshing acidity too. It's medium-bodied but meaty; tannic but juicy; substantially flavoured but spicy. Great food wine. Ninety per cent tempranillo. **DRINK** 2009–2015.

Price	$29.95
Region	Barossa
Value	♦♦♦
Auction	N/A
Score	93

WINE GLOSSARY

Aromatic
When you stick your nose in the glass you can smell lots and lots of fruity aroma. This is an aromatic wine – full of good, fresh, fruity smells. An aromatic wine is a smelly wine, in a good way.

Austere
The opposite of fruity and flavoursome. Lean and tight, maybe even a bit unripe. Can be both a positive and a negative – young riesling and young chardonnay are often described as austere in a positive sense. Most often though, it refers to wines that are a bit lacking in flavour.

Body
The body of the wine mostly relates to the intensity of flavour – if the wine is rich and seems to fill your mouth with flavour, then it's called 'full-bodied' (eg Barossa Valley shiraz). If it's rich but slightly lighter, and less intense, then it's called 'medium-bodied' (eg pinot noir or traditional Hunter Valley shiraz). And if it's lighter still, it's called 'light-bodied' (eg rosé or the lighter styles of gamay or pinot noir). A lot of people find full-bodied wines simply too intense (too much); while others find that only a full-bodied wine will satisfy.

Bottle-aged
When a wine is first made it is usually stored in a stainless steel tank or a wooden oak barrel. From here it is transferred into the wine bottle that it will be sold in. Bottled-aged refers to how much time the wine has spent in the bottle – for some wines, this improves them, making them seem softer and more interesting. The vast majority of wines though, are made better by a short period of bottle ageing but are made worse by extended bottle ageing.

Blockbuster
Refers to an intensely flavoured (usually high in alcohol) red wine. A wine that relies on intensity of flavour, rather than subtlety or finesse. Penfolds Grange was arguably Australia's first blockbuster red; Kaesler, Torbreck, Noon, Saltram and many Heathcote shiraz producers are among the leaders of the style today.

Chalky
Yes, some wines taste and feel (on your tongue) like chalk. This can occur in both white and red wines, and while it's more common in white wines, an increasing number of red wines (particularly from the cooler regions) have a chalky feel to their tannins (see Tannins). The taste and feel of chalk in a wine is usually regarded as a positive thing.

Chewy
Some wines grip your mouth in the same way that chewing the last remnants of a grape-skin can. It is all to do with the tannin in grapes (and hence in wine) – that drying, mouth-puckering substance also found in most tea. Lots of thick, fruity flavour plus lots of dry tannin usually makes for a 'chewy' wine.

Clean
A clean wine is one that seems to have kept all its pure, sunny, fruit flavour intact. It relates to a wine being sound and fresh and free of unpleasant bacterial infection or spoilage.

Closed
Some wines offer up all their charms from the moment you open them, while others take a long time to reveal their full personality, and need either to be decanted (see Decant) or aged for a further amount of time. A closed wine keeps its cards close to its chest, holding its best flavours back. The opposite to a closed wine is an open, or forward, wine.

Coarse
In some ways it's another word for 'sharp' or unpleasant, though the best way to describe it is that a coarse wine usually tastes a bit rough. Not a good quality wine.

Complex
The ultimate goal of all the best wines. A wine with various flavours, textures, experiences or delights is a complex wine. The opposite of a simple wine. Complex is always a positive way to describe a wine.

Corked
It has nothing to do with pieces of cork crumbling and floating in the wine – in which case, just strain it and the wine is fine. A corked wine has been attacked by a specific chemical compound (and it gets there via the cork), which deadens the flavour and can give the wine a dank, wet-hessian, chlorine-like smell. A badly corked wine tastes unpleasant, while a slightly corked wine tasted duller than it should. It has been estimated that nearly ten per cent of cork-sealed wines are to some degree corked. Bottles sealed with a screwcap cannot be corked (or it is extremely unlikely). There is no cure for a corked wine, and no telling whether a wine is corked or not without opening and smelling/tasting it. A corked wine is specific to each bottle – it says nothing of the quality of other like bottles.

Drinkability
You would hope that all wines are drinkable, but some wines are easier to drink than others. Drinkability, or how easy the wine is to drink, is an increasing phenomenon in wine; wines are becoming more and more drinkable, making cellaring less and less necessary.

Elegant
Some wines are brash and bold, others are stylish and elegant – Pamela Anderson versus Juliet Binoche, or Steven Segal versus Jude Law. An elegant wine relies on more subtle, even wry pleasures. Almost always nowadays, elegant in regards to wine is a positive description (though sometimes it is used facetiously to infer a lack of flavour or intensity).

Fat
Yes, fat, though this does not mean that the wine is fattening. A fat wine is a wine that feels wide and flabby in the mouth, like it's lost its verve and energy. Clumsy, floppy, and weighty, and lacking vigour. Of course, a blockbuster shiraz that is 'fat with flavour', and intentionally so, can be a big ball of fun.

Finish
How long the flavours of the wine linger in your mouth after you've swallowed. The length, in time, of the aftertaste. The best wines have a long, lingering, satisfying finish. The longer, the better – it's one of the key indicators of a quality wine.

Firm
Lots of tight, strong tannin, so that the wine's flavours seem bunched, almost to the point of being locked in.

Fleshy
It's a bit like saying that the wine tastes like alcoholic grape pulp, in that there's lots of fruit flavour and texture to wrap your tongue around. Almost always guarantees that the wine will be an enjoyable experience.

Floral
The wine smells like flowers, dried or fresh.

Green
This refers to the fact that the grapes that made the wine were picked when they weren't fully ripe. As a result, there are 'green', unripe flavours, most often bitter and unpleasant. Often heard in the phrase 'green and mean'.

Hot
In some wines the level of alcohol is so high that it seems to dominate the wine – by dominating the drinker's first and last impressions of it. A hot wine usually smells excessively alcoholic and leaves a burning sensation in the drinker's throat after the wine is swallowed. A negative description of a wine. A wine that is 'warm' with flavour also refers to its alcohol, but in a more positive sense.

Lifted
Another word for 'aromatic' (see Aromatic).

NV Release
Refers (most commonly) to sparkling wines that are a blend of various vintages (rather than being the result of a single year). Literally, non-vintage.

Nose
The way a wine smells. When you 'nose' a wine, you smell it.

Oaky
When a wine is matured in an oak barrel, an oak-barrel flavour becomes part of the wine – brand new barrels impart more flavour in the wine than used or old oak barrels (though most oak barrels are retired to the nursery once they are five or six years old). An 'oaky' wine is a wine that has an excessive amount of this oak flavour.

Palate
You can roughly break the taste of a wine into three parts. The entry – the first impression, as it hits your mouth. The palate – the bulk of the wine, as it passes through your mouth. And the finish – the way the wine leaves your mouth, and the aftertaste it leaves. The palate is what most people focus on, and quite rightly; it's the main player of all wine. 'Mid-palate' is a loose term to describe the middle of the wine's flavour, as it passes through your mouth.

Rich
It's got nothing to do with how much the wine cost, or how prestigious it is. A rich wine is an intensely flavoured wine.

Spicy
It doesn't mean that it'll burn your mouth, and it has nothing to do with curry. Spicy usually means that the wine smells or tastes a little like white or black pepper, though other spices are possible – these flavours usually come from the grape variety (shiraz/syrah grown in a cool climate is a classic for exhibiting smells and tastes of pepper spice) or sometimes from the

type of oak barrel used. When successful, 'spice' is seen to be the height of sophistication in a wine.

Stalky (Sappy)
When grapes are fermented into wine there are two essential ways to start the process – by removing the grapes from the stems that hold them, and then fermenting the grapes only; or by fermenting the grapes and their stems all in together. If the stems are included, it can add intriguing complexity to the wine, and a dose of extra, natural tannin too. The risk though, is that the stems will impart an excessive, and unpleasant, stalkiness in the wine – like a kind of green sap. A 'stalky' wine is a wine that has been made with the grape stems intact. It's a flavour that polarises opinion.

Tannins
A tannic wine is full of tannins. Most red wines have them, particularly varieties such as nebbiolo and cabernet sauvignon. Tannins create the dry, mouth-puckering effect, and come not from the juice of the wine grapes but from the grape skins (and sometimes from the oak the wine has been matured in). Tannins help a wine to age – they are a naturally occurring preservative. The way the tannins feel in the mouth is highly important to its ageing ability, quality, and sense of structure – they are the frame that hold the flavours of the wine in place.

Thin
A wine lacking in flavour. This is a negative trait.

Varietal
It is seen as important in wine that shiraz tastes like shiraz and chardonnay like chardonnay. Were a shiraz to taste like cabernet sauvignon, for instance, it would be deemed to be a bit odd, and a negative. 'Varietal character' is a sign of a grape being grown and made to taste true to itself.

WINERY CONTACT DETAILS

Adam's Rib
(03) 5728 2888
www.castagna.com.au

Alkoomi Wines
(08) 9855 2229
www.alkoomiwines.com.au

Allira (Elgo Estate) Wines
(03) 5798 5563
www.elgoestate.com.au

Amberley Estate
(08) 9750 1113
www.amberleyestate.com.au

Angove's
(08) 8580 3100 (office)
(08) 8580 3148 (Renmark cellar door)
(08) 8264 2366 (Tea Tree Gully cellar door)
www.angoves.com.au

Angus the Bull
(02) 8966 9020
www.angusthebull.com

Annie's Lane
(08) 8843 2204
www.annieslane.com.au

Anvers
(08) 8323 9603
www.anvers.com.au

Arrivo
(08) 8370 8072
No website.

Ashton Hills
(08) 8390 1243
No website.

Ata Rangi
64 6 306 9570 (New Zealand)
www.atarangi.co.nz

Au
(07) 5545 2000
www.aussievineyards.com.au

Baileys of Glenrowan
(03) 5766 2392
www.baileysofglenrowan.com.au

Balgownie Estate
(03) 5449 6222 (Bendigo cellar door)
(03) 9730 0700 (Yarra Valley cellar door)
www.balgownieestate.com.au

Balnaves
(08) 8737 2946
www.balnaves.com.au

Bannockburn
(03) 5281 1363
www.bannockburnvineyards.com

Barossa Old Vine Wine Company (Langmeil Winery)
(08) 8563 2595
www.langmeilwinery.com.au

Bass Phillip
(03) 5664 3341
No website.

Battely
(03) 5727 0505
www.battelywines.com.au

Battle of Bosworth
(08) 8556 2441
www.battleofbosworth.com.au

Bay of Fires
(03) 6382 7622
www.bayoffireswines.com.au

Bilancia
64 6 879 9711 (New Zealand)
www.bilancia.co.nz

Black Chook
(08) 8556 4460
www.woopwoop.com.au

Blackjack Wines
(03) 5474 2355
www.blackjackwines.net.au

Blue Poles
0408 096 411
www.bluepolesvineyard.com.au

Blue Pyrenees Estate
(03) 5465 1120
www.bluepyrenees.com.au

Bowen Estate
(08) 8737 2229
www.bowenestate.com.au

Brand's of Coonawarra
(08) 8736 3260
www.mcwilliams.com.au

Bremerton
(08) 8537 3093
www.bremerton.com.au

Bridgewater
(08) 8339 9222
www.bridgewatermill.com.au

Brini Estate
(08) 8383 0080
www.briniwines.com.au

Brokenwood
(02) 4998 7559
www.brokenwood.com.au

Brown Brothers
(03) 5720 5457
www.brownbrothers.com.au

Burge Family Winemakers
(08) 8524 4644
www.burgefamily.com.au

By Farr
(03) 5281 1979
www.byfarr.com.au

Campbell's Wines
(02) 6032 9458
www.campbellswines.com.au

Cape Mentelle
(08) 9757 0888
www.capementelle.com.au

Capel Vale
(08) 9727 1986
www.capelvale.com

Carlei Wines
(03) 5944 4599
www.carlei.com.au

Carrick
64 3 445 3480 (New Zealand)
www.carrick.co.nz

Cascabel
(08) 8557 4434
No website.

Castagna
(03) 5728 2888
www.castagna.com.au

Chapel Hill
(08) 8323 8429
www.chapelhillwine.com.au

Charles Cimicky Wines
(08) 8524 4025
Email: charlescimickywines@bigpond.com

Charles Melton Wines
(08) 8563 3606
www.charlesmeltonwines.com.au

Chatto
(02) 4998 7293
www.chattowines.com.au

Chrismont
(03) 5729 8220
www.chrismont.com.au

Clonakilla
(02) 6227 5877
www.clonakilla.com.au

Clos Pierre
No phone.
www.clospierre.com

Coldstream Hills
(03) 5964 9410
www.coldstreamhills.com.au

Cookoothama (Nugan Estate)
(02) 9362 9993
www.nuganestate.com.au

Coriole
(08) 8323 8305
www.coriole.com

Crackerjack Wines
(03) 9682 5000
www.crackerjackwines.com.au

Craggy Range
64 06 873 7126 (New Zealand)
www.craggyrange.com

Craiglee
(03) 9744 4489
www.craiglee.com.au

Cullen Wines
(08) 9755 5277
www.cullenwines.com.au

Curly Flat
(03) 5429 1956
www.curlyflat.com

Dalwhinnie
(03) 5467 2388
www.dalwhinnie.com.au

D'Arenberg
(08) 8329 4888
www.darenberg.com.au

David Hook Wines
(02) 4998 7121
www.davidhookwines.com.au

De Bortoli
(03) 5965 2271
www.debortoli.com.au

De Iuliis
(02) 4993 8000
www.dewine.com.au

Devil's Lair
(08) 9757 7573
www.devils-lair.com

Donny Goodmac
Email: thepig@donnygoodmac.com.au
www.donnygoodmac.com.au

Dowie Doole
(08) 8323 7428
www.dowiedoole.com

Dutschke Wines
(08) 8524 5485
www.dutschkewines.com

Edwards
(08) 9755 5999
www.edwardsvineyard.com.au

Elderton Wines
(08) 8568 7878
www.eldertonwines.com.au

Eldridge Estate
(03) 5989 2644
www.eldridge-estate.com.au

(Domaine) Epis
(03) 5427 1204
No website.

Escarpment
64 6 306 8305 (New Zealand)
www.escarpment.co.nz

Euroa Creeks (Eldridge Estate)
(03) 5989 2644
www.eldridge-estate.com.au

Evans and Tate
(08) 9755 6244
www.evansandtate.com.au

Fairbank (Sutton Grange winery)
(03) 5474 8285
www.suttongrangewines.com

Fifth Leg
(08) 9757 7573
www.fifthleg.com.au

Fox Creek
(08) 8556 4779
www.foxcreekwines.com

Fox Gordon
(08) 8361 8136
www.foxgordon.com.au

Frogmore Creek
(03) 6248 5844
www.hoodwines.com.au

Galli Estate
(03) 9747 1444
www.galliestate.com.au

Gapsted
(03) 5751 1383
www.gapstedwines.com.au

Gemtree
(08) 8323 7428
www.gemtreevineyards.com.au

Geoff Merrill
(08) 8381 6877
www.geoffmerrillwines.com

Giaconda
(03) 5727 0246
www.giaconda.com.au

Giant Steps
(03) 5962 6111
www.giant-steps.com.au

Gilligan
0412 423 131
www.gilligan.com.au

Glaetzer
(08) 8563 0288
www.glaetzer.com

Gramp's (Orlando Wines)
(08) 8521 3000
www.orlandowines.com.au

Grant Burge
(08) 8563 7471
www.grantburgewines.com.au

Grosset
(08) 8849 2175
www.grosset.com.au

Grove Estate
(02) 6382 6999
www.groveestate.com.au

Hardy's
(08) 8392 2222
www.hardywines.com.au

Heartland
(02) 4938 6272
www.heartlandvineyard.com.au

Hewitson
(08) 8443 6466
www.hewitson.com.au

Higher Plane
(08) 9755 9000
www.higherplanewines.com.au

Hillcrest Vineyard
(03) 5964 6689
www.hillcrestvineyard.com.au

Hoddles Creek Estate
(03) 5967 4692
www.hoddlescreekestate.com.au

Houghton
(08) 9274 9540
www.houghton-wines.com.au

Howard Park
(08) 9423 1200 (office)
(08) 9756 5200 (Margaret River cellar door)
(08) 9848 2345 (Denmark cellar door)
www.howardparkwines.com.au

Hugh Hamilton Wines
(08) 8323 8689
www.hughhamiltonwines.com.au

Ingoldby (Foster's)
1300 651 650
(08) 8383 0005
www.ingoldby.com.au

Innocent Bystander
(03) 5962 6111
www.innocentbystander.com.au

Izway
(08) 8367 0002
No website.

J & J Wines
(08) 8323 9888
www.jjwines.com.au

Jacob's Creek
(08) 8521 3000
www.jacobscreek.com.au

Jamieson's Run
(08) 8737 3250
www.jamiesonsrun.com.au

Jim Barry
(08) 8842 2261
www.jimbarry.com

John Duval Wines
(08) 8563 2591
www.johnduvalwines.com

Kaesler Wines
(08) 8562 4488
www.kaesler.com.au

Kalleske
0403 811 433
www.kalleske.com

Katnook Estate
(08) 8737 2394
www.katnookestate.com.au

Kilikanoon
(08) 8843 4206
www.kilikanoon.com.au

Kooyong
(03) 5989 2708
www.kooyong.com

Kurtz
(08) 8564 3217
www.kurtzfamilyvineyards.com.au

Lake Breeze
(08) 8537 3017
www.lakebreeze.com.au

Langmeil
(08) 8563 2595
www.langmeilwinery.com.au

Lazy Ballerina
0400 656 350
www.lazyballerina.com

Leaping Lizard (Ferngrove)
(08) 9855 2378
www.ferngrove.com.au

Leasingham
(08) 8842 2785
www.leasingham-wines.com.au

Leconfield
(08) 8323 8830
(office and McLaren Vale cellar door)
www.leconfieldwines.com.au

Lenton Brae
(08) 9755 6255
www.lentonbrae.com

Lillydale Estate
(03) 5964 2016
www.mcwilliams.com.au

Lindemans
(03) 9633 2000
www.lindemans.com.au

Longhop
0407 605 601
www.oldplains.com

Longview
(08) 8388 9694
www.longviewvineyard.com.au

Luke Lambert
(03) 9730 2944
www.lukelambertwines.com.au

McKellar Ridge
(02) 6258 1556
www.mckellarridgewines.com.au

McWilliam's Hanwood
(02) 6963 0001
www.mcwilliams.com.au

Mad Fish
(08) 9423 1200
www.madfishwines.com.au

Maglieri of McLaren Vale (Foster's)
(08) 8383 0177
www.maglieri.com.au

Matua Valley
64 9 411 8301 (New Zealand office)
64 3 572 8642 (Marlborough cellar door)
64 9 411 8301 (Auckland cellar door)
www.matua.co.nz

Maude Wines
64 3 443 2959 (New Zealand)
www.maudewines.com

Maxwell
(08) 8323 8200
www.maxwellwines.com.au

Majella
(08) 8736 3055
www.majellawines.com.au

Marius
(08) 8556 2421
www.mariuswines.com.au

Mayer
(03) 5967 3779
No website.

Mayford Wines
(03) 5756 2528
www.mayfordwines.com

Meerea Park
0417 693 310
www.meereapark.com.au

Metala
(08) 8564 3355
www.saltramwines.com.au

Mike Press Wines
(08) 8389 5546
www.topdropwines.com.au

Mildara
(03) 5025 2303
www.fosters.com.au

Mitchelton
(03) 5736 2221
www.mitchelton.com.au

Mitolo
(08) 8282 9012
www.mitolowines.com.au

Mollydooker
(08) 8323 7708
www.mollydookerwines.com

Moondah Brook
(08) 9274 9540
www.houghton-wines.com.au

Moss Wood
(08) 9755 6266
www.mosswood.com.au

Mount Langi Ghiran
(03) 5354 3207
www.langi.com.au

Mount Majura
(02) 6262 3070
www.mountmajura.com.au

Mount Pleasant
(02) 4998 7505
www.mountpleasantwines.com.au

Mountadam
(08) 8564 1900
www.mountadam.com.au

Mr Riggs
(08) 8556 4460
www.mrriggs.com.au

Ngeringa
(08) 8398 2867
www.ngeringa.com

Noon
(08) 8323 8290
www.noonwinery.com.au

Nugan Estate
(02) 6962 1822
www.nuganestate.com.au

Oliver's Taranga
(08) 8323 8498
www.oliverstaranga.com

Orlando
(08) 8521 3000
www.orlandowines.com.au

Over the Shoulder
(03) 9739 1920
www.oakridgeestate.com.au

Paringa Estate
(03) 5989 2669
www.paringaestate.com.au

Parker Coonawarra Estate
(08) 8737 3525
www.parkercoonawarraestate.com.au

Paxton Vineyards
(08) 8323 8645
www.paxtonvineyards.com

Penfolds
(08) 8301 5569
www.penfolds.com.au

Penley
(08) 8736 3211
www.penley.com.au

Penny's Hill
(08) 8556 4460
www.pennyshill.com.au

Pepperjack
(03) 8564 3355
www.saltramwines.com.au

Petaluma
(08) 8339 9222
www.petaluma.com.au

Peter Lehmann Wines
(08) 8563 2100
www.peterlehmannwines.com

Pfeiffer
(02) 6033 2805
www.pfeifferwinesrutherglen.com.au

PHI
(03) 5433 5188
www.phiwines.com

Philip Shaw
(02) 6365 2334
www.philipshaw.com.au

Picardy
(08) 9776 0036
www.picardy.com.au

Pillar Box
(08) 8765 5251
www.henrysdrive.com

Pizzini
(03) 5729 8278
www.pizzini.com.au

Plantagenet
(08) 9851 3131
www.plantagenetwines.com

Poacher's Ridge
(08) 9387 5003
www.prv.com.au

Polleters
(03) 9569 5030
www.polleters.com

Port Phillip Estate
(03) 5989 2708
www.portphillip.net

Primo Estate
(08) 8323 6800
www.primoestate.com.au

Punch
(03) 9710 1155
www.punched.com.au

Punt Road
(03) 9739 0666
www.puntroadwines.com.au

Pyrette
(03) 5428 2564
No website.

Ravensworth
(02) 6226 8368
www.ravensworthwines.com.au

Red Knot
(08) 8323 9919
www.shingleback.com.au

Reilly's
(08) 8834 9013
www.reillyswines.com

Reynella
(08) 8392 2300
www.hardyswines.com.au

Richard Hamilton
(08) 8323 8830
www.leconfieldwines.com

Ring Bolt
(08) 8561 3200
www.ringbolt.com

Riposte
(08) 8389 8149
No website.

Rockbare
(08) 8389 5192
www.rockbare.com.au

Rockford
(08) 8563 2720
No website.

Rolf Binder
(08) 8562 3300
www.rolfbinder.com

Rosemount
(03) 8626 3300
(02) 4998 6670
(Lower Hunter Valley cellar door)
www.rosemountestates.com

Rutherglen Estates
(02) 6032 7999
www.rutherglenestates.com.au

S. C. Pannell
(08) 8299 9256
No website.

St Hallett
(08) 8563 7000
www.sthallett.com.au

St Hubert
(03) 9739 1118
www.sthuberts.com.au

Saltram
(08) 8564 3355
www.saltramwines.com.au

Savaterre
(03) 5727 0551
www.savaterre.com

Scarpantoni Wines
(08) 8383 0186
www.scarpantoni-wines.com.au

Scotchmans Hill
(03) 5251 3176
www.scotchmanshill.com.au

Seppelt
(03) 5361 2239
www.seppelt.com

Setanta
(08) 8380 5516
www.setantawines.com.au

Shadowfax
(03) 9731 4420
www.shadowfax.com.au

Shaw and Smith
(08) 8398 0500
www.shawandsmith.com

Skillogalee
(08) 8843 4311
www.skillogalee.com

Squitchy Lane
(03) 5964 9114
www.squitchylane.com.au

Stefano Lubiana
(03) 6263 7457
www.slw.com.au

Smithbrook
(08) 9772 3557
www.smithbrook.com.au

Stanton and Killeen
(02) 6032 9457
www.stantonandkilleenwines.com.au

Starvedog Lane
(08) 8392 2222
www.starvedoglane.com.au

Stella Bella
(08) 9757 6377
www.stellabella.com.au

Stonier
(03) 5989 8300
www.stoniers.com.au

Suckfizzle
(08) 9757 6377
www.stellabella.com.au

Tahbilk
(03) 5794 2555
www.tahbilk.com.au

Talinga Park (Nugan Estate)
(02) 6962 1822
www.nuganestate.com.au

Taltarni
(03) 5459 7900
www.taltarni.com.au

Tapanappa Wines
0418 818 223
www.tapanappawines.com.au

Tarrington
(03) 5572 4509
www.tarrington.com.au

Taylors
(08) 8849 1111
www.taylorswines.com.au

Temple Bruer
(08) 8431 0911
www.templebruer.com.au

Ten Minutes by Tractor
(03) 5989 6080
www.tenminutesbytractor.com.au

T'Gallant
(03) 5989 6565
www.tgallant.com.au

The Pawn
0438 373 247
www.thepawn.com.au

The Story Wines
No phone.
www.thestorywines.com.au

(Andrew) Thomas Wines
(02) 6574 7371
www.thomaswines.com.au

Tim Adams
(08) 8842 2429
www.timadamswines.com.au

Tollana
(03) 8626 3300
www.fosters.com.au

Toolangi
(03) 9822 9488
www.toolangi.com

Torbreck
(08) 8562 4155
www.torbreck.com

Torzi Matthews
0412 323 486
www.edenvalleyshiraz.com.au

Turkey Flat
(08) 8563 2851
www.turkeyflat.com.au

Tyrrell's
(02) 4993 7000
www.tyrrells.com.au

Ulithorne
0419 040 670
www.ulithorne.com.au

Valhalla Wines
(02) 6033 1438
www.valhallawines.com.au

Vasse Felix
(08) 9756 5055
www.vassefelix.com.au

Victorian Alps Winery
(03) 5751 1383
www.victorianalpswinery.com

Vinea Marson
0417 035 673
www.vineamarson.com

Voyager Estate
(08) 9385 3133
www.voyagerestate.com.au

Wanderer Wines
Email: andrew@wandererwines.com
www.wandererwines.com

Wanted Man
(03) 9654 4664
www.wantedman.com.au

Warburn Estate
(02) 6963 8325
www.warburnestate.com.au

Warrabilla Wines
(02) 6035 7242
www.warrabillawines.com.au

Water Wheel
(03) 5437 3060
www.waterwheelwine.com

West Cape Howe
(08) 9848 2959
www.westcapehowewines.com.au

William Downie
(03) 5634 2216
www.williamdownie.com.au

Wine by Brad
0409 572 957
www.winebybrad.com.au

Wirra Wirra
(08) 8323 8414
www.wirrawirra.com

Wolf Blass
(03) 8568 7311
www.wolfblass.com.au

Woodlands
(08) 9755 6226
www.woodlandswines.com

Woodstock
(08) 8383 0156
www.woodstockwine.com.au

Woop Woop
(08) 8556 4460
www.woopwoop.com.au

Wynns
(08) 8736 2225
www.wynns.com.au

Yalumba
(08) 8561 3200
www.yalumba.com

Yering Station
(03) 9730 0100
www.yering.com

Zema
(08) 8736 3219
www.zema.com.au

WINE INDEX

A

Adam's Rib The Red 2005 **211**
Adam's Rib The Red 2006 **127**
Alkoomi Cabernet Sauvignon 2005 **153**
Alkoomi Jarrah Shiraz 2003 **21**
Alkoomi Shiraz Viognier 2005 **21**
Allira Shiraz 2006 **21**
Amberley Shiraz Viognier 2005 **22**
Andrew Thomas Kiss Shiraz 2006 **22**
Andrew Thomas Sweetwater Shiraz 2006 **22**
Angove's Long Row Cabernet Sauvignon 2006 **153**
Angove's Long Row Shiraz 2006 **23**
Angus The Bull Cabernet Sauvignon 2006 **153**
Annie's Lane Cabernet Merlot 2005 **154**
Annie's Lane Shiraz 2006 **23**
Anvers Razorback Road Shiraz Cabernet Sauvignon 2005 **211**
Anvers Shiraz 2005 **23**
Arrivo Nebbiolo 2005 **211**
Arrivo Rosato di Nebbiolo 2007 **212**
Ashton Hills Estate Pinot Noir 2006 **127**
Ashton Hills Reserve Pinot Noir 2006 **128**
Ata Rangi Crimson Pinot Noir 2006 **128**
Ata Rangi Pinot Noir 2006 **129**
Au Cabernet Sauvignon 2004 **154**

B

Baileys of Glenrowan 1904 Block Shiraz 2004 **24**
Baileys of Glenrowan 1920s Block Shiraz 2006 **24**
Baileys of Glenrowan Cabernet Sauvignon 2006 **154**
Baileys of Glenrowan Shiraz 2006 **24**
Balgownie White Label Cabernet Sauvignon 2005 **155**
Balgownie White Label Shiraz 2005 **25**
Balnaves of Coonawarra Cabernet Merlot 2005 **155**
Balnaves of Coonawarra Cabernet Sauvignon 2005 **156**
Balnaves of Coonawarra Reserve The Tally Cabernet Sauvignon 2005 **156**
Balnaves of Coonawarra Shiraz 2005 **25**
Balnaves of Coonawarra The Blend 2005 **157**
Bannockburn Pinot Noir 2005 **129**
Bannockburn Range Shiraz 2005 **26**
Bannockburn Serre Pinot Noir 2005 **130**
Banrock Station Reserve Sparkling Shiraz NV **26**
Barossa Old Vine Company Shiraz 2003 & 2004 **26**
Bass Phillip 'The 21' Pinot Noir 2006 **130**
Battely Syrah 2005 **27**
Battle of Bosworth Cabernet Sauvignon 2005 **157**
Battle of Bosworth Shiraz 2005 **27**
Bay of Fires Tigress Pinot Noir 2006 **131**
Bilancia La Collina Syrah 2005 **27**
Black Chook Shiraz Viognier 2006 **28**
Black Chook Sparkling Shiraz NV **28**
Blackjack Block 6 Shiraz 2005 **28**
Blackjack Major's Line Shiraz 2005 **29**
Blackjack Shiraz 2005 **29**
Bleasdale Sparkling Shiraz NV **29**
Blue Poles Merlot Cabernet Franc 2005 **212**

Blue Pyrenees Estate Richardson
   Cabernet Sauvignon 2004 **157**
Bowen Estate Cabernet Sauvignon
   2005 **158**
Bowen Estate Shiraz 2005 **30**
Brands of Coonawarra Laira Cabernet
   Sauvignon 2004 **158**
Bremerton Old Adam Shiraz 2004 **30**
Bremerton Selkirk Shiraz 2005 **31**
Bridgewater Mill Shiraz 2005 **31**
Brini Blewitt Springs Shiraz 2004 **31**
Brokenwood Graveyard Shiraz 2005 **32**
Brokenwood Shiraz 2005 **32**
Brown Brothers Barbera 2005 **213**
Brown Brothers Dolcetto
   Syrah 2007 **213**
Brown Brothers Everton Red 2006 **213**
Brown Brothers Zibibbo Rosa NV **214**
Burge Family Winemakers Draycott
   Shiraz 2005 **33**
Burge Family Winemakers Garnacha
   Dry Grown Grenache 2005 **214**
Burge Family Winemakers Olive Hill
   Shiraz Mourvedre Grenache 2005 **215**
By Farr Pinot Noir 2005 **131**
By Farr Sangreal Pinot Noir 2005 **131**
By Farr Shiraz 2005 **33**

C

Campbells Bobbie Burns Shiraz
   2004 & 2005 **34**
Cape Mentelle Cabernet
   Sauvignon 2003 **159**
Cape Mentelle Marmaduke 2005 **34**
Cape Mentelle Shiraz 2005 **35**
Cape Mentelle Zinfandel 2005 **215**
Capel Vale Debut Cabernet Merlot
   2005 **159**
Carlei Green Vineyards Cabernet
   Sauvignon 2004 **160**
Carlei Green Vineyards Shiraz 2004 **35**
Carrick Pinot Noir 2006 **132**
Cascabel Tempranillo 2007 **215**

Castagna Genesis Sparkling
   Syrah 2005 **36**
Castagna Genesis Syrah 2005 **36**
Castagna Un Segreto Sangiovese
   Syrah 2005 **216**
Chapel Hill Cabernet Sauvignon
   2004 & 2005 **160**
Chapel Hill Il Vescovo Tempranillo
   2006 **216**
Chapel Hill Sangiovese 2005 **216**
Chapel Hill Shiraz 2005 **37**
Charles Cimicky Trumps Shiraz 2005 **37**
Charles Melton Cabernet
   Sauvignon 2005 **160**
Charles Melton Nine Popes 2005 **217**
Charles Melton Shiraz 2005 **38**
Chatto Pinot Noir 2005 **132**
Chatto Shiraz 2005 **38**
Chrismont Cabernet
   Sauvignon 2004 **161**
Clonakilla Ballinderry Cabernet
   Sauvignon Merlot Cabernet
   Franc 2005 **161**
Clonakilla Shiraz 2006 **39**
Clonakilla Shiraz Viognier
   2006 & 2007 **39**
Clos Pierre Reserve Pinot Noir
   2005 **132**
Clos Pierre Reserve Shiraz 2005 **40**
Coldstream Hills Amphitheatre
   Pinot Noir 2006 **133**
Coldstream Hills Cabernet
   Sauvignon 2005 **161**
Coldstream Hills Pinot Noir 2007 **133**
Coldstream Hills Reserve Cabernet
   Sauvignon 2005 **162**
Coldstream Hills Reserve
   Pinot Noir 2006 **133**
Cookoothama Darlington Point
   Shiraz 2005 **40**
Coriole Nebbiolo Rose 2007 **217**
Coriole Sangiovese 2006 **217**
Crackerjack Shiraz Viognier 2005 **40**
Craggy Range Gimblett Gravels Le Sol
   Syrah 2005 **41**

Craggy Range Sophia Merlot Cabernet Franc 2005 **218**
Craiglee Shiraz 2005 **41**
Cullen Diana Madeline Cabernet Merlot 2005 **162**
Cullen Mangan 2006 **218**
Curly Flat Pinot Noir 2004 & 2005 **134**
Curly Flat Williams Crossing Pinot Noir 2005 **134**

D

Dalwhinnie Moonambel Cabernet Sauvignon 2005 **163**
Dalwhinnie Moonambel Pinot Noir 2005 **135**
Dalwhinnie Moonambel Shiraz 2005 **42**
Dalwhinnie South West Rocks Shiraz 2005 **42**
D'Arenberg Dead Arm Shiraz 2005 **43**
D'Arenberg Derelict Vineyard Grenache 2005 & 2006 **219**
D'Arenberg Laughing Magpie Shiraz Viognier 2006 **43**
D'Arenberg The Ironstone Pressings Grenache Shiraz Mourvedre 2005 **220**
D'Arenberg The Peppermint Paddock Sparkling Red Chambourcin NV **219**
D'Arenberg Twentyeight Road Mourvedre 2005 **220**
D'Arenberg Vintage Fortified Shiraz 2006 **44**
David Hook The Gorge Shiraz 2006 **44**
De Bortoli Estate Grown Pinot Noir 2006 **135**
De Bortoli Estate Grown Shiraz Viognier 2006 **44**
De Bortoli Gulf Station Pinot Noir 2006 **135**
De Bortoli Gulf Station Shiraz Viognier 2006 **45**
De Bortoli Merlot Sangiovese 2006 **220**
De Bortoli Windy Peak Pinot Noir 2007 **136**

De Iuliis Charlie Shiraz 2006 **45**
De Iuliis Limited Release Shiraz 2006 **45**
Devil's Lair Cabernet Sauvignon Merlot 2005 **163**
Donny Goodmac Shiraz 2006 **46**
Dowie Doole Shiraz 2005 **46**
Dutschke GHR Four Vineyards Shiraz 2005 **46**
Dutschke Sami Cabernet Sauvignon 2005 **164**

E

Edwards Cabernet Sauvignon 2005 **164**
Elderton 'Friends' Cabernet Sauvignon 2005 **164**
Elderton 'Friends' Shiraz 2005 **47**
Elderton Estate Shiraz 2005 **47**
Eldridge Estate Clonal Blend Pinot Noir 2006 **136**
Eldridge Estate Gamay 2006 **221**
Eldridge Pinot Noir 2006 **136**
Epis Pinot Noir 2006 **137**
Epis The Williams Vineyard Cabernet Merlot 2006 **165**
Escarpment Pinot Noir 2006 **137**
Euroa Creeks Shiraz 2006 **47**
Evans and Tate Shiraz 2004 **48**

F

Fairbank Syrah 2004 **48**
Fifth Leg 2006 **221**
Fox Creek Red Baron Shiraz 2006 **48**
Fox Creek Reserve Cabernet Sauvignon 2005 **165**
Fox Creek Reserve Shiraz 2005 **49**
Fox Creek Shadow's Run Shiraz Cabernet Sauvignon 2006 **49**
Fox Gordon By George Cabernet Tempranillo 2005 **221**
Frogmore Creek Reserve Pinot Noir 2005 **138**

G

Galli Estate Tempranillo Grenache Mourvedre 2006 **222**
Gapsted Cabernet Sauvignon 2005 **165**
Gemtree Tadpole Shiraz Cabernet Sauvignon 2006 **222**
Gemtree Uncut Shiraz 2006 **50**
Geoff Merrill Cabernet Sauvignon 2004 **166**
Geoff Merrill Shiraz 2004 **50**
Giaconda Warner's Vineyard Shiraz 2005 **51**
Giant Steps Harry's Monster 2005 **166**
Giant Steps Sexton Pinot Noir 2006 **138**
Gilligan Shiraz Grenache Mourvedre 2006 **51**
Glaetzer Anaperenna Cabernet Sauvignon Shiraz 2006 **167**
Glaetzer Bishop Shiraz 2006 **52**
Glaetzer Wallace Shiraz Grenache 2006 **222**
Gralyn Unoaked Cabernet Sauvignon 2007 **167**
Gramp's Grenache 2006 **223**
Gramp's Shiraz 2004 & 2005 **52**
Grant Burge Shadrach Cabernet Sauvignon 2004 **167**
Grosset Gaia Cabernet Sauvignon 2004 & 2005 **168**
Grosset Pinot Noir 2006 **138**
Grove Estate Cellar Block Reserve Shiraz 2006 **53**
Grove Estate The Partners Cabernet Sauvignon 2006 **168**

Hardy's Tintara Tempranillo 2004 **224**
Heartland Cabernet Sauvignon 2006 **169**
Heartland Director's Cut Shiraz 2006 **54**
Heartland Shiraz 2006 **54**
Hewitson Baby Bush Mourvedre 2006 **224**
Hewitson Miss Harry 2006 **224**
Hewitson Ned and Henry's Shiraz 2006 **55**
Hewitson Old Garden Mourvedre 2006 **225**
Higher Plane Cabernet Sauvignon 2004 **170**
Higher Plane South by Southwest Cabernet Merlot 2004 **170**
Hillcrest Reserve Pinot Noir 2006 **139**
Hoddles Creek Estate Cabernet Sauvignon 2006 **171**
Hoddles Creek Pinot Noir 2006 **139**
Houghton Gladstones Shiraz 2003 **55**
Houghton Jack Mann Cabernet Sauvignon 2001 **171**
Houghton Shiraz 2003 **56**
Howard Park Cabernet Sauvignon Merlot 2004 **172**
Howard Park Leston Cabernet Sauvignon 2005 **172**
Howard Park Leston Shiraz 2005 **56**
Howard Park Mad Fish Premium Red 2005 **173**
Howard Park Scotsdale Shiraz 2005 **57**
Hugh Hamilton The Mongrel Sangiovese 2006 **225**

H

Hardy's Oomoo Grenache Shiraz Mourvedre 2006 **223**
Hardy's Oomoo Shiraz 2006 **53**
Hardy's Tintara Cabernet Sauvignon 2005 **169**
Hardy's Tintara Grenache 2004 **223**
Hardy's Tintara Shiraz 2005 **54**

I

Ingoldby Cabernet Sauvignon 2004 **173**
Ingoldby Shiraz 2005 **57**
Innocent Bystander Pinot Noir 2006 **139**
Innocent Bystander Sangiovese Merlot 2006 **226**
Innocent Bystander Shiraz 2006 **58**
Izway Mates GMS 2006 **226**

J

J & J Shiraz 2006 **58**
Jacob's Creek Centenary Hill Shiraz 2002 & 2003 **59**
Jacob's Creek Reserve Cabernet Sauvignon 2005 **173**
Jacob's Creek Reserve Shiraz 2005 **59**
Jacob's Creek Shiraz 2006 **60**
Jacob's Creek St Hugo Cabernet Sauvignon 2004 & 2005 **174**
Jamieson's Run Cabernet Sauvignon 2004 **174**
Jamieson's Run Cabernet Shiraz Merlot 2004 **175**
Jim Barry McRae Wood Shiraz 2004 **60**
Jim Barry Three Little Pigs Shiraz Cabernet Malbec 2004 **226**
John Duval Wines Entity Shiraz 2005 **60**
John Duval Wines Plexus Shiraz Grenache Mourvedre 2005 **227**

K

Kaesler Old Vine Shiraz 2006 **61**
Kalleske Basket Press Clarry's Red 2006 **227**
Kangarilla Road Cabernet Sauvignon 2006 **175**
Katnook Estate Founder's Block Cabernet Sauvignon 2005 **175**
Kilikanoon Covenant Shiraz 2005 **61**
Kilikanoon Parable Shiraz 2005 **61**
Kilikanoon Testament Shiraz 2005 **62**
Kooyong Haven Pinot Noir 2005 **140**
Kooyong Meres Pinot Noir 2005 **140**
Kooyong Pinot Noir 2006 **140**
Kurtz Boundary Row Grenache Shiraz Mataro 2005 **227**
Kurtz Boundary Row Shiraz 2005 **62**
Kurtz Siebenschlafer Seven Sleepers 2005 **228**

L

Lake Breeze Bernoota Shiraz Cabernet 2005 **62**
Lake Breeze Cabernet Sauvignon 2004 & 2005 **176**
Langmeil Fifth Wave Grenache 2005 **228**
Langmeil Hangin' Snakes Shiraz Viognier 2006 **63**
Langmeil Jackaman's Cabernet 2005 **176**
Langmeil Orphan Bank Shiraz 2005 **63**
Langmeil The Freedom 1843 Shiraz 2005 **63**
Lazy Ballerina Shiraz 2006 **64**
Leaping Lizard Shiraz 2006 **64**
Leasingham Bin 61 Shiraz 2005 **64**
Leconfield Cabernet Sauvignon 2005 **176**
Leeuwin Estate Art Series Cabernet Sauvignon 2004 **177**
Lenton Brae Cabernet Merlot 2006 **177**
Lillydale Estate Pinot Noir 2006 **141**
Lindemans Limestone Ridge Shiraz Cabernet Sauvignon 2004 & 2005 **65**
Lindemans Pyrus 2004 & 2005 **177**
Lindemans Reserve Cabernet Sauvignon 2005 **178**
Lindemans Reserve Shiraz 2005 **65**
Lindemans St George Cabernet Sauvignon 2004 & 2005 **178**
Longhop Old Vine Grenache 2006 **228**
Longhop Old Vine Shiraz 2006 & 2007 **66**
Longview Yakka Shiraz 2006 **66**
Luke Lambert Nebbiolo 2006 **229**
Luke Lambert Syrah 2006 **67**

M

Mad Fish Gold Turtle Shiraz 2005 **67**
Maglieri Shiraz 2006 **68**
Majella Cabernet Sauvignon 2005 **179**
Majella Shiraz 2005 **68**

Majella The Musician Cabernet Shiraz 2006 **180**
Marius Symphony Shiraz 2005 **69**
Marius Symposium Shiraz Mourvedre 2006 **69**
Matua Valley Pinot Noir 2006 **141**
Maude Pinot Noir 2006 **141**
Maxwell Four Roads Shiraz Grenache Viognier 2005 **229**
Maxwell Little Demon Cabernet Merlot 2005 **180**
Mayer Big Betty Shiraz 2006 **69**
Mayer Pinot Noir 2006 **142**
Mayford Tempranillo 2006 **230**
McKellar Ridge Cabernet Sauvignon Cabernet Franc 2006 **178**
McWilliam's Hanwood Estate Cabernet Sauvignon 2006 **179**
McWilliam's Hanwood Estate Merlot 2006 **229**
McWilliam's Hanwood Estate Shiraz 2006 **67**
Meerea Park Alexander Munro Shiraz 2006 **70**
Meerea Park Hell Hole Shiraz 2006 **70**
Meerea Park Shiraz 2006 & 2007 **71**
Metala White Label Shiraz Cabernet Sauvignon 2005 **71**
Mike Press Cabernet Sauvignon 2006 **180**
Mike Press Shiraz 2006 **71**
Mildara Cabernet Sauvignon 2006 **181**
Mildara Cabernet Shiraz 2004 **181**
Mildara Rothwell Cabernet Sauvignon 2004 **181**
Mitchelton Parish Shiraz Viognier 2005 **72**
Mitchelton Print Shiraz 2003 & 2004 **72**
Mitolo Reiver Shiraz 2005 **73**
Mitolo Savitar Shiraz 2005 **73**
Mitolo Serpico Cabernet Sauvignon 2005 **182**
Mollydooker Goosebumps Sparkling Shiraz 2006 **74**

Mollydooker The Boxer Shiraz 2006 **74**
Moondah Brook Cabernet Sauvignon 2005 **182**
Moondah Brook Shiraz 2005 **74**
Moss Wood Amy's Cabernet Sauvignon 2006 **183**
Moss Wood Cabernet Sauvignon 2004 **183**
Mount Langi Ghiran Bradach Vineyard Pinot Noir 2006 **142**
Mount Langi Ghiran Cliff Edge Shiraz 2004 & 2005 **75**
Mount Langi Ghiran Langi Shiraz 2005 **75**
Mount Majura Shiraz 2006 **76**
Mount Pleasant Maurice O'Shea Shiraz 2005 **76**
Mount Pleasant Old Paddock & Old Hill Shiraz 2003 **77**
Mount Pleasant Philip Shiraz 2005 **77**
Mount Pleasant Rosehill Shiraz 2003 **77**
Mountadam Shiraz 2006 **78**
Mountadam Shiraz Viognier 2006 **78**
Mr Riggs The Gaffer Shiraz 2006 **78**

N

Ngeringa J.E. Pinot Noir 2005 **142**
Ngeringa Syrah 2005 **79**
Noon Eclipse 2006 **230**
Noon Reserve Cabernet Sauvignon 2006 **184**
Noon Reserve Shiraz 2006 **79**
Nugan Estate Frasca's Lane Vineyard Sangiovese Merlot 2005 **230**
Nugan Estate Parish Vineyard Shiraz 2005 **80**

O

O'Leary Walker Pinot Noir 2006 **143**
Oliver's Taranga Vineyards HJ Reserve Shiraz 2005 **80**

Oliver's Taranga Vineyards Shiraz 2005 **80**
Oliver's Taranga Vineyards Vine Dried Cabernet Sauvignon 2006 **184**
Orlando Jacaranda Ridge Cabernet Sauvignon 2003 **185**
Over The Shoulder Cabernet Merlot 2005 **185**
Over The Shoulder Pinot Noir 2006 **143**

P

Paringa Estate 'Estate' Shiraz 2005 **81**
Paringa Estate Peninsula Shiraz 2005 **81**
Paringa Estate Reserve Shiraz 2005 **81**
Parker Coonawarra Estate Cabernet Sauvignon 2004 **185**
Paxton Vineyards AAA Shiraz Grenache 2006 **82**
Paxton Vineyards Jones Block Shiraz 2004 **82**
Penfolds Bin 138 Shiraz Grenache Mourvedre 2005 **231**
Penfolds Bin 28 Shiraz 2005 **82**
Penfolds Bin 389 Cabernet Shiraz 2005 **186**
Penfolds Bin 407 Cabernet Sauvignon 2005 **186**
Penfolds Bin 707 Cabernet Sauvignon 2005 **187**
Penfolds Coonawarra Bin 128 Shiraz 2006 **83**
Penfolds Grange Shiraz 2003 **84**
Penfolds Koonunga Hill Shiraz 2005 **84**
Penfolds Koonunga Hill Shiraz Cabernet 2005 **85**
Penfolds RWT Barossa Shiraz 2005 **85**
Penfolds St Henri Shiraz 2004 **86**
Penfolds Thomas Hyland Shiraz 2005 **86**
Penley Estate Hyland Shiraz 2005 **87**
Penley Estate Phoenix Cabernet Sauvignon 2005 **188**
Penny's Hill Red Dot Shiraz Viognier 2006 **87**

Penny's Hill Specialized Shiraz Cabernet Merlot 2005 **231**
Pepperjack Cabernet Sauvignon 2006 **188**
Pepperjack Shiraz 2006 **87**
Pepperjack Shiraz Grenache Mourvedre 2006 **232**
Pepperjack Shiraz Viognier 2006 **88**
Petaluma Cabernet Merlot 2004 & 2005 **189**
Petaluma Shiraz 2005 **88**
Peter Lehmann Cabernet Sauvignon 2005 **189**
Peter Lehmann Clancy's 2005 **232**
Peter Lehmann Futures Shiraz 2005 **89**
Peter Lehmann Shiraz 2005 **89**
Pfeiffer Sparkling Pinot Noir 2004 **143**
PHI Lusatia Park Vineyard Pinot Noir 2006 **144**
Philip Shaw No. 8 Pinot Noir 2006 **144**
Picardy Merlot Cabernet Sauvignon Cabernet Franc 2005 **232**
Picardy Tete de Cuvée Pinot Noir 2005 **144**
Pillar Box Red 2006 **233**
Pirathon by Kalleske Shiraz 2005 **89**
Pizzini Il Barone 2004 **233**
Pizzini Nebbiolo 2003 **233**
Pizzini Sangiovese 2005 & 2006 **234**
Plantagenet Lioness Shiraz Viognier 2005 **90**
Plantagenet Omrah Shiraz 2005 **90**
Poacher's Ridge Vineyard Louis Block Cabernet Sauvignon 2005 **190**
Poacher's Ridge Vineyard Louis Block Merlot 2005 **234**
Polleters Cabernet Sauvignon 2005 **190**
Polleters Moonambel Shiraz 2005 **90**
Port Phillip Estate Quartier Barbera 2006 **235**
Port Phillip Estate Tete De Cuvee Rimage Syrah 2005 **91**
Primo Estate Il Briccone Sangiovese Shiraz 2005 **235**
Primo Estate Merlesco Merlot 2006 **235**

WINE INDEX **267**

Punch Close Planted
   Pinot Noir 2005 **145**
Punch Lance's Vineyard
   Pinot Noir 2005 **145**
Punt Road Yarra Valley
   Pinot Noir 2006 **145**
Pyrette Shiraz 2005 **91**

R

Ravensworth Sangiovese 2006 **236**
Ravensworth Shiraz Viognier 2006 **91**
Red Knot Cabernet Sauvignon 2006 **190**
Red Knot Shiraz 2006 **92**
Reilly's Barking Mad Shiraz 2006 **92**
Reynella Basket Pressed Shiraz 2005 **92**
Richard Hamilton Gumprs'
   Shiraz 2006 **93**
Richard Hamilton Hut Block Cabernet
   Sauvignon 2006 **191**
Riddoch Cabernet Shiraz 2004 **191**
Ring Bolt Cabernet Sauvignon 2005 **191**
Riposte The Sabre Pinot Noir 2006 **146**
Rockbare Shiraz 2006 **93**
Rockford Basket Press Shiraz 2005 **94**
Rolf Binder Bulls Blood Shiraz
   Mourvedre 2005 **94**
Rolf Binder Christa Rolf Shiraz
   Grenache 2005 **236**
Rolf Binder Hanisch Shiraz 2005 **95**
Rosemount Diamond Label Cabernet
   Sauvignon 2005 **192**
Rosemount Diamond Label
   Shiraz 2006 **95**
Rosemount Show Reserve Cabernet
   Sauvignon 2005 **192**
Rosemount Show Reserve
   GSM 2004 **236**
Rosemount Show Reserve
   Shiraz 2004 **95**
Rutherglen Estates 'Red' 2006 **96**
Rutherglen Estates Durif 2006 **237**
Rymill MC² 2004 **237**

S

S.C. Pannell Nebbiolo 2005 **237**
S.C. Pannell Pronto Red 2006 **238**
S.C. Pannell Shiraz 2005 **96**
S.C. Pannell Shiraz Grenache 2005 **238**
Saltram Maker's Table Cabernet
   Sauvignon 2007 **193**
Saltram Mamre Brook Cabernet
   Sauvignon 2005 **193**
Saltram Mamre Brook Shiraz 2005 **98**
Saltram No. 1 Shiraz 2004 **98**
Saltram Winemaker Selection Cabernet
   Sauvignon 2004 **193**
Savaterre Pinot Noir 2005 **146**
Scarpantoni School Block Shiraz
   Cabernet 2004 **99**
Scarpantoni The Brothers Block
   Cabernet Sauvignon 2004 **194**
Scotchmans Hill Cornelius
   Syrah 2005 **99**
Scotchmans Hill Swan Bay
   Pinot Noir 2007 **147**
Seppelt Benno Shiraz 2005 **99**
Seppelt Cabernet Sauvignon 2005 **194**
Seppelt Chalambar Shiraz 2006 **100**
Seppelt Mount Ida Shiraz 2005 **100**
Seppelt Silverband Shiraz 2005 **101**
Seppelt Silverband Sparkling
   Shiraz NV **102**
Seppelt St Peters Shiraz 2005 **101**
Seppelt Victoria Shiraz 2005 **102**
Setanta Cuchulain Shiraz 2005 **102**
Shadowfax Pinot Noir 2004 **147**
Shaw & Smith Shiraz
   2005 & 2006 **103**
Skillogalee Basket Pressed Cabernet
   Sauvignon Cabernet Franc
   Malbec 2004 **194**
Smithbrook Merlot 2005 **239**
Squitchy Lane Vineyard
   Cabernets 2005 **195**
St Hallett Blackwell Shiraz
   2005 & 2006 **97**
St Hallett GST 2007 **238**

St Hallett Old Block Shiraz
    2004 & 2005 **97**
St Hubert Cabernet Sauvignon 2005 **192**
Stanton & Killeen Shiraz Durif 2005 **103**
Starvedog Lane Cabernet
    Merlot 2005 **195**
Starvedog Lane Shiraz
    Viognier 2005 **104**
Stefano Lubiana Primavera
    Pinot Noir 2006 **147**
Stella Bella Cabernet Sauvignon
    Merlot 2005 **195**
Stella Bella Shiraz 2006 **104**
Stoney Rise Pinot Noir 2006 **148**
Stonier Pinot Noir 2006 **148**
Stonier Reserve Pinot Noir 2005 **148**
Stonier Windmill Vineyard
    Pinot Noir 2005 **149**
Suckfizzle Cabernet Sauvignon 2005 **196**

T

T'Gallant Juliet Pinot Noir 2006 **149**
Tahbilk Cabernet Sauvignon 2004 **196**
Tahbilk Reserve Shiraz 2002 **104**
Talinga Park Cabernet Merlot 2005 **196**
Taltarni Cabernet Sauvignon 2004 **197**
Tapanappa Whalebone Vineyard
    Cabernet Shiraz 2005 **197**
Tarrington Artemisia Shiraz 2006 **105**
Taylors Cabernet Sauvignon
    2005 & 2006 **198**
Taylors Eighty Acres Cabernet Shiraz
    Merlot 2005 **239**
Taylors Eighty Acres Shiraz
    Viognier 2005 **105**
Taylors Jaraman Cabernet
    Sauvignon 2005 **198**
Taylors Jaraman Shiraz 2005 **105**
Taylors St Andrews Shiraz 2003 **106**
Temple Bruer Preservative Free Shiraz
    Malbec 2007 **106**
Ten Minutes by Tractor
    Pinot Noir 2006 **149**

The Pawn En Passant
    Tempranillo 2006 **239**
The Pawn The Gambit
    Sangiovese 2006 **240**
The Story Shiraz 2005 & 2006 **106**
The Story Westgate Vineyard
    Shiraz 2006 **107**
Tim Adams Cabernet Sauvignon 2004
    & 2005 **199**
Tim Adams The Fergus 2005 & 2006 **240**
Tollana Bin TR16 Shiraz 2006 **107**
Toolangi Estate Shiraz 2005 **107**
Toolangi Shiraz 2005 **108**
Torbreck Juveniles 2007 **240**
Torbreck Run Rig Shiraz 2005 **108**
Torbreck The Gask Shiraz 2006 **109**
Torbreck The Struie Shiraz 2005 **109**
Torzi Matthews Frost Dodger
    Shiraz 2005 **110**
Torzi Matthews Schist Rock Shiraz
    2006 & 2007 **110**
Turkey Flat Grenache 2006 **241**
Turkey Flat Shiraz 2005 **111**
Turkey Flat Sparkling Shiraz NV **111**
Tyrrell's Four Acres Shiraz 2007 **112**
Tyrrell's Reserve Stevens Vineyard
    Shiraz 2005 **112**
Tyrrell's Rufus Stone Shiraz 2005 **112**
Tyrrell's Vat 9 Shiraz 2005 & 2006 **113**

U

Ulithorne Flamma Sparkling Shiraz
    Disgorged 2007 **113**
Ulithorne Frux Frugis Shiraz 2005 **114**
Ulithorne Paternus Cabernet
    Shiraz 2006 **199**

V

Valhalla Wines Shiraz 2005 **114**
Vasse Felix Cabernet
    Sauvignon 2005 **200**

Vasse Felix Shiraz 2005 **115**
Victorian Alps Dividing Range Shiraz Cabernet 2006 **115**
Vinea Marson Nebbiolo 2006 **241**
Vinea Marson Sangiovese 2006 **241**
Vinea Marson Syrah 2006 **116**
Voyager Estate Cabernet Merlot 2004 **200**
Voyager Estate Girt by Sea Cabernet Merlot 2005 **201**
Voyager Estate Shiraz 2006 **116**

W

Wanderer Shiraz 2006 **117**
Wanted Man Shiraz 2006 **117**
Warburn Estate Premium Reserve Cabernet Merlot 2006 **201**
Warburn Estate Premium Reserve Shiraz 2006 **117**
Warburn Estate Stephendale Shiraz 2006 **118**
Warrabilla Reserve Cabernet Sauvignon 2006 **201**
Warrabilla Reserve Shiraz 2006 **118**
Water Wheel Memsie 2006 **118**
Water Wheel Shiraz 2006 **119**
West Cape Howe Two Steps Shiraz Viognier 2005 **119**
William Downie Pinot Noir 2006 **150**
Wine by Brad Cabernet Merlot 2005 **202**
Wirra Wirra Catapult Shiraz Viognier 2006 **119**
Wirra Wirra Church Block 2006 **242**
Wirra Wirra RSW Shiraz 2005 **120**
Wirra Wirra Scrubby Rise Red 2006 **242**
Wirra Wirra The Angelus Cabernet Sauvignon 2005 **202**
Wirra Wirra Woodhenge Shiraz 2006 **120**
Wolf Blass Gold Label Pinot Noir 2005 **150**
Wolf Blass Gold Label Shiraz 2005 **120**
Wolf Blass Grey Label Cabernet Sauvignon 2006 **202**
Woodlands Cabernet Merlot 2005 & 2006 **203**
Woodstock Cabernet Sauvignon 2005 **203**
Woodstock Shiraz 2005 **121**
Woop Woop Shiraz 2006 **121**
Wrattonbully Vineyards Tempranillo 2006 **242**
Wynns Coonawarra Estate Black Label Cabernet Sauvignon 2005 **204**
Wynns Coonawarra Estate John Riddoch Cabernet Sauvignon 2005 **205**
Wynns Coonawarra Estate Messenger Cabernet Sauvignon 2005 **205**
Wynns Coonawarra Estate Michael Shiraz 2005 **121**
Wynns Coonawarra Estate White Label Shiraz 2006 **122**

X

Xanadu Dragon Cabernet Merlot 2006 **206**

Y

Yalumba Bush Vine Grenache 2005 **243**
Yalumba Hand-picked Shiraz & Viognier 2005 **122**
Yalumba Menzies Cabernet Sauvignon 2004 & 2005 **206**
Yalumba Mourvedre Grenache Shiraz 2006 **243**
Yalumba Octavius Shiraz 2004 **123**
Yalumba Shiraz & Viognier 2005 **123**
Yalumba Signature Cabernet Sauvignon Shiraz 2004 **207**
Yalumba Tempranillo Grenache Viognier 200 **243**

Yalumba Y Series Shiraz
    Viognier 2006 **123**
Yering Station Pinot Noir 2006 **150**
Yering Station Shiraz Viognier 2006 **124**

Z

Zema Estate Cabernet Sauvignon
    2004 **207**

WHY THE FRENCH HATE US
BY CAMPBELL MATTINSON

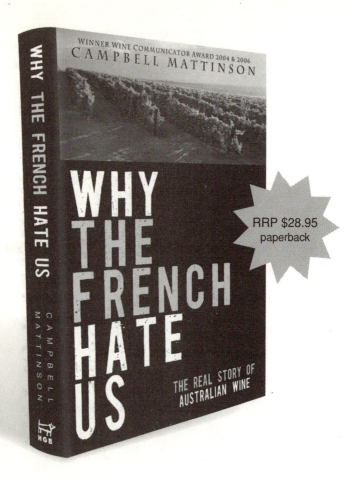

RRP $28.95 paperback

'This is a book full of entirely new insights into Australian wine, the way it is made, the way it is marketed (or mis-marketed), and where it should head. And you don't have to be a wine-nerd to enjoy every page.'

James Halliday

Hardie Grant Books